Workplace Skills

Applied Mathematics

Career Readiness Preparation

 **Contemporary**

The *McGraw·Hill* Companies

www.mhcontemporary.com

 **Contemporary**

Copyright © 2011 by The McGraw-Hill Companies, Inc.

Printed in the United States of America.

WORKKEYS® is the registered trademark of ACT, Inc.
The McGraw-Hill Companies, Inc. have no affiliation with
ACT, Inc., and this publication is not approved, authorized
or endorsed by ACT, Inc.

Send all inquiries to:
McGraw-Hill/Contemporary
130 East Randolph, Suite 400
Chicago, IL 60601

ISBN 978-0-07-657481-0
MHID 0-07-657481-4

6 7 8 9 QDB 16 15 14 13 12 11

Contents ...

Introduction ...

Today's employers want to know if you have the skills and knowledge needed to be productive in the 21st Century workplace. *Workplace Skills* is designed to help you to certify the career readiness skills that you already have and to help you to improve your skill levels for greater career success and mobility. By completing this series, you will be better prepared to take a career readiness test and receive a Career Readiness Certificate.

The *Workplace Skills* series provides instruction and practice in three skill areas identified by employers as holding the key to your success in more than 85 percent of current and emerging careers. These areas are: Applied Mathematics, Reading for Information, and Locating Information. The questions you are asked in each of these areas are taken from actual workplace situations. They are designed to help you to identify, understand, and solve problems that you may encounter on the job.

Each book contains lessons that include a step-by-step example to introduce the skill and *On Your Own* problems to practice the skill. The lessons in the book will guide you through progressively higher skill levels, from those needed for entry-level employment to those required in higher-level jobs. Foundational skills are listed in the *Remember!* notes included in each lesson. *Performance Assessment* problems with answers and explanations at the end of each skill level allow you to review and assess your mastery of the skills at that level. In each of the three subject areas, employers have determined the skill level required for a job, and you may ask for that information from your instructor.

Workplace Skills: Applied Mathematics ■ ■ ■

Applying mathematics in the workplace is an essential skill. While the required level of mathematical knowledge is often basic, the work-based context and application of that knowledge is sometimes more complex. For example, you might be required to perform a straightforward mathematical task such as giving change for a purchase. However, you may also need to perform more complex tasks such as finding the percentage of a number or converting units of measurement.

Workplace Skills: Applied Mathematics contains lessons that will help you develop and improve your ability to apply mathematical skills. Realistic scenarios, practice exercises, and assessment problems taken from workplace situations help you to develop a problem-solving approach to mathematical situations.

Two-Step Approach ■ ■ ■

Knowing how to approach Applied Mathematics problems will give you confidence when solving them. Though different problems require application of different skills, the problem-solving process can be summarized in two essential steps.

Step 1 — Understand the Problem ■ ■ ■

Before approaching any problem, you must be sure you understand what you are being asked to do. You can use the *Plan for Successful Solving* to organize the information presented in a problem and then plan how to solve it. The plan includes five questions:

Plan for Successful Solving	
What am I asked to do?	Determine what solution it is you are being asked to find. This is usually found in the question posed at the end of the problem.
What are the facts?	Identify what information provided in the problem may help lead you to a solution. This may include both numbers and facts.
How do I find the answer?	Determine what operations and steps will help you solve the problem. Refer to the Formula Sheet on page 265 if necessary.
Is there any unnecessary information?	Review the problem and decide if any information is not needed. Some problems include unnecessary numbers or facts.
What prior knowledge will help me?	Think about personal background knowledge and experience you have that might help you better understand the problem and what steps are needed to find a solution.

Find Key Terms and Phrases

Applying mathematical skills to solve word problems can be like decoding a message or solving a puzzle. In addition to needing the necessary skills and a plan for solving the problem, you must also recognize how to determine which mathematical expression or procedure should be used. Below are examples of key terms or phrases often used in problems that will help you decide which operation is needed to solve the problem.

Operation	Key Term(s) or Phrases	
Addition	· Find the *total*. · *How many* or *how much*?	· Find the *sum*. · Find the *perimeter*.
Subtraction	· Find the *difference*. · How much *greater*?	· How much *more*? · How much *less*?
Multiplication	· Find the *total* (of a number of equal groups). · Find the *area* or *volume*.	· Find *percent* of. · Find the *circumference*.
Division	· How many *sets* or *groups*? · How many in each *set* or *group*?	· Find the *average*. · Find the *decimal equivalent* of a fraction.

Step 2 Find and Check Your Answer ▪ ▪ ▪

Sometimes finding the right answer may require you to adjust your initial plan. Once you have identified the best answer choice, it is a good idea to review the original problem to be sure your understanding of what you are being asked to do is correct and that your answer makes sense. If you determine that your answer may be incorrect, you should look back at your plan and revise it. Then perform the steps needed to arrive at and check your revised answer.

The two-step approach to problem solving is an easy-to-follow model for you to use as you develop the confidence needed to successfully approach problems you will encounter both in the workplace and on a Career Readiness Certificate test. *Do not worry yet about memorizing the steps.* With practice, you will naturally learn and remember this extremely useful approach. Over time, learning this model and using it carefully in your preparation for the test will provide you with a reliable approach to problem solving.

Remember!

If necessary, revise your *Plan for Successful Solving.*

· Determine and apply your solution approach.
· Check your answer.
· Select the correct answer.

Applied Mathematics

Level 3 Introduction ...

The lesson and practice pages that follow will give you the opportunity to develop and practice the mathematical skills needed to solve work-related problems at a Level 3 rating of difficulty. The *On Your Own* practice problems provide a review of math skills and instruction for specific problem-solving strategies. The *Performance Assessment* provides problems similar to those you will encounter on a Career Readiness Certificate test. By completing the Level 3 *On Your Own* and *Performance Assessment* problems, you will gain the ability to confidently approach workplace scenarios that require understanding and application of the skills featured in the following lessons:

Lesson 1: Solve Problems with Math Operations

Lesson 2: Convert Money and Time

Lesson 3: Change Numbers from One Form to Another

Lesson 4: Add and Subtract Negative Numbers

These skills are intended to help you successfully understand and solve problems requiring mathematics in the workplace that involve addition, subtraction, multiplication, and division; conversion of time and money; and changing numbers into equivalent forms. Solving these types of problems often requires the ability to:

- convert the information presented in word problems and workplace situations into a math equation,
- locate and understand information presented in a logical order,
- determine what information is needed in order to find a solution.

Through solving problems at this level, you will begin to develop problem-solving approaches and strategies that will help you determine the correct answer in real-world and test-taking situations.

Lesson 1 ■ ■ ■
Solve Problems with Math Operations

Skill: Solve problems with single math operations using whole numbers

When using numbers in the workplace, you will likely need to use each of the four mathematical operations—addition, subtraction, multiplication, and division. These operations help you calculate things such as the amount of material needed for a project; how much money is left in a budget; and how to divide time, money, or supplies equally.

Skill Examples

Example 1
Add two or more numbers.

Add: $114 + 108 + 4$

Line up the numbers in a column by aligning their place values. If the sum of one column is 10 or more, "carry" the tens digit of the sum to the next column.

$$\begin{array}{r} 1 \quad \\ 114 \\ 108 \\ +4 \\ \hline 226 \end{array}$$

◄····· Carried 10s digit from $4 + 8 + 4 = 16$

Example 2
Subtract one number from another.

Subtract: $156 - 27$

Line up the numbers in a column by aligning their place values. The larger of the two numbers should be on top. If the top number in a column is less than the number below it, "borrow" from the column to its left.

$$\begin{array}{r} 4\;16 \\ 1\cancel{5}\cancel{6} \\ -27 \\ \hline 129 \end{array}$$

◄····· "Borrow" one 10 from 50 to make the ones column equal to 16 and the 10s column equal to 40.

Skill Practice

A. Add two whole numbers. $\qquad$ $18 + 25$ = _____

B. Subtract a smaller whole number from a larger whole number. $\qquad$ $144 - 36$ = _____

C. Multiply one whole number by another whole number. $\qquad$ 8×15 = _____

D. Divide a whole number by a smaller whole number. $\qquad$ $72 \div 9$ = _____

Try It Out! ▪ ▪ ▪

As part of your job as a child care worker, you must keep track of all the children in your care. At the end of a day-long outing, each driver reports the number of children on his or her van. The number of children on the three vans is 17, 15, and 12. How many children are aboard the vans?

A. 29   B. 32   C. 34   D. 44   E. 47

 Step 1 ## Understand the Problem ▪ ▪ ▪

Complete the *Plan for Successful Solving.*

Plan for Successful Solving				
What am I asked to do?	**What are the facts?**	**How do I find the answer?**	**Is there any unnecessary information?**	**What prior knowledge will help me?**
Find the total number of children aboard the vans.	Van 1 = 17 children Van 2 = 15 children Van 3 = 12 children	Add the numbers of children in the three vans.	No.	To combine numbers, add or multiply.

Step 2 ## Find and Check Your Answer ▪ ▪ ▪

- Confirm your understanding of the problem and revise your plan as needed.
- Based on your plan, determine your solution approach: *I'm going to add the number of children in all the vans to find the total.*

```
  17
  15
+ 12
```
◄······ Place the numbers in a column with the ones lined up.

```
  1
  17
  15
+ 12
   4
```
◄······ Add the ones and regroup, or carry, if necessary.

```
  1
  17
  15
+ 12
  44
```
◄······ Add the tens.

- Check your answer. Check addition by subtracting.
  44 – 12 = 32; 32 – 15 = 17; There are 17 children in the first van.
- **Select the correct answer:**   D. 44
  By adding the number of children in each van, you find that the sum, or total number of children aboard the vans, is 44.

Problem Solving Tip

In order to solve most mathematics problems, you must first know how to choose an operation. Since you are asked to calculate the total number of children, and you know the number of children in each van, you must combine, or add, the three amounts.

Remember!

Addition and subtraction are opposite operations. Because of this, you can check addition results by subtracting. If you subtract two of the three numbers from the sum, the result will be the third number.

On Your Own ■ ■ ■

1. As a brickmason's apprentice, you need to move the correct number of bricks. The mason needs enough bricks to lay the next 4 rows. Each row is 24 bricks long. How many bricks do you need to move to complete the four rows?

   A. 6

   B. 20

   C. 28

   D. 96

   E. 120

2. One of your responsibilities as a line cook is to make sandwiches during lunch hour. People have ordered three types of sandwiches. Each sandwich is served with a slice of cheese. There are 28 orders for ham sandwiches, 14 orders for tuna sandwiches, and 30 orders for chicken sandwiches. How many slices of cheese do you need to make all of the sandwich orders?

   F. 42

   G. 54

   H. 62

   J. 72

   K. 78

3. You are a technician in a biology lab. You need to separate mice into equal groups. There are 84 mice altogether. You are instructed to place 12 mice in each cage. How many cages do you need?

   A. 6

   B. 7

   C. 72

   D. 96

   E. 1,008

4. As a janitorial supervisor, part of your job is to keep track of cleaning supplies. Yesterday you had 105 gallons of floor wax. The overnight crew used 15 gallons last night. How much floor wax is left?

   F. 7 gallons

   G. 80 gallons

   H. 85 gallons

   J. 90 gallons

   K. 120 gallons

5. At the hotel where you are a clerk at the front desk, there are 260 rooms. They are all reserved. The tracking sheet shows that guests have checked into 146 of the rooms. How many more guests do you expect?

    A. 14

    B. 96

    C. 114

    D. 124

    E. 406

6. You are a cabinetmaker who is installing new kitchen cabinets. You need 6 screws for each cabinet door. How many screws will you need to install 20 cabinet doors?

    F. 24

    G. 120

    H. 144

    J. 240

    K. 2,400

7. As a manager for a construction company, you are currently supervising workers at four sites. You plan to spend the same amount of time at each site. You will spend 196 hours supervising sites during the next few weeks. How many hours will you work at each site?

    A. 10

    B. 16

    C. 40

    D. 49

    E. 98

8. You are a stonecutter. A mason orders capstones for a wall. The wall is 12 inches wide. The capstones extend an extra 2 inches on each side of the wall. To what width should you cut the capstones?

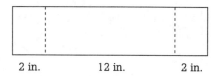

2 in.   12 in.   2 in.

    F. 12 inches

    G. 14 inches

    H. 16 inches

    J. 20 inches

    K. 24 inches

9. One of your responsibilities as a dental assistant is to prepare materials for the day. You need a set of four sterilized dental instruments for each patient. The chart shows that 13 checkups are on the schedule. How many dental instruments do you need?

   A. 13

   B. 17

   C. 36

   D. 48

   E. 52

10. As a surgical technician, you are responsible for stocking surgical supplies. You bring 144 surgical sponges from the supply room. The surgeons use 96 of them. How many sponges are left?

    F. 38

    G. 48

    H. 58

    J. 64

    K. 240

11. You are a veterinary technologist preparing a large dog for surgery. For every 8 pounds of the dog's weight, you need one unit of anesthetic. The dog weighs 48 pounds. How many units of anesthetic do you need?

    A. 4

    B. 6

    C. 8

    D. 40

    E. 396

12. As a bank teller, you count and record the total dollar amount of the coins in your drawer at the end of each day. Today you count 110 quarters. Which dollar amount do you record?

    F. $5.50

    G. $22.00

    H. $25.00

    J. $27.50

    K. $110.00

13. You work as a dishwasher in a large cafeteria. Clean trays are placed in stacks of 35. You count the stacks to be sure there are enough trays for the next meal. There are 22 stacks of trays. How many clean trays are available?

    A. 23

    B. 47

    C. 70

    D. 770

    E. 900

14. As a counter clerk for a dry cleaner, you keep track of the number of customers. Below is the record you kept of this morning's customers. How many customers dropped off clothes before noon today?

8:00 A.M. to 9:00 A.M.	⫽⫻ ///	8
9:00 A.M. to 10:00 A.M.	⫽⫻ ⫽⫻ //	12
10:00 A.M. to 11:00 A.M.	⫽⫻ /	6
11:00 A.M. to 12:00 P.M.	⫽⫻ ⫽⫻ ⫽⫻	15

    F. 20

    G. 26

    H. 35

    J. 41

    K. 45

15. You install solar energy systems on buildings. Each system has 4 sensor inputs that connect to a control unit. You need to install 6 solar energy systems this month. How many sensor inputs will you need?

    A. 10

    B. 18

    C. 24

    D. 42

    E. 48

16. As a meter reader for the electric company, the number that you read on the meter represents the amount of power used. Last month, a customer's meter reading was 34,510 kilowatt hours. This month it is 35,312 kilowatt hours. How much more power did the customer use this month than last month?

    F.   198 kilowatt hours

    G.   802 kilowatt hours

    H.   1,802 kilowatt hours

    J.   35,312 kilowatt hours

    K.   69,822 kilowatt hours

Answers are on page 233.

Money Units		
Unit	**Value**	
penny	1 cent	$0.01
nickel	5 cents	$0.05
dime	10 cents	$0.10
quarter	25 cents	$0.25
dollar	100 cents	$1.00
five dollar bill	500 cents or 5 dollars	$5.00
ten dollar bill	1,000 cents or 10 dollars	$10.00
twenty dollar bill	2,000 cents or 20 dollars	$20.00

Time Units	
Unit	**Value**
1 minute	60 seconds
1 hour	60 minutes
1 day	24 hours
1 week	7 days
1 year	365 days

Lesson 2 ▪▪▪
Convert Money and Time

Skill: Convert simple money and time units

Many jobs require that you handle money. You might need to purchase items for your work. In other jobs, you may need to accept money from customers. It is important to know how to calculate correctly in situations that involve money.

A number of jobs also require that you keep track of time. Sometimes you will fill out a timecard or timesheet to show how long you worked at a task. Some job tasks must start or stop at a certain time. In other tasks, you will need to figure out when a certain amount of time has passed. You may need to convert seconds to minutes or minutes to hours.

Skill Examples

Example 1
Convert total value (in cents) to dollars and cents.

What is the total value of 3 quarters, 3 dimes, and 2 nickels?

Add:

3 quarters	75 cents
3 dimes	30 cents
2 nickels	+ 10 cents
	115 cents

Since 100 cents = $1.00, the total value of the coins is $1.15.

Example 2
Convert total amount of time (in minutes) to hours and minutes.

How much time is 40 minutes + 50 minutes?

Add:

    40 minutes
  + 50 minutes
    90 minutes

Since 60 minutes = 1 hour, the total time is 1 hour, 30 minutes.

Skill Practice

A. Add money.   90¢ + 75¢ = _____

B. Subtract money. $2.25 – $0.75 = _____

C. Convert hours to minutes.   2 hours, 15 minutes = _____ minutes

D. Convert minutes to hours.   100 minutes = _____ hour,
                                      _____ minutes

Try It Out! ■ ■ ■

You are a mold maker at a foundry. For one of your procedures, the mold must cure for 2 hours and 15 minutes before it can be used. You start the curing at 1:50 P.M. When will the mold finish curing?

A. 3:15 P.M.   **B.** 3:55 P.M.   **C.** 4:05 P.M.   **D.** 4:25 P.M.   **E.** 5:05 P.M.

 Step 1 ## Understand the Problem ■ ■ ■

Complete the *Plan for Successful Solving.*

Plan for Successful Solving				
What am I asked to do?	**What are the facts?**	**How do I find the answer?**	**Is there any unnecessary information?**	**What prior knowledge will help me?**
Find the time when the mold will finish curing.	Curing starts at 1:50 P.M. Curing takes 2 hours, 15 minutes.	Add the curing time to 1:50 P.M.	No.	There are 60 minutes in 1 hour.

 Step 2 ## Find and Check Your Answer ■ ■ ■

- Confirm your understanding of the problem and revise your plan as needed.
- Based on your plan, determine your solution approach: *I'm going to add the hours and minutes needed for curing to the starting time.*

    1:50 P.M. = 1 hour, 50 minutes past noon

    1 hour   50 minutes
    + 2 hours 15 minutes
    ――――――――――――――
    3 hours 65 minutes   ◄······ Add the number of hours and minutes it takes to cure to the initial start time.

    65 minutes = 1 hour 5 minutes   ◄······ If the total number of minutes is greater than 60, convert to hours and minutes.

    3 hours + 1 hour 5 minutes = 4 hours 5 minutes   ◄······ Add to find the number of hours and minutes past noon.

- Check your answer. Check addition by subtracting.

    4 hours 5 minutes − 2 hours = 2 hours 5 minutes;

    2 hours 5 minutes − 5 minutes = 2 hours;

    2 hours − 10 minutes = 1 hour 50 minutes. The mold began curing at 1:50 P.M.

- **Select the correct answer:**   **C.** 4:05 P.M.
    By adding the cure time to the start time, you find curing ended at 3 hours and 65 minutes past noon. Converting this helps you find that the mold finished curing at 4 hours and 5 minutes past noon, or 4:05 P.M.

Problem Solving Tip

When solving problems that involve time, using a visual aid such as an analog clock can be helpful.

Remember!

When adding time, be careful to distinguish between A.M. and P.M. If you begin at a P.M. time and the elapsed time takes you past midnight, the ending time will likely be in A.M. If you start from an A.M. time and the elapsed time takes you past noon, the ending time will likely be in P.M. time. For instance, if you start sleeping at 10 P.M. and you sleep for 8 hours, the time you wake up is in A.M. time. To calculate, add the hours as in the *Try It Out!* example to the left, then subtract 12 from the total. (10 + 8 = 18 hours; 18 hours − 12 = 6 hours past *midnight,* or 6 A.M.)

1. You are working as a clerk at a rental car company. A customer asks for change for a $1 bill because the vending machine only accepts coins. You do not have any quarters, so you give the customer change in dimes and nickels. Which of these combinations totals the correct amount?

    A. 5 dimes, 5 nickels

    B. 6 dimes, 4 nickels

    C. 6 dimes, 6 nickels

    D. 8 dimes, 2 nickels

    E. 7 dimes, 6 nickels

2. The construction crew you manage is framing walls. Each wall will take 45 minutes to frame. How much time should you allow for framing 6 walls?

    F. 3 hours, 30 minutes

    G. 4 hours

    H. 4 hours, 30 minutes

    J. 5 hours, 15 minutes

    K. 6 hours

3. As a loan officer at a bank, you need to schedule a mortgage closing. A closing occurs about 6 weeks after the loan approval. A loan is approved on August 1. Which date would be best for the closing?

    A. August 15

    B. August 27

    C. September 1

    D. September 13

    E. October 8

4. One of your responsibilities as an administrative assistant in an architect's office is to count the money in the petty cash box and update the tally sheet on a daily basis. Today you counted one $20 bill, five $5 bills, and six $1 bills. You also counted 9 quarters, 8 dimes, and 3 nickels. What amount should you write on the tally sheet?

    F. $41.40

    G. $44.20

    H. $52.20

    J. $54.20

    K. $62.80

5. At the convenience store where you work as a clerk, a customer buys two candy bars that cost 75 cents each. Which of the following is the exact payment?

    A. 1 dollar bill

    B. 1 dollar bill and 5 nickels

    C. 6 quarters

    D. 5 quarters and 3 dimes

    E. 1 dollar bill and 3 quarters

6. You are working as a floral designer. A customer wants an arrangement of 6 roses and 2 sprays of baby's breath. Roses cost $1.50 each. Each spray of baby's breath costs $1. What is the cost of the flower arrangement?

    F. $9.00

    G. $10.00

    H. $10.50

    J. $11.00

    K. $12.00

7. You are a maintenance worker at a factory. After you repair a pump motor, it must be tested. Your work order calls for a $1\frac{1}{2}$-hour test period. You start the test at 1:15 P.M. When will the test be done?

    A. 2:15 P.M.

    B. 2:45 P.M.

    C. 3:00 P.M.

    D. 3:30 P.M.

    E. 3:45 P.M.

8. As a computer operator who works for several companies, you must bill each company for the time you spend maintaining their computer hardware. You started work on a task at 2:00 A.M. and finished at 4:30 A.M. How much time should be billed to the company?

    F. 2 hours

    G. $2\frac{1}{2}$ hours

    H. 3 hours

    J. 4 hours

    K. $4\frac{1}{2}$ hours

9. As a nursing attendant at a nursing home, you must make certain that patients take their medication. One of your patients needs medication every 4 hours. You gave the patient his last dose at 10:00 A.M. At what time should you give him the next dose?

    A. 12:00 A.M. (midnight)

    B. 2:00 A.M.

    C. 12:00 P.M. (noon)

    D. 2:00 P.M.

    E. 4:00 P.M.

10. You are a cashier at a restaurant. A customer owes $19.72. Which of these is correct change for a $20 bill?

    F. 2 dimes and 3 pennies

    G. 1 quarter and 3 pennies

    H. 1 quarter, 1 dime, and 3 pennies

    J. 2 quarters and 3 pennies

    K. 2 quarters, 2 dimes and 3 pennies

11. As a dental lab technician, you are responsible for making crowns. The procedure for making a dental crown says it should rest for 150 seconds after coming out of a high–heat furnace. How long should you let the crown rest?

    A. 1 minute, 30 seconds

    B. 2 minutes

    C. 2 minutes, 30 seconds

    D. 3 minutes, 20 seconds

    E. 5 minutes

12. Your shift as a switchboard operator at a large animal hospital lasts $3\frac{1}{2}$ hours. You start working at 8:15 A.M. When will you finish your shift?

    F. 10:45 A.M.

    G. 11:00 A.M.

    H. 11:15 A.M.

    J. 11:45 A.M.

    K. 12:45 P.M.

13. As a night security guard, you are scheduled to move to a different location every 40 minutes. You arrive at a site at 3:25 A.M. When should you travel to the next site?

    A. 3:55 A.M.

    B. 3:65 A.M.

    C. 4:05 A.M.

    D. 4:25 A.M.

    E. 5:05 A.M.

14. You are a library technician. A patron owes a 42-cent overdue fine. Which of the following coin combinations totals the exact amount owed?

    F. 2 dimes, 1 nickel, and 2 pennies

    G. 1 quarter, 1 dime, and 2 pennies

    H. 1 quarter, 2 nickels, and 2 pennies

    J. 1 quarter, 1 dime, 1 nickel, and 2 pennies

    K. 2 quarters, 1 nickel, and 2 pennies

15. As an environmental compliance inspector, you are responsible for recording data. The pump counter on a smokestack shows that an air sample was in place for 130 minutes. Which sampling time should you record?

    A. 1 hour, 30 minutes

    B. 1 hour, 50 minutes

    C. 2 hours, 10 minutes

    D. 2 hours, 30 minutes

    E. 2 hours, 40 minutes

16. You are a truck driver on a delivery between cities. At a toll booth, you must pay $1.75. You don't have any dollar bills. How many quarters should you pay?

    F. 5

    G. 6

    H. 7

    J. 9

    K. 13

Answers are on page 233.

Lesson 3 ■ ■ ■
Change Numbers from One Form to Another

Skill: Change numbers from one form to another using whole numbers, fractions, decimals, or percentages

Many jobs require you to use quantities that cannot be represented using whole numbers. For instance, if a job involves money, you will likely need to use decimal numbers. Often, cooks follow recipes that use fractions of ingredient amounts. Retail jobs use percents to find tax and discounts.

The table on the lower left shows the value of some common fractions as decimals and as percents. The ability to change numbers from one form to another is extremely important when using numbers in the workplace.

Skill Examples

Example 1

Convert a fraction to a decimal.

What is $\frac{1}{4}$ as a decimal?

Divide the top number by the bottom number.

$$1 \div 4 = 0.25$$
$$\frac{1}{4} = 0.25$$

Example 2

Convert a percentage to a decimal.

$$89\% = \frac{89}{100}$$

Divide 89 by 100.

$$89 \div 100 = 0.89$$
$$89\% = 0.89$$

Example 3

Convert a percentage to a fraction.

What is 30% as a fraction?

Divide the percent value by 100.

$$30\% = \frac{30}{100} = \frac{3}{10}$$

Example 4

Convert an improper fraction to a mixed number.

What is $\frac{9}{4}$ as a mixed number?

Divide 9 by 4.

$$9 \div 4 = 2 \text{ with a remainder of } 1$$
$$\frac{9}{4} = 2\frac{1}{4}$$

Skill Practice

A. Convert a fraction to a decimal. $\frac{1}{5}$ = _____

B. Convert a percent to a fraction. 50% = _____

C. Convert a fraction greater than 1 to a mixed number. $\frac{10}{3}$ = _____

D. Convert a decimal to a fraction. 0.6 = _____

Try It Out! ▪ ▪ ▪

You are a data entry keyer at a doctor's clinic. The doctor tells you that a patient should exercise for $2\frac{1}{2}$ hours each week. The program only allows for numbers to be entered in decimal form. What number should you use to record the time?

A. 0.25 hour   **B.** 0.5 hour   **C.** 2.12 hours   **D.** 2.5 hours   **E.** 2.75 hours

Understand the Problem ▪ ▪ ▪

Complete the *Plan for Successful Solving.*

Plan for Successful Solving

What am I asked to do?	What are the facts?	How do I find the answer?	Is there any unnecessary information?	What prior knowledge will help me?
Find the decimal number that shows the exercise time.	The total exercise time is $2\frac{1}{2}$ hours.	Change $2\frac{1}{2}$ to a decimal.	No.	Convert fractions by dividing the top number (numerator) by the bottom number (denominator).

Find and Check Your Answer ▪ ▪ ▪

- Confirm your understanding of the problem and revise your plan as needed.

- Based on your plan, determine your solution approach: *I am first going to convert the fraction part of the mixed number into a decimal. I will do this by dividing the numerator (top number) by the denominator (bottom number). The decimal number I get as a result, plus the 2 wholes, is the correct answer.*

$2\frac{1}{2} = 2 + \frac{1}{2}$ ◄······ Separate the whole number and the fraction.

$\frac{1}{2} = 1 \div 2 = 0.5$ ◄······ Divide the numerator by the denominator to convert the fraction to a decimal.

$2 + 0.5 = 2.5$ ◄······ Add the original whole number to the decimal.

- Check your answer. Check by converting 2.5 to a fraction.

$2.5 = 2\frac{5}{10} = 2\frac{1}{2}$

- **Select the correct answer:**   **D.** 2.5 hours

By converting $\frac{1}{2}$ to a decimal, you find that it equals 0.5. By adding 0.5 to 2, you find that the patient should exercise for 2.5 hours each week.

Remember!

A decimal number reads the same as its fraction equivalent. For example:

$0.4 = $ "four-tenths" $= \frac{4}{10}$

$0.15 = $ "fifteen hundredths" $= \frac{15}{100}$

Problem Solving Tips

When working with fraction and decimal quantities that are greater than 1, remember that these numbers can be written as the number of wholes plus the number of parts. In the *Try It Out!* example, 2.5 can be written as 2 + 0.5 ("two wholes plus five-tenths of another whole"). Similarly, the mixed number $2\frac{1}{2}$ can be written as $2 + \frac{1}{2}$ ("two wholes plus half of another whole"). When converting these numbers, the whole number stays the same. Always remember to add the whole number back to the fraction or decimal after you have completed converting.

On Your Own ■ ■ ■

1. You are painting the walls of three units in an apartment building. Your supervisor says you will need $5\frac{3}{4}$ gallons of paint for the three units. The amount of paint in each can is written in decimals. Which of these is the same as $5\frac{3}{4}$ gallons?

    A.   0.575 gallon

    B.   5.34 gallons

    C.   5.75 gallons

    D.   53.4 gallons

    E.   534 gallons

2. As a parts salesperson, one of your jobs is keeping track of the total cost of parts used for a client's project. Your expense sheet shows that the cost of steel beams will be $30\frac{1}{2}\%$ of the budget for parts needed for the job. You need to enter this amount on your client's software using a decimal amount. Which of these should you enter?

    F.   0.0305

    G.   0.0312

    H.   0.035

    J.   0.305

    K.   3.5

3. You are a home health care aide. Your employer pays you for travel time to the patient's home. Today, your travel time was $1\frac{1}{3}$ hours. You report your time as a decimal number on your timesheet. How should you report your travel time?

    A.   0.13 hour

    B.   1.13 hours

    C.   1.33 hours

    D.   11.3 hours

    E.   13.3 hours

4. In your job as a cutter for a plastic factory, you trim parts to the correct length. You are instructed to leave an extra 0.25 inches on a product. Your ruler is marked in fractions of an inch. How much extra length should you measure?

    F. $\frac{1}{16}$ inch

    G. $\frac{1}{8}$ inch

    H. $\frac{1}{4}$ inch

    J. $\frac{3}{8}$ inch

    K. $\frac{3}{4}$ inch

5. At the department store where you work as a counter clerk, every purchase is discounted by 15% today. How much will customers save on each $1 purchase?

    A. $0.05

    B. $0.10

    C. $0.15

    D. $0.25

    E. $0.85

6. You work as a cook in a school cafeteria. A recipe you are making calls for 4 cups + $1\frac{3}{4}$ cups of sugar. How much total sugar will you need?

    F. $\frac{3}{414}$ cup

    G. $\frac{3}{4}$ cup

    H. $4\frac{3}{14}$ cups

    J. $4\frac{13}{14}$ cups

    K. $5\frac{3}{4}$ cups

7. In your job as a housekeeping cleaner, you record the time spent on cleaning each house on your weekly timesheet. You spend $1\frac{1}{4}$ hours cleaning one house. What time should you enter on your timesheet?

    A.   1.00 hour

    B.   1.05 hours

    C.   1.25 hours

    D.   1.50 hours

    E.   1.75 hours

8. As an equipment cleaner for a large company, you need to divide your time equally among several jobs. You decide that 20% of the time should be spent on each job. What fraction of your time will be spent on each job?

    F. $\frac{1}{6}$

    G. $\frac{1}{5}$

    H. $\frac{1}{4}$

    J. $\frac{1}{3}$

    K. $\frac{1}{2}$

9. You are a lathe operator making posts for a wooden bed frame. The widest part of each post is $3\frac{3}{4}$ inches. Your lathe is calibrated in decimal units. Which setting should you use for the widest part of the post?

A. 0.375 inch

B. 3.075 inches

C. 3.25 inches

D. 3.5 inches

E. 3.75 inches

10. As a cashier at a department store, you notice that your register adds a state sales tax of $0.06 for each dollar purchased. What is the state sales tax rate?

F. 0.06%

G. 1%

H. 6%

J. 60%

K. 600%

11. You work as a packager in a warehouse. Your supervisor tells you that a box should be no more than 90% full. What is this fill level as a fraction?

A. $\frac{9}{100}$

B. $\frac{1}{10}$

C. $\frac{1}{9}$

D. $\frac{9}{10}$

E. $1\frac{1}{9}$

12. As a machine operator, you use equipment that measures length in meters. You are asked to make a cut of $4\frac{1}{2}$ meters. The controls on the table show length in decimals. How should you set the machine table?

F. 0.412 meter

G. 0.45 meter

H. 4.12 meters

J. 4.5 meters

K. 45 meters

13. As a truck driver, you deliver bread to grocery stores. You deliver 75% of the bread in your truck today. What fraction of your load did you deliver today?

- A. $\frac{1}{2}$
- B. $\frac{1}{4}$
- C. $\frac{3}{4}$
- D. $\frac{2}{5}$
- E. $\frac{4}{5}$

14. The advertising company at which you work as a sales agent offers a 20% discount to clients who pay in advance. By what decimal should you multiply the price to find the amount of the discount?

- F. 0.1
- G. 0.2
- H. 0.25
- J. 0.33
- K. 0.5

15. As an electronic equipment assembler, you need to report the percentage of faulty computer chips. In one batch of chips, you found 2 out of the 100 chips did not work. What fault rate do you report?

- A. 2%
- B. 5%
- C. 20%
- D. 25%
- E. 200%

16. You work as a control panel operator at an oil refinery. When a tank reaches 90% of its volume, you switch the flow to the next tank. The control panel shows the amount of liquid in a tank using a scale of 0 to 1.00. At which reading should you switch to the next tank?

- F. 0.09
- G. 0.10
- H. 0.50
- J. 0.90
- K. 0.99

Answers are on page 233.

Lesson 4 ∎∎∎
Add and Subtract Negative Numbers

Skill: Add or subtract negative numbers

In performing workplace calculations, you may need to add and subtract negative numbers. For example, in business, negative numbers may take the form of a discount, a net loss, or a shortfall in revenue or available merchandise.

When adding or subtracting negative numbers, the answer may be positive or negative.

Remember!

When you add two or more numbers together, the order of the numbers does not matter.

$$2 + 3 = 5$$
$$3 + 2 = 5$$

Since adding a negative number is the same thing as subtraction, it can be helpful to always list the negative number second.

$$(-4) + 6 = 2$$
$$6 + (-4) = 2$$
$$6 - 4 = 2$$

When you need to find the *difference* between two numbers, you always subtract. So, the larger number should be listed first in your equation. To find the difference between −4 and −2, you would calculate

$$-2 - (-4) = 2$$
$$\text{not}$$
$$-4 - (-2) = -2.$$

Skill Examples

Example 1
Add a negative number to a positive number.

Add: 7 + (−4)

Adding a negative number to a positive number is the same thing as subtraction. If you start at 7 on the number line and add −4, the result is 3.

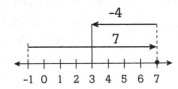

Example 2
Subtract a negative number.

Subtract: −2 − (− 5)

Subtracting a negative number is the same as adding the opposite of the negative number being subtracted.

$$-2 - (- 5) = -2 + 5 = 3$$

Example 3
Add a negative number to a negative number.

Add: (−3) + (− 4)

To add two negative numbers, add the numbers and then insert a negative sign in the answer.

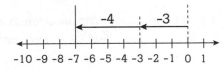

$$(-3) + (- 4) = (-7)$$

Skill Practice

A. Add two negative numbers.   −21 + −17   =   _____

B. Add a positive number and a negative number   −28 + 75   =   _____
   where the sum is positive.

C. Add a positive number and a negative number   19 + (−38)   =   _____
   where the sum is negative.

D. Add a positive number and a negative number   11 + (−11)   =   _____
   where both numbers are the same.

Try It Out! ▪ ▪ ▪

You are a sales clerk at a camera store. A customer buys a digital camera for $120. The customer has a coupon for $30. What is the final cost of the camera?

A. $40   **B.** $90   **C.** $120   **D.** $150   **E.** $3,600

Step 1 Understand the Problem ▪ ▪ ▪

Complete the *Plan for Successful Solving*.

\multicolumn{5}{c}{Plan for Successful Solving}				
What am I asked to do?	What are the facts?	How do I find the answer?	Is there any unnecessary information?	What prior knowledge will help me?
Find the final cost of the camera.	The cost of the camera is $120. The coupon is for $30 off of the price, so its net value is (−$30).	Add a negative number to a positive number.	No.	Adding a negative number to a positive number is the same as subtracting that number.

Step 2 Find and Check Your Answer ▪ ▪ ▪

- Confirm your understanding of the problem and revise your plan as needed.
- Based on your plan, determine your solution approach: *I'm going to add the cost of the camera and the amount of the coupon.*

   120 + (−30)   ◄······ Write the problem.

   120 + (−30) = 90   ◄······ Add the numbers.

- Check your answer. If you take the final price and add the discounted amount, then you should get the original price. $90 + $30 = $120
- **Select the correct answer:**   **B.** $90
   By adding the net value of the coupon ($−30) to the total cost ($120), you are actually taking $30 off of the price, or subtracting $30 from $120.
   $120 − $30 = $90

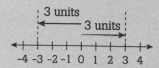

On Your Own ▪ ▪ ▪

1. In your role as an executive secretary, you are helping to prepare the year-to-date profit and loss statement for the first half of this year. The company had a $15,000 loss in the first quarter. This was followed by a $27,000 loss in the second quarter. What is the year-to-date net loss after the first two quarters?

    A. −$42,000

    B. −$32,000

    C. −$12,000

    D. $12,000

    E. $42,000

2. One of your tasks as a respiratory therapy technician is to check a patient's breathing. A patient moves the lever to 550 when blowing into a meter. You know to call the doctor if the patient's lever reading falls 115 points. At what meter reading should you call the doctor?

    F. −665

    G. −435

    H. 435

    J. 445

    K. 665

3. At the warehouse where you work, you are in charge of the inventory of math books. You have 725 books in stock. You receive an order for 1,162 books. How many books are now on back order?

    A. −1,887

    B. −437

    C. 437

    D. 447

    E. 1,887

4. You are working as a groundskeeper installing a border of granite bricks. The height of the brick is 5 inches. The brick is marked at 1 inch from the bottom to show how much of the brick is below ground. What is the height of the brick above ground?

    F. −6 inches

    G. −4 inches

    H. 4 inches

    J. 5 inches

    K. 6 inches

5. In your role as a clerk for a jewelry store, you need to pay the store's bills. The account has a starting balance of $3,578. You write checks totaling $4,173. What is the ending balance in the account?

    A.   −$7,751

    B.   −$595

    C.   −$405

    D. $595

    E. $7,751

6. As a forest ranger at a state park, you monitor the temperature of a nearby mountain summit. One morning the low temperature at the summit is −15°F. The temperature rises to a high of 3°F during the day. What is the difference between the high and low temperatures at the summit for the day?

    F.   −18°F

    G.   −12°F

    H.   3°F

    J.   12°F

    K.   18°F

7. You are a bookbinder who makes covers for books. You cut 6 millimeters from the left side of a cover. You add 8 millimeters to the right side of a cover. What is the total gain or loss to the size of the new book cover?

    A.   −14 millimeters

    B.   −2 millimeters

    C.   1 millimeter

    D.   2 millimeters

    E.   14 millimeters

8. You are employed as a media consultant. A client wants to place an advertisement in a local magazine. The magazine's guidelines state that the ad can be no larger than 6 inches wide. Your client's ad is 12 inches wide. By how much will you need to reduce the ad so that it will fit in the magazine?

    F.   −6 inches

    G.   6 inches

    H.   9 inches

    J.   12 inches

    K.   18 inches

9. As a health care worker in a weight loss clinic, you keep track of weight loss for clients. One client has had a net weight change of −52 pounds. Her chart shows a weight of 237 pounds before beginning the program. What is the current weight of the client?

    A.   −289 pounds

    B.   −185 pounds

    C.   175 pounds

    D.   185 pounds

    E.   285 pounds

10. As a food service provider, you write diet plans for patients. One patient normally eats 3,500 calories a day. The plan you write is for 2,200 calories. What is the difference in the daily caloric intake between your diet plan and the patient's normal eating routine?

    F.   −1,300 calories

    G.   −1,200 calories

    H.   1,200 calories

    J.   1,300 calories

    K.   1,700 calories

11. You own a mechanical inspection company. Your company had a $24,000 profit in the first quarter of the year. It then had a $35,000 loss in the second quarter. What is the net profit or loss for the first two quarters?

    A.   −$11,000

    B.   −$9,000

    C. $9,000

    D. $11,000

    E. $59,000

12. As a warehouse manager, one of your jobs is to monitor inventory. The warehouse has 217 gym bags in stock. You receive an order for 538 bags. How many bags are now on back order?

    F.   −775 bags

    G.   −321 bags

    H.   321 bags

    J.   467 bags

    K.   775 bags

13. As a research assistant, one of your important responsibilities is to closely monitor a cooling chamber. The temperature of the cooling chamber is currently −8°C. The researcher asks that you lower the temperature 12 degrees. At what temperature should the cooling chamber be after you lower the temperature?

    A. −20°C

    B. −16°C

    C. −4°C

    D. 4°C

    E. 20°C

14. Another one of your responsibilities as a research assistant is to monitor the temperature of a heating machine. You notice the temperature is 16° below the standard 121°C setting. What is the temperature of the machine?

    F. −137°C

    G. −105°C

    H. 16°C

    J. 105°C

    K. 137°C

15. You write mortgage loans for home buyers. A buyer is purchasing a house for $325,000. The buyer makes a down payment of $65,000. What is the amount of the mortgage loan you write?

    A. $260,000

    B. $270,000

    C. $318,500

    D. $380,000

    E. $390,000

16. You work in the billing department at a utility company. A customer mistakenly writes a check for $582, but the amount that they owed was actually $528. What balance is now shown in your records for this customer?

    F. −$54

    G. −$46

    H. $46

    J. $54

    K. $1,110

Answers are on page 233.

Level 3 Performance Assessment

The following problems will test your ability to answer questions at a Level 3 rating of difficulty. These problems are similar to those that appear on a Career Readiness Certificate test. For each question, you can refer to the answer key for answer justifications. The answer justifications provide an explanation of why each answer option is either correct or incorrect and indicate the skill lesson that should be referred to if further review of a particular skill is needed.

1. As a bench carpenter, you are building a shelf unit that will be placed in a 37 inch wide opening. You need to leave 6 inches on one side. What is the widest shelf unit that you can build for the space?

    A. 25 inches

    B. 31 inches

    C. 35 inches

    D. 37 inches

    E. 43 inches

2. You are a clerk at a grocery store. After a customer pays for a grocery order, the register shows that you owe the customer 87 cents in change. Which combination of coins totals the correct change?

    F. 2 quarters, 2 dimes, and 2 pennies

    G. 2 quarters, 3 dimes, and 2 pennies

    H. 3 quarters, 1 nickel, and 2 pennies

    J. 3 quarters, 1 dime, and 2 pennies

    K. 4 quarters, 1 dime, and 2 pennies

Penny 1¢ $0.01
Nickel 5¢ $0.05
Dime 10¢ $0.10
Quarter 25¢ $0.25

3. As a sales associate at an electronics store, a customer presents you with a coupon for 60% off. You need to input the discount percent as a decimal on your cash register. Which is the correct decimal?

    A. 0.06

    B. 0.60

    C. 6.0

    D. 60.0

    E. 600.0

4. You work as a candy maker. One of your recipes calls for $2\frac{2}{3}$ cups of chocolate syrup. You are making a batch that is 4 times the size of the recipe. After calculating, you realize you need $8\frac{8}{3}$ cups of chocolate syrup. How much chocolate syrup should you measure?

    F. $10\frac{2}{3}$ cups

    G. 11 cups

    H. $11\frac{2}{3}$ cups

    J. $12\frac{2}{3}$ cups

    K. $13\frac{1}{3}$ cups

5. As a forest technician, you need to find the number of trees that can be harvested in a large forest. The forest is divided into 25 equal sized areas. You count 40 trees in one area. What is the best estimate of the number of trees in the forest?

A. 15

B. 65

C. 100

D. 1,000

E. 10,000

6. As a park ranger, you monitor the daily temperature. Today's high temperature was 34°F. After taking the last temperature reading of the day, a fellow ranger comments that the temperature has dropped 16°F from the high. What is the temperature at the end of the day?

F. −50°F

G. −28°F

H. −18°F

J. 18°F

K. 50°F

7. As an operator in a chemical plant, you tend a separating machine. After you fill the tank, the content settles for $1\frac{1}{2}$ hours before the liquid is removed. You fill the tank at 1:45 A.M. When do you remove the liquid?

A. 2:15 A.M.

B. 2:45 A.M.

C. 3:00 A.M.

D. 3:15 A.M.

E. 3:45 A.M.

8. You are a textile cutter making a jacket. You need three sections of fabric for the jacket pattern. The lengths of these sections are 35 inches, 28 inches, and 12 inches. What is total length of fabric that you need?

F. 35 inches

G. 47 inches

H. 63 inches

J. 75 inches

K. 105 inches

9. You are a customer service representative for an online store. You have to add 5% for sales tax. How much tax do you add for each dollar of the purchase?

    A. $0.05

    B. $0.07

    C. $0.10

    D. $0.15

    E. $0.50

10. As a butcher in a grocery store, you need to package ground beef. You have 72 pounds of beef. Each package holds 3 pounds. How many packages will you make?

    F. 24

    G. 69

    H. 72

    J. 75

    K. 216

11. As a farmworker, you are loading a spreader with fertilizer. Each bag holds 60 pounds. You need 420 pounds to treat the whole field. How many bags should you load?

    A. 6

    B. 7

    C. 8

    D. 70

    E. 480

12. You recently opened a new checking account for your furniture finishing business. Today you make two withdrawals of $120 and $275 from the account. What is the net total of your transactions today?

    F. −$395

    G. −$155

    H. $155

    J. $395

    K. $405

13. Your job in a plastics factory is to heat treat the final products. You must start by treating a particular part at 150°C. Then the temperature is decreased by 35°C. What is the second treatment temperature?

    A. 35°C

    B. 115°C

    C. 125°C

    D. 150°C

    E. 185°C

14. You are a medical secretary in a doctor's office. A patient has insurance that covers a visit with the doctor. The insurance requires a payment of 20% of the total bill by the patient. What fraction of the bill do you collect from the patient?

    F. $\frac{1}{6}$

    G. $\frac{1}{5}$

    H. $\frac{1}{4}$

    J. $\frac{1}{3}$

    K. $\frac{1}{2}$

15. You are a landscaper who is planting a flower garden. You need 9 small bulbs for each square foot. The area of the garden is 27 square feet. How many bulbs will you plant?

    A. 3

    B. 18

    C. 36

    D. 81

    E. 243

16. You are a health care worker who works in a cardiologist's office. The doctor orders a cardiac stress test for a patient where the patient will exercise on a treadmill while being monitored by an EKG. The intensity of the exercise should be increased every 1 minute, 20 seconds. Your stopwatch only records time in seconds. Which is the same as that amount of time?

    F. 20 seconds

    G. 60 seconds

    H. 80 seconds

    J. 120 seconds

    K. 140 seconds

17. You work as a cashier at a roadside produce stand. When you close the stand, you count the money in the cash box. You count two $20 bills, six $5 bills, twelve $1 bills, and 13 quarters. What amount should you record for the day's sales?

    A. $65.25

    B. $82

    C. $84.25

    D. $85.25

    E. $85.75

18. In your role as a claims examiner, you are responsible for paying claims. The account balance is $7,924. You write checks totaling $8,126. What is the ending net balance in the account?

    F. −$16,050

    G. −$1,808

    H. −$202

    J. $202

    K. $16,050

Penny 1¢ $0.01
Nickel 5¢ $0.05
Dime 10¢ $0.10
Quarter 25¢ $0.25

19. You are a clerk at a souvenir store. A customer buys three postcards that come to a total of $1.50. Which of the following is the correct payment for the purchase?

    A. 8 dimes and 3 nickels

    B. 3 quarters and 5 nickels

    C. 3 quarters and 3 dimes

    D. 1 dollar bill and 4 dimes

    E. 6 quarters

20. As a maintenance worker, you are installing a fence post for a fence that is 4 feet tall. The fence post is 6 feet. If the top of the fence is supposed to be in line with the top of the fence post, how deep should you dig the hole for the post?

    F. −10 feet

    G. −2 feet

    H. 2 feet

    J. 4 feet

    K. 10 feet

21. You are working as an order clerk for a sheet metal shop. The sheet metal workers need a special nut and bolt combination. Each bolt costs 85 cents. The nut that fits the bolt costs 50 cents. What is the cost of each nut and bolt pair?

    A. $0.35

    B. $1.00

    C. $1.35

    D. $1.70

    E. $2.20

22. As a tire builder, you add new tread to used tires. You check the tread on a tire before the rubber is treated. The tread must be 1.25 inches deep. Your gauge shows measurements as a fraction of an inch. What is the correct tread depth?

    F. $1\frac{1}{16}$ inches

    G. $1\frac{1}{8}$ inches

    H. $1\frac{1}{4}$ inches

    J. $1\frac{3}{8}$ inches

    K. $1\frac{1}{2}$ inches

23. In your work as a crane operator, you require that clients schedule your service in advance. A client asks you to come to a job site in two weeks. Today is April 5. On what day should you go to the job site?

    A. April 12

    B. April 14

    C. April 19

    D. April 21

    E. April 26

24. You work as a ship loader. One bag of sand weighs 100 pounds. You must pour out some sand into a second bag so that the first bag weighs 85 pounds. What is the weight of the sand that must be poured out?

    F. −15 pounds

    G. −14 pounds

    H. −10 pounds

    J. 10 pounds

    K. 15 pounds

25. You are a mixing machine setter for a company that makes food for livestock. One recipe for a large batch of feed uses $4\frac{1}{4}$ pounds of dry milk powder. Your machine controls use decimal numbers. What setting do you use for the scale that measures the milk powder?

    A.   4.20 pounds

    B.   4.25 pounds

    C.   4.40 pounds

    D.   4.50 pounds

    E.   4.75 pounds

26. You work as a stock clerk in an office supply warehouse. At the beginning of the week, you had 20 televisions in stock. During the week, 10 televisions were shipped out of the warehouse to a local store. How many televisions will show up on the end-of-week inventory printout?

    F.   −20

    G.   −10

    H.   10

    J.   20

    K.   30

27. As part of your job as a nursing aide in a hospital, you record how much water a patient drinks. This morning you refill the water container 3 times and record the amount that the patient drinks each time. You write down $1\frac{1}{2}$ cups, 2 cups, and $1\frac{1}{2}$ cups. You add the amounts and get $4\frac{2}{2}$ cups. What number should you report?

    A.   3 cups

    B.   4 cups

    C. $4\frac{1}{4}$ cups

    D.   5 cups

    E. $5\frac{1}{2}$ cups

28. The classrooms in the building where you teach preschool are rented by the school. You are allowed to keep pets in your classroom for a rent increase of 10%. Which fraction shows the amount of the extra charge?

    F. $\frac{1}{1,000}$

    G. $\frac{1}{100}$

    H. $\frac{1}{10}$

    J. $\frac{1}{5}$

    K.   1

Answers are on page 233.

Level 4 Introduction ...

The lesson and practice pages that follow will give you the opportunity to develop and practice the mathematical skills needed to solve work-related problems at a Level 4 rating of difficulty. The *On Your Own* practice problems provide a review of math skills and instruction for specific problem-solving strategies. The *Performance Assessment* provides problems similar to those you will encounter on a Career Readiness Certificate test. By completing the Level 4 *On Your Own* and *Performance Assessment* problems, you will gain the ability to confidently approach workplace scenarios that require understanding and application of the skills featured in the following lessons:

Lesson 5: Add Fractions, Decimals, and Percents

Lesson 6: Add Fractions in Common Terms

Lesson 7: Multiply Mixed Numbers

Lesson 8: Find Averages, Ratios, Proportions, and Rates

Lesson 9: Solve Problems Using One or Two Operations

Lesson 10: Put Information in the Right Order

Lesson 11: Multiply Negative Numbers

These skills are intended to help you successfully understand and solve problems requiring mathematics in the workplace that involve using fractions, decimals, and percents; performing one or two operations and putting information in the correct order before performing calculations; and performing calculations using negative numbers. Solving these types of problems often requires the ability to:

- reorder information presented in the question to solve the problem,
- identify and exclude unnecessary information,
- read and use information from charts, graphs, or diagrams.

Through solving problems at this level, you will continue to develop problem-solving approaches and strategies that will help you determine the correct answer in real-world and test-taking situations.

Converting a Percentage to a Fraction

A percentage is a number that tells a part of a whole in which the whole is always 100. To convert a percentage to a fraction, simply write the percentage (numerator) over 100 (denominator).

$$50\% = \frac{50}{100}$$

Converting a Percentage to a Decimal

To convert a percentage to a decimal, you follow the same steps as when converting a percentage to a fraction. Once you have set up the fraction, simply divide the numerator by the denominator.

$$25\% = 25 \div 100 = 0.25$$

Note that the decimal is "twenty-five hundredths," which is equal to $\frac{25}{100}$.

$$25\% = 0.25 = \frac{25}{100}$$

Lesson 5 ∎∎∎
Add Fractions, Decimals, and Percents

Skill: Add commonly known fractions, decimals, or percentages

In performing workforce calculations, you may need to add common fractions, decimals, or percentages. When adding money, such as items listed on an invoice, you are adding decimals. When adding measured amounts, such as recipe ingredients or construction materials, you may be adding fractions. Knowing how to calculate with fractions, decimals, and percentages is an important workplace skill.

Skill Examples

Example 1
Add fractions with like terms.

Add: $\frac{1}{4} + \frac{1}{4}$

To add fractions, make sure the bottom numbers, or denominators, are the same. Remember that the numerator tells the number of "parts" you have, so only the numerators are added. You may need to simplify the answer to lowest terms. This should be done whenever both the numerator and denominator can be divided by the same number.

$$\frac{1}{4} + \frac{1}{4} = \frac{2 \div 2}{4 \div 2} = \frac{1}{2}$$

Example 2
Add decimals.

Add: 0.25 + 2.75

To add decimals, first align the numbers by place value. The digit to the left of the decimal is the one's place value and the digit to the right of the decimal is the tenth's place value. Then, add the numbers as you would any other numbers.

$$
\begin{array}{r}
0.25 \\
+\ 2.75 \\
\hline
3.00 \text{ or } 3
\end{array}
$$

Skill Practice

A. Add two common fractions whose sum is greater than 1. $\frac{1}{2} + \frac{3}{4}$ = _____

B. Add common decimals.   0.25 + 0.50 = _____

C. Add percentages.   25% + 15% = _____

Try It Out! ▪ ▪ ▪

In your position as a cost estimator, you determine the cost of installing carpet. This month only, the company is offering a huge savings of half off the total cost of installation. A customer who is purchasing installation has a coupon for 15% off the total cost of installation. After reviewing the restrictions of both offers, you determine that the two offers can be combined. What is the total percent off the customer will receive for the total cost of installation?

A. 20%   B. 35%   C. 40%   D. 50%   E. 65%

Step 1 Understand the Problem ▪ ▪ ▪

Complete the *Plan for Successful Solving*.

Plan for Successful Solving

What am I asked to do?	What are the facts?	How do I find the answer?	Is there any unnecessary information?	What prior knowledge will help me?
Find the total percent off the cost of installation.	Coupon is 15% off. Company discount is half off. Offers can be combined.	I need to add the two amounts. I first need to convert the fraction to a percentage.	The company offer is for this month only.	One-half is written as $\frac{1}{2}$. Divide the numerator by the denominator to convert a fraction to a decimal.

Step 2 Find and Check Your Answer ▪ ▪ ▪

- Confirm your understanding of the problem and revise your plan as needed.

- Based on your plan, determine your solution approach: *I will first convert the fraction ($\frac{1}{2}$) to a decimal and then the decimal to a percent so that my numbers are in the same terms. I will then add the percent discount of the coupon and the percent discount the company is offering to find the total discount.*

  $\frac{1}{2} = 1 \div 2 = 0.5$ ◄----- Convert the fraction to a decimal.

  $0.5 \times 100\% = 50\%$ ◄----- Multiply by 100% to convert the decimal to a percentage.

  $50\% + 15\% = 65\%$ ◄----- Add the percentages and solve.

- Check your answer. The answer is written as a percent.

- **Select the correct answer:** E. 65%

  By converting the company discount to a percentage and adding this to the percentage discount offered by the coupon, you find the total percentage off the original price.

Problem Solving Tip

Key words within word problems often give clues about which operation should be used. In the *Try It Out!* example, the word *combined* indicates that addition should be used to find the answer.

Remember!

To convert fractions to percentages, first divide the numerator by the denominator to find the decimal equivalent. The decimal can then be multiplied by 100% to find the equivalent percentage.

On Your Own ▪ ▪ ▪

1. You are employed as a private chef. You are making a recipe that calls for $1\frac{1}{2}$ cups white flour and $\frac{1}{2}$ cup wheat flour. What is the total amount of flour in the recipe?

    A. $\frac{3}{4}$ cup

    B. 1 cup

    C. $1\frac{2}{4}$ cups

    D. 2 cups

    E. 6 cups

2. As the owner of a pottery studio, you have asked your assistant to make a clay pot for a customer. The total diameter of the pot must be 6 inches. The inside diameter of the finished pot measures 5 inches. The rim of the pot measures $\frac{1}{4}$ inch. Does the finished pot meet the customer's guidelines?

    F. No, the pot has a total diameter of $5\frac{1}{4}$ inches.

    G. No, the pot has a total diameter of $5\frac{1}{2}$ inches.

    H. Yes, the pot has a total diameter of 6 inches.

    J. No, the pot has a total diameter of $6\frac{1}{2}$ inches.

    K. No, the pot has a total diameter of 7 inches.

3. You are an assistant to the head of the history department at the local college. Freshmen at your school are required to take one history class during their first year. This chart shows the percentage of freshmen in each of the three introductory history courses. What is the total percentage of freshmen enrolled in American History and European History?

Course	Percentage of Freshmen
American History	35%
European History	40%
Ancient History	25%

    A. 25%

    B. 35%

    C. 40%

    D. 65%

    E. 75%

4. You work as a licensed practical nurse and must monitor the weight loss of patients. One patient lost 5.75 pounds in the first month. He lost 4.5 pounds in the second month. What is his total weight loss after 2 months?

    F. 1.25 pounds

    G. 1.5 pounds

    H. 9.25 pounds

    J. 10.20 pounds

    K. 10.25 pounds

5. As a tool grinder, you make sure tools meet specifications. You use a grinding machine to take off 0.75 millimeter of metal from a tool. Then you grind off another 0.25 millimeter. By how much did you reduce the size of the tool?

    A. 0.25 millimeter

    B. 0.75 millimeter

    C. 0.9 millimeter

    D. 1 millimeter

    E. 1.5 millimeters

6. Part of your work as a design consultant is to provide cost estimations for landscape projects. A customer wants two pansy shrubs and one rose shrub. What is the estimated cost?

Shrub	Cost (Estimate)
Daisy	$18.50
Lilac	$15.25
Pansy	$13.75
Rose	$10.25

    F. $24.00

    G. $25.50

    H. $34.25

    J. $37.75

    K. $40.75

7. You are a production inspector. In a batch of 1,000 units, 15% of the units have bad wiring. An additional 5% of the units lack insulation. Also, 5% of the units have loose computer chips. What percent of the units are defective?

    A. 20%

    B. 25%

    C. 75%

    D. 200%

    E. 1,975%

8. As a head baker for a catering company, you are making three different desserts. The cupcakes require $4\frac{1}{2}$ cups flour. The brownies require $3\frac{1}{4}$ cups flour. The cookies require $4\frac{1}{4}$ cups sugar. How much flour do you need?

    F. $7\frac{1}{3}$ cups

    G. $7\frac{1}{2}$ cups

    H. $7\frac{3}{4}$ cups

    J. $8\frac{5}{6}$ cups

    K. $12\frac{1}{2}$ cups

9. You are cutting out a pattern for a box. What size of cardboard do you need to make the box shown?

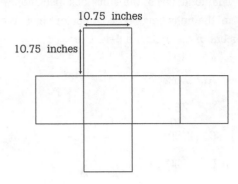

10.75 inches

10.75 inches

- A. 10.75 inches × 10.75 inches
- B. 21.50 inches × 32.25 inches
- C. 32.25 inches × 41.5 inches
- D. 43 inches × 32.25 inches
- E. 64.5 inches × 43 inches

10. As an accounting clerk at a bank, you need to know the prime rate. It is currently 3.25%. It is expected to increase 0.25% each month. What will the prime rate be 3 months from today?

- F. 3.5%
- G. 4%
- H. 4.25%
- J. 5%
- K. 9.75%

11. You are a construction worker building a fence around a rectangular area that is 6.25 meters × 8.50 meters. How much fencing do you need to enclose the area?

- A. 14.75 meters
- B. 15 meters
- C. 21 meters
- D. 23.5 meters
- E. 29.5 meters

12. One of your responsibilities as a statistical assistant is to monitor an area of growth of chestnut plants. How many pounds of the plant were removed in Connecticut (CT)?

Lake	State	Pounds removed
Blue Cove	MA	1,000.05
West River	MA	945.25
East River	MA	189.00
Mill Pond	CT	565.75
Fast Brook	CT	445.50

- F. 1,011.25 pounds
- G. 1,134.25 pounds
- H. 2,134.30 pounds
- J. 2,579.80 pounds
- K. 3,145.55 pounds

13. You are a boilermaker working with sheet metal. You are measuring the sheet metal to locate and mark bend and cut marks. From the edge of a sheet of metal, you measure 63.25 centimeters to mark a bend. You measure another 15.50 centimeters to mark a cut. What is the total length from the edge of the sheet to the cut mark?

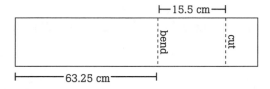

    A. 47.45 centimeters

    B. 78.25 centimeters

    C. 78.50 centimeters

    D. 78.75 centimeters

    E. 79 centimeters

14. You work as a quality control inspector of shirts for a clothing manufacturing company. Today, you examine one batch and 15% fail because of holes or tears. An additional 5% fail because the color is off and 3% more fail because of missing buttons. What percent of the products failed inspection?

    F. 8%

    G. 18%

    H. 20%

    J. 23%

    K. 25%

15. One of your responsibilities as an architectural drafter is to determine the percent of open space on the second level of an office building. The level has been designed to have four zones of equal size. Zone 1 has 15% open space, Zone 2 has 5%, Zone 3 has 10%, and Zone 4 has 20%. What percent of the second level is open space?

    A. 20%

    B. 25%

    C. 30%

    D. 35%

    E. 50%

16. As a baker, you measure ingredients to make batters. You need $2\frac{1}{2}$ cups flour for each batch. You need 1 cup butter for each batch. How many cups of flour do you need for three batches?

    F. $2\frac{1}{2}$ cups

    G. 4 cups

    H. $4\frac{1}{2}$ cups

    J. 5 cups

    K. $7\frac{1}{2}$ cups

Answers are on page 237.

A fraction is a number that tells how much of a whole you have. The denominator is the bottom number of a fraction and tells the total number of parts in one whole. The numerator is the top number of a fraction and tells the number of parts.

Fractions can be used to describe:

Part of a whole

The whole is divided into 12 equal-sized pieces.

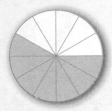

$\frac{5}{12}$ of the whole is not shaded

$\frac{7}{12}$ of the whole is shaded

Part of a set

There are 8 circles in the whole set.

$\frac{6}{8}$ of the circles are shaded

$\frac{2}{8}$ of the circles are not shaded

Distance along a number line

An inch is often divided into sixteenths.

0    $\frac{1}{4}$ $\frac{1}{2}$ $\frac{3}{4}$ 1 inch

The bar is $\frac{9}{16}$ inch long.

Lesson 6
Add Fractions in Common Terms

Skill: Add up to three fractions that share a common denominator

In performing workplace calculations, you may need to add fractions. Fractions are commonly used when measuring length, weight, and volume. They also are sometimes used when dividing something such as land or materials into equal portions.

When adding fractions, you must first be certain that the fractions all share a common denominator.

Skill Examples

Example 1
Add fractions with like terms.

Add: $\frac{3}{9} + \frac{1}{9} + \frac{4}{9}$

All of these fractions are in equal or "like" terms because they are all written in ninths. The whole is divided into nine equal parts, and each fraction tells how many of those parts you have. To add these fractions, add the numerators to find the total number of ninths.

$$\frac{3}{9} + \frac{1}{9} + \frac{4}{9} = \frac{3 + 1 + 4}{9} = \frac{8}{9}$$

Example 2
Add fractions with unlike terms.

Add: $\frac{1}{4} + \frac{1}{2}$

These fractions are not written in the same terms. Before adding them, they must be put into equal terms.

$$\frac{1}{2} = \frac{2}{4}, \text{ so}$$

$$\frac{1}{4} + \frac{1}{2} = \frac{1}{4} + \frac{2}{4}$$

$$\frac{1}{4} + \frac{2}{4} = \frac{1 + 2}{4} = \frac{3}{4}$$

Skill Practice

A. Add fractions with common denominators (like terms).

$\frac{2}{5} + \frac{2}{5}$ = _____

B. Add fractions without common denominators (unlike terms).

$\frac{3}{8} + \frac{1}{4}$ = _____

C. Add fractions that add up to a total greater than 1.

$\frac{2}{9} + \frac{5}{9} + \frac{4}{9}$ = _____

Try It Out! ■ ■ ■

As part of your work in the business office of a large corporation, you are responsible for drafting leases on a vacant piece of land in Center City. Center City has a vacant piece of land that residents can lease to plant a garden. The land includes a patch of blueberry bushes covering $\frac{2}{16}$ of the land. Amy decides to lease $\frac{1}{16}$ of the land, Jona leases $\frac{1}{2}$ of the land, and Roy leases $\frac{5}{16}$ of the land. How much of the land is leased for gardening?

A. $\frac{40}{4,096}$ B. $\frac{8}{50}$ C. $\frac{15}{64}$ D. $\frac{7}{16}$ E. $\frac{7}{8}$

Step 1 Understand the Problem ■ ■ ■

Complete the *Plan for Successful Solving.*

Plan for Successful Solving

What am I asked to do?	What are the facts?	How do I find the answer?	Is there any unnecessary information?	What prior knowledge will help me?
Find how much of the land is leased.	Amy: $\frac{1}{16}$ Jona: $\frac{1}{2}$ Roy: $\frac{5}{16}$	Add the fractions.	Blueberry patch covers $\frac{2}{16}$ of the land	Fractions must be in equal terms before calculating.

Step 2 Find and Check Your Answer ■ ■ ■

- Confirm your understanding of the problem and revise your plan as needed.

- Based on your plan, determine your solution approach: *I am going to put all fractions into like terms. Then I am going to add the amount of space each person has leased.*

Blueberry Patch	Amy's Garden	Jona's Garden	
Roy's Garden			

$\frac{1}{2} = \frac{8}{16}$ ◄······ Convert fractions to like terms.

$\frac{1}{16} + \frac{8}{16} + \frac{5}{16} = \frac{1 + 8 + 5}{16} = \frac{14}{16}$ ◄······ Add the numerators and solve.

$\frac{14}{16} = \frac{7}{8}$ ◄······ If necessary, simplify to lowest terms.

- Check your answer. Refer to your diagram and count how many of the 16 sections are leased to Amy, Roy, and Jona. The total should be 14 of the 16 sections.

- **Select the correct answer:** E. $\frac{7}{8}$
  By converting all fractions to like terms, you can add the numerators. By simplifying the answer to lowest terms, you find that $\frac{7}{8}$ of the land is leased.

Problem Solving Tip

Drawing a diagram may help you solve the problem. In the *Try It Out!* example, the diagram shows the piece of land divided into 16 equally sized sections.

Remember!

When working with problems involving fractions, the answers will most likely be listed in lowest terms.

On Your Own ▪ ▪ ▪

1. You work in a photography studio framing pictures. A customer has asked you to frame a square photograph with overlapping border mats. The visible width of the blue mat is $\frac{5}{16}$ inch and the visible width of the beige mat is $\frac{9}{16}$ inch. What is the total width of the visible border mats?

   A. $\frac{45}{256}$ inch

   B. $\frac{1}{4}$ inch

   C. $\frac{7}{16}$ inch

   D. $\frac{21}{25}$ inch

   E. $\frac{7}{8}$ inch

2. You are a pastry chef at a bakery. The apple pie recipe you are following uses $\frac{3}{4}$ teaspoon cinnamon. Today you have to complete orders for three apple pies, but you first want to see if you have enough cinnamon to fulfill the orders. How much cinnamon will you need to make the three pies?

   F. $\frac{3}{12}$ teaspoon

   G. $\frac{9}{12}$ teaspoon

   H. $\frac{6}{8}$ teaspoon

   J. $\frac{6}{4}$ teaspoons

   K. $2\frac{1}{4}$ teaspoons

Use the following information for items 3–5:

As the carpenter on a project, you have been asked to drill holes in studs for pipes and wires to pass through. There needs to be $\frac{1}{4}$-inch clearance around the pipes and wires.

3. The main hot and cold water pipes have a diameter of $\frac{3}{4}$ inch. What is the diameter of the holes you will need to drill to run these pipes?

   A. $\frac{5}{12}$ inch

   B. $\frac{1}{2}$ inch

   C. $\frac{3}{4}$ inch

   D. 1 inch

   E. $1\frac{1}{4}$ inches

4. The smaller supply line pipes have a diameter of $\frac{3}{8}$ inch. What is the diameter of the holes you will need to drill to run these pipes?

   F. $\frac{5}{16}$ inch

   G. $\frac{4}{12}$ inch

   H. $\frac{5}{8}$ inch

   J. $\frac{7}{8}$ inch

   K. 1 inch

5. The wiring used for the house's sound system has a diameter of $\frac{1}{4}$ inch. What is the diameter of the holes you need to drill to pass the wire through?

A. $\frac{1}{4}$ inch

B. $\frac{3}{8}$ inch

C. $\frac{1}{2}$ inch

D. $\frac{3}{4}$ inch

E. 1 inch

6. As a metal fabricator, you have just shaped a piece of 13 gauge aluminum into a can. The two ends overlap slightly to make the cylinder. The thickness of the 13 gauge aluminum is $\frac{72}{1,000}$ inch. What is the thickness at the overlap?

F. 0 inch

G. $\frac{26}{1,000}$ inch

H. $\frac{144}{2,000}$ inch

J. $\frac{144}{1,000}$ inch

K. 26 inches

Use the table below for items 7–8.

You are inspecting sheets of metal. The thickness of the sheet should be within $\frac{100}{10,000}$ of the indicated thickness for each gauge.

Gauge	Thickness	
	inch	**mm**
6	$\frac{2,031}{10,000}$	5.16
7	$\frac{1,875}{10,000}$	4.76
8	$\frac{1,719}{10,000}$	4.37
9	$\frac{1,563}{10,000}$	3.97

7. What is the maximum thickness of a 6 gauge sheet of metal?

A. $\frac{2,131}{20,000}$ inches

B. $\frac{1,663}{10,000}$ inches

C. $\frac{1,931}{10,000}$ inches

D. $\frac{1,975}{10,000}$ inches

E. $\frac{2,131}{10,000}$ inches

8. What is the maximum thickness of an 8 gauge sheet of metal?

F. $\frac{1,819}{20,000}$ inch

G. $\frac{2,131}{20,000}$ inch

H. $\frac{1,619}{10,000}$ inch

J. $\frac{1,819}{10,000}$ inch

K. $\frac{1,931}{10,000}$ inch

9. You work as an upholsterer. The chair you are upholstering needs its seat cushion replaced. The original cushion was $2\frac{1}{4}$ inches thick. Currently you have foam padding in three thicknesses: $\frac{3}{4}$ inch, $1\frac{1}{2}$ inch, and $\frac{3}{8}$ inch. What combination of padding should you use to make a new seat cushion with the same thickness as the old?

   A. $\frac{3}{4}$ inch + $\frac{3}{4}$ inch + $\frac{3}{8}$ inch

   B. $\frac{3}{4}$ inch + $\frac{3}{4}$ inch

   C. $\frac{3}{4}$ inch + $\frac{3}{8}$ inch

   D. $1\frac{1}{2}$ inches + $\frac{3}{8}$ inch + $\frac{3}{8}$ inch

   E. $1\frac{1}{2}$ inches + $1\frac{1}{2}$ inches

10. As an upholsterer, you need to determine how much fabric is needed to make seat covers. You are covering a piece of wood that is 10 inches × 10 inches × $2\frac{1}{4}$ inches. You need at least $\frac{5}{8}$ inch of extra fabric on all sides. What are the minimum dimensions needed for the piece of fabric that will be used to cover the top (10 inches × 10 inches) part of the wood?

   F.   10 inches × 10 inches

   G. $10\frac{5}{8}$ inches × $10\frac{5}{8}$ inches

   H. $11\frac{1}{4}$ inches × $11\frac{1}{4}$ inches

   J. $12\frac{1}{4}$ inches × $12\frac{1}{4}$ inches

   K. $20\frac{5}{8}$ inches × $20\frac{5}{8}$ inches

11. You work at an engine assembly facility. You are responsible for checking the gap distance in spark plugs. The gap for spark plugs cannot be more than $\frac{3}{10}$ millimeter over or under the specification gap. The specifications for spark plugs set the gap at $\frac{7}{10}$ millimeter. What is the acceptable maximum gap distance?

   A. $\frac{21}{100}$ millimeter

   B. $\frac{2}{5}$ millimeter

   C. $\frac{1}{2}$ millimeter

   D.   1 millimeter

   E. $\frac{7}{3}$ millimeters

12. You are a carpenter building a railing for a piece of a deck. The four balusters are each 3 inches wide. The gap between each baluster is $2\frac{5}{16}$ inch. Based on the diagram below, what length will you need to cut the wood for rail A if this side will contain 4 balusters?

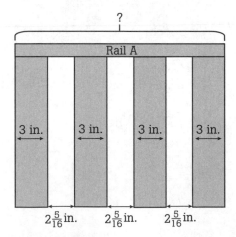

   F. $5\frac{5}{16}$ inches

   G. $6\frac{15}{16}$ inches

   H.   12 inches

   J. $18\frac{15}{16}$ inches

   K. $21\frac{1}{4}$ inches

Use the following graph for items 13 and 14.

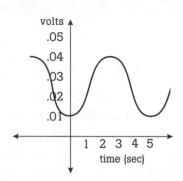

13. You are an electric line installer. You use an oscilloscope to read the electrical signal in an electrical circuit. The maximum amplitude of the curve for an acceptable signal is .040 volt with a tolerance of $\pm\frac{3}{1,000}$ volt. What is the maximum amplitude of the curve?

    A. $\frac{120}{100,000}$ volt

    B. $\frac{43}{2,000}$ volt

    C. $\frac{37}{1,000}$ volt

    D. $\frac{43}{1,000}$ volt

    E. $\frac{43}{100}$ volt

14. As an electric line installer, you use an oscilloscope to read the electrical signal in an electrical circuit. The minimum amplitude of the curve for an acceptable signal is .010 volt with a tolerance of $\pm\frac{3}{1,000}$ volt. What is the highest tolerance for the minimum amplitude of the curve?

    F. $\frac{30}{100,000}$ volt

    G. $\frac{13}{2,000}$ volt

    H. $\frac{7}{1,000}$ volt

    J. $\frac{13}{1,000}$ volt

    K. $\frac{13}{100}$ volt

15. You are the chef at a local restaurant. Tonight's special entrée calls for $\frac{1}{4}$ pound of cubed filet. You have just received 9 orders for the special entrée. How much filet will you need to fulfill the orders?

    A. $\frac{1}{36}$ pound

    B. $\frac{9}{36}$ pound

    C. $2\frac{1}{4}$ pounds

    D. 9 pounds

    E. $9\frac{1}{4}$ pounds

16. You work for a jeweler who is setting a triangular shaped stone for a necklace. The stone measures $\frac{1}{2}$ inch on two sides and $\frac{5}{8}$ inch on the third side. He asks you to cut him a piece of silver to go around the stone. How long is the piece of silver?

    F. $\frac{13}{24}$ inch

    G. $\frac{7}{12}$ inch

    H. $\frac{6}{10}$ inch

    J. $1\frac{1}{8}$ inches

    K. $1\frac{5}{8}$ inches

Answers are on page 237.

Remember!

Decimals are named by their ending place value (tenths, hundredths, thousandths, etc.). This makes it easy to convert decimals to fractions.

0.3	"3 tenths"	$\frac{3}{10}$
0.76	"76 hundredths"	$\frac{76}{100}$
0.923	"923 thousandths"	$\frac{923}{1,000}$
1.7	"1 and 7 tenths"	$1\frac{7}{10}$

Multiply Fractions by Fractions

When you multiply a fraction by another fraction, the result is the product of the numerators over the product of the denominators.

$$\frac{4}{5} \times \frac{2}{3} = \frac{4 \times 2}{5 \times 3} = \frac{8}{15}$$

Multiply Fractions by Whole Numbers

A whole number is the same as a fraction whose denominator is 1.

$$\frac{4}{5} \times 2 = \frac{4}{5} \times \frac{2}{1} = \frac{4 \times 2}{5 \times 1} = \frac{8}{5} = 1\frac{3}{5}$$

Multiply Fractions by Decimals

To multiply a fraction by a decimal, convert the fraction to a decimal.

$$\frac{1}{2} \times .25 = .5 \times .25 = .125$$

Lesson 7 ■ ■ ■
Multiply Mixed Numbers

Skill: Multiply a mixed number by a whole number or decimal

A mixed number is a number that includes a whole number and a fraction, such as $2\frac{1}{3}$. In many jobs, you may have to multiply mixed numbers by whole numbers, fractions, or decimals. For example, when ordering products, you may need to multiply a specific amount of money, written as decimal numbers, by the number of items. When making multiple batches of a recipe, a baker may need to multiply mixed numbers, such as the number of cups of flour in a cake, by the number of batches that are being made.

Skill Examples

Example 1
Multiply a mixed number by a whole number.

Multiply: $4 \times 2\frac{1}{8}$

$$2\frac{1}{8} = \left(2 + \frac{1}{8}\right)$$ ◄····· Convert the mixed number to a whole number plus a fraction.

$$4 \times \left(2 + \frac{1}{8}\right) = (4 \times 2) + \left(4 \times \frac{1}{8}\right) =$$ ◄····· Multiply each by 4.

$$(4 \times 2) + \left(\frac{4}{1} \times \frac{1}{8}\right) = 8 + \frac{4}{8}$$

$$8 + \frac{4}{8} = 8\frac{4}{8} = 8\frac{1}{2}$$ ◄····· Add and simplify to lowest terms.

Example 2
Multiply a mixed number by a decimal.*

Multiply: $4\frac{1}{2} \times 0.75$

$$4\frac{1}{2} = 4.5$$ ◄····· Convert the mixed number to a decimal. The fraction portion of the mixed number is converted by dividing the numerator by the denominator.

$$4.5 \times 0.75 = 3.375$$ ◄····· Multiply.

If the answer options are listed as fractions or mixed numbers, convert the product back to a mixed number and simplify to lowest terms.

Skill Practice

A. Multiply a mixed number by a fraction.

$$5\frac{1}{2} \times \frac{1}{5} = \underline{\quad\quad}$$

B. Multiply a mixed number by a whole number.

$$3\frac{3}{4} \times 2 = \underline{\quad\quad}$$

C. Multiply a mixed number by a decimal.

$$2\frac{1}{2} \times \$1.50 = \underline{\quad\quad}$$

Applied Mathematics

Try It Out! ■ ■ ■

You are an assembler cutting a base for a wall frame. You know the length of the wall. For the length of the base, you need to add $1\frac{3}{4}$ inches at each end for an additional stud. What is the total length that you need to add to the length of the wall for the base?

A. $1\frac{3}{4}$ inches   B. $3\frac{1}{2}$ inches   C. $3\frac{3}{4}$ inches   D. 4 inches   E. $4\frac{1}{2}$ inches

 Step 1 **Understand the Problem** ■ ■ ■

Complete the *Plan for Successful Solving.*

Plan for Successful Solving				
What am I asked to do?	**What are the facts?**	**How do I find the answer?**	**Is there any unnecessary information?**	**What prior knowledge will help me?**
Find the total length that needs to be added to the wall length for the base.	The additional length needed on each end of the base is $1\frac{3}{4}$ inches.	Multiply $1\frac{3}{4}$ inches by 2.	No.	$1\frac{3}{4}$ is a mixed number that can be converted into an improper fraction.

Step 2 **Find and Check Your Answer** ■ ■ ■

- Confirm your understanding of the problem and revise your plan as needed.

- Based on your plan, determine your solution approach: *I am going to convert $1\frac{3}{4}$ to a whole number plus a fraction and multiply each by 2.*

$1\frac{3}{4} = \left(1 + \frac{3}{4}\right)$ ◄······ Convert the mixed number to a whole number plus a fraction.

$2 \times \left(1 + \frac{3}{4}\right) = (2 \times 1) + \left(2 \times \frac{3}{4}\right) = (2 \times 1) + \left(\frac{2}{1} \times \frac{3}{4}\right) = 2 + \frac{6}{4}$ ◄ Multiply each by 2.

$2 + \frac{6}{4} = 2 + 1\frac{2}{4}$ ◄······ Convert the improper fraction to a mixed number.

$2 + 1\frac{2}{4} = 3\frac{2}{4} = 3\frac{1}{2}$ ◄······ Add and simplify to lowest terms.

- Check your answer. Convert $3\frac{1}{2}$ to an improper fraction and multiply by $\frac{1}{2}$, which is the opposite of multiplying by 2.

$3\frac{1}{2} = \frac{7}{2}; \frac{7}{2} \times \frac{1}{2} = \frac{7}{4} = 1\frac{3}{4}$ inches

The base must be $3\frac{1}{2}$ inches longer than the wall.

- **Select the correct answer:** B. $3\frac{1}{2}$ inches
By multiplying $1\frac{3}{4}$ inches by 2, you find that you must cut the base to be $3\frac{1}{2}$ inches longer than the wall.

Problem Solving Tip

Sometimes you can eliminate answers by checking to see if they are reasonable. For the *Try It Out!* example, you know that $1\frac{3}{4}$ is less than 2, and you know that $2 \times 2 = 4$. Because of this, you can estimate that the product of $2 \times 1\frac{3}{4}$ must be *less than* 4. Since answers D and E are both *equal to or greater than* 4, you now know these answers cannot be correct.

Remember!

You can also multiply a whole number by a mixed number by converting the mixed number to an improper fraction.

$1\frac{3}{4} = \frac{7}{4}$

Once you have converted to an improper fraction, multiply the fraction by the whole number.

$\frac{7}{4} \times 2 = \frac{7}{4} \times \frac{2}{1} = \frac{14}{4} = 3\frac{2}{4} = 3\frac{1}{2}$

On Your Own ■ ■ ■

1. You are a cake decorator at a large bakery. One batch of your chocolate frosting recipe uses $1\frac{1}{2}$ cups butter. How many cups of butter will you need to make 4 batches of the recipe?

   A. 3 cups

   B. 4 cups

   C. $4\frac{1}{2}$ cups

   D. $4\frac{3}{4}$ cups

   E. 6 cups

2. As an automotive mechanic, you are balancing a set of replacement tires. The label on the box of weights shows that each weight is $1\frac{1}{4}$ ounces. How much weight do you put on the wheels if you use 4 weights?

   F. 4 ounces

   G. $4\frac{1}{4}$ ounces

   H. $4\frac{3}{4}$ ounces

   J. 5 ounces

   K. $5\frac{1}{2}$ ounces

3. You work as a chemical technician in a manufacturing plant. You are using a pump that delivers $8\frac{1}{3}$ gallons per minute of solvent to a reaction tank. You run the pump for exactly 5 minutes. How many gallons of solvent do you transfer into the tank?

   A. 10 gallons

   B. $13\frac{1}{3}$ gallons

   C. $40\frac{1}{3}$ gallons

   D. 41 gallons

   E. $41\frac{2}{3}$ gallons

4. You are a lead carpenter repairing an old house. The original structure was made with lumber dimensions that are no longer standard measures. One beam has 5 stacked boards that are each $1\frac{3}{4}$ inches thick. What is the thickness of the beam?

   F. $4\frac{3}{4}$ inches

   G. 6 inches

   H. 7 inches

   J. $7\frac{1}{2}$ inches

   K. $8\frac{3}{4}$ inches

5. As an environmental engineering technician, you are doing a study of a toxic waste site. In the study, the waste is extracted for 24 hours using an acid solution. You extract $1\frac{1}{2}$ milliliters of waste each hour during the study. How many total milliliters of waste are extracted during the entire study?

    A. $1\frac{1}{2}$

    B. 12

    C. 24

    D. 36

    E. 48

6. You are a secretary for a floral business. You need to deposit coins from petty cash. You have $1\frac{1}{2}$ rolls of dimes. Each roll of dimes is equal to $5. What will your total deposit be?

    F. $1.50

    G. $3.00

    H. $5.00

    J. $6.50

    K. $7.50

7. In your job as a radiographer, you must set an instrument to obtain the correct image density. You use a setting of 8 for each inch thickness of tissue to be imaged. You measure the thickness of a patient's arm as $3\frac{1}{4}$ inches. What instrument setting will you use?

    A. 22

    B. 24

    C. 26

    D. 30

    E. 34

8. You are a process control programmer setting a machine to drill holes in a sheet of metal. The drill must go $\frac{3}{8}$ of the way through the sheet. The sheet is 2.5 centimeters thick. How deep should the drill be set?

    F. 0.375 centimeter

    G. 0.9375 centimeter

    H. 2.25 centimeters

    J. 2.375 centimeters

    K. 3 centimeters

9. You work as a billing clerk for a consulting company. Your company bills clients for service based on quarter-hour time units. The rate for a consulting engineer is $80 per hour. How much should you bill the client for $1\frac{3}{4}$ hours of engineering time?

    A. $60

    B. $90

    C. $100

    D. $120

    E. $140

10. You are an insulation installer. You are installing insulation that comes in bats that are $3\frac{1}{2}$ inches thick. How much clearance do you need to install 5 layers of batting?

    F. $10\frac{1}{2}$ inches

    G. $12\frac{1}{2}$ inches

    H. 16 inches

    J. $17\frac{1}{2}$ inches

    K. 19 inches

11. Working as an industrial engineering technician, you are checking the operation of a hand-operated cutting machine. An employee moves a handle on the machine to start the cutter. The operating manual says that the handle must be at least 7 inches from the blade. The company safety policy uses a distance that is $1\frac{1}{2}$ times the minimum. What distance should be between the handle and the blade?

    A. $7\frac{1}{2}$ inches

    B. $8\frac{1}{2}$ inches

    C. 9 inches

    D. $10\frac{1}{2}$ inches

    E. 11 inches

12. As a pipe fitter, you are responsible for joining two sections of pipe together. When you measure a section of pipe, you need to add enough length to fit inside the joint. The joint measures $3\frac{1}{2}$ inches. The pipe should extend $\frac{1}{4}$ of the way into the joint. How much should you add to the pipe length for the fitting?

    F. $\frac{1}{4}$ inch

    G. $\frac{7}{8}$ inch

    H. $1\frac{1}{8}$ inches

    J. $1\frac{1}{4}$ inches

    K. $1\frac{3}{4}$ inches

13. As a payroll clerk, you calculate the pay for overtime work. Overtime pay is $1\frac{1}{2}$ times the normal rate. What is the overtime pay rate for an employee whose normal rate is $16.50 per hour?

    A. $17.00

    B. $22.00

    C. $24.50

    D. $24.75

    E. $33.00

14. You work as the assistant to a project architect. Part of your job is to prepare invoices for the architect with whom you work. The architect bills clients on an hourly basis. He spends $38\frac{1}{6}$ hours on one job and charges $60 per hour. How much will you bill the client for this job?

    F. $229

    G. $2,280

    H. $2,290

    J. $2,390

    K. $22,900

15. As a medical assistant, you need to draw blood from a patient for testing. The lab runs three different tests. Each test requires $2\frac{1}{4}$ cubic centimeters of blood. What is the minimum amount of blood needed?

    A. $3\frac{1}{12}$ cubic centimeters

    B. $6\frac{1}{4}$ cubic centimeters

    C. $6\frac{1}{2}$ cubic centimeters

    D. $6\frac{3}{4}$ cubic centimeters

    E. $7\frac{1}{2}$ cubic centimeters

16. You are a dispatcher for a company that sells landscape stones. Each of your small delivery trucks can carry $5\frac{1}{2}$ tons of stone. A driver can make 6 local deliveries in the small delivery truck in one day. How much stone can the driver deliver to a local worksite today?

    F. $11\frac{1}{2}$ tons

    G. $30\frac{1}{2}$ tons

    H. 33 tons

    J. $33\frac{1}{2}$ tons

    K. 38 tons

Answers are on page 237.

Understanding Average

In math problems, the term *average* usually refers to the arithmetic mean, as in *Skill Example 2*. It is found by adding a set of data, or values, and then dividing the sum by the number of data. By finding an average, you find the result that is typical or most expected.

Sometimes the term *average* is also used when describing a rate, such as speed. For instance, if you drive 100 miles in two hours, your average speed is 50 miles per hour (mph), which is found by dividing the total number of miles driven (100) by the number of hours (2).

Lesson 8 ...
Find Averages, Ratios, Proportions, and Rates

Skill: Calculate averages, simple ratios, simple proportions, or rates using whole numbers and decimals

In many jobs, you will work with numbers using averages, ratios, proportions, and rates. Averages are commonly used when determining how much of an item to prepare. Ratios are commonly used to show the relationship between two comparable things, such as number of students per teacher. Proportions can be used to determine if a larger item is the better deal.

Skill Examples

Example 1
Find the value of the missing term n in a proportion.

Solve for the missing term n.

$$\frac{n}{5} \times \frac{12}{30}$$ ◀······ Multiply to find equal cross products.

$$30 \times n = 60$$

$$\frac{30 \times n}{30} = \frac{60}{30}$$ ◀······ To solve for n, divide both sides of the equation by the factor being multiplied by n.

$$n = 2$$

Example 2
Find the average of a set of data.

What is the average high temperature for the week, given the following high temperatures (in °F): 94, 87, 86, 86, 80, 92, 91.

$$94 + 87 + 86 + 86 + 80 + 92 + 91 = 616$$ ◀······ Find the sum of the values.

$$616 \div 7 = 88°F$$ ◀······ Divide by the total number of values to find the average high temperature.

Skill Practice

A. Find the average of a set of numbers.

Average of 28, 34, and 40   = _____

B. Find the unknown value in a proportion.

$\frac{n}{3} = \frac{45}{9}$; $n =$ _____

C. Find a value using a rate.

How much do you make if you work 8 hours at $9.50/hour?   = _____

Applied Mathematics

Try It Out! ■ ■ ■

You are a doctor's assistant. You collect information about each patient's heart rate. You count 17 heartbeats in 15 seconds. What heart rate do you record?

A. 15 beats/minute

D. 68 beats/minute

B. 17 beats/minute

E. 110 beats/minute

C. 34 beats/minute

Step 1 Understand the Problem ■ ■ ■

Complete the *Plan for Successful Solving.*

Plan for Successful Solving

What am I asked to do?	What are the facts?	How do I find the answer?	Is there any unnecessary information?	What prior knowledge will help me?
Find the patient's heart rate.	The patient's heart beat 17 times in 15 seconds.	Set up a proportion using beats to seconds.	No.	There are 60 seconds in a minute.

Step 2 Find and Check Your Answer ■ ■ ■

- Confirm your understanding of the problem and revise your plan as needed.

- Based on your plan, determine your solution approach: *To find the number of beats per minute, I will write a proportion statement of two equal rates of beats to seconds, where one of the rates is the unknown number of beats (b) to 60 seconds. By finding the cross products and solving for b, I will know the number of times this patient's heart will beat in one minute.*

$$\frac{17 \text{ (beats)}}{15 \text{ (seconds)}} \times \frac{b \text{ (beats)}}{60 \text{ (seconds)}}$$ ◄······ Write the proportion statement for two equal ratios of beats to seconds.

$$15 \times b = 17 \times 60$$ ◄······ Multiply to find equal cross products.

$$15 \times b = 1{,}020$$ ◄······ Multiply 17×60.

$$\frac{15 \times b}{15} = \frac{1{,}020}{15}$$ ◄······ Divide both sides by 15 to solve for b.

$$b = 68 \text{ beats}$$

- Check your answer. To check this answer, replace b in the original equation with 68. The cross products should be equal.

- **Select the correct answer:**   D. 68 beats/minute
  By writing a proportion statement and multiplying to find equal cross products, you find the patient's heart rate is 68 beats per minute.

Remember!

If you calculate the per unit amount first for a single unit, you can multiply by whatever number of units you are asked to find. In the *Try It Out!* example, you know that there are 17 beats per 15 seconds. By dividing 17 by 15, you can find the number of beats per second, which is 1.13 beats/second. Knowing this rate allows you to multiply the heart rate by the number of seconds to find the number of beats for any period of time (i.e., multiply by 30 to find the number of beats in 30 seconds, by 60 to find the number of beats in 60 seconds).

Problem Solving Tip

To check the answer to proportion problems or any problem that involves solving for a missing value, replace the missing value in the original equation with the answer. If the two sides are not equal, then the answer is incorrect. The original proportion may have been set up incorrectly, or you may have calculated incorrectly.

On Your Own ■ ■ ■

1. You are a computer-aided design technician preparing a scale drawing of an office building. The scale of the drawing is 1 inch = 4 feet. The front of the building will be 120 feet long. What is the length of the building front on your drawing?

    A.   4 inches

    B.   8 inches

    C.   10 inches

    D.   30 inches

    E.   40 inches

2. As a cook in a restaurant, you have a recipe that uses 4 cups flour to make 3 dozen cookies. You want to make 15 dozen cookies. How many cups of flour will you need?

    F.   8 cups

    G.   10 cups

    H.   15 cups

    J.   18 cups

    K.   20 cups

3. In your job as an insurance sales agent, you work out the cost of life insurance. The best rate for one client is $240 per year for $100,000 of life insurance. What is the cost per year for $300,000 of life insurance for this client?

    A. $80

    B. $120

    C. $480

    D. $720

    E. $1,000

4. You are a plumber installing a pipe. The ratio of the outside diameter to the inside diameter is 1.5 to 1. You use a pipe with a 0.5-inch inside diameter. What is the smallest diameter that you will need to drill to allow the pipe to pass through a wall?

    F.   0.375 inch

    G.   0.75 inch

    H.   0.875 inch

    J.   1 inch

    K.   1.5 inches

5. In an office, you work as the purchasing manager. You are responsible for buying printer paper. Your last order of 12 cases cost $240. You will need 30 cases for this upcoming order. Assuming that the cost per case is the same as the previous order, how much will your upcoming paper order cost?

    A. $20

    B. $300

    C. $600

    D. $720

    E. $7,200

6. You work at a college cafeteria as the food service manager. You need to decide how much food to make for breakfast each day. On Monday 235 students come to breakfast. On Tuesday there are 250. On Wednesday there are 248. On Thursday there are 206. On Friday there are 236. What is the daily average number of students eating breakfast?

    F. 224

    G. 235

    H. 236

    J. 250

    K. 1,175

7. You work as a machine operator on a glass fiber extruder. The machine produces 2.6 kilometers of fiber per hour. How much fiber will the machine produce during 10 hours of a process run?

    A. 0.26 kilometer

    B. 2.6 kilometers

    C. 3.8 kilometers

    D. 26 kilometers

    E. 38 kilometers

8. You are working as an emergency medical technician. You need to give medication to a patient. The label instructs you to use 0.25 milligram for each pound of body weight. The patient weighs 150 pounds. How much medication should you give him?

    F. 3.75 milligrams

    G. 37 milligrams

    H. 37.5 milligrams

    J. 75 milligrams

    K. 150 milligrams

9. As a mechanical engineer, you are preparing a scale drawing of a machine design. Your drawing uses a scale ratio of 1 inch = 8 feet. A connecting rod in the machine is 4 feet long. How long will you make the rod in your drawing?

   A. 0.25 inch

   B. 0.5 inch

   C. 0.75 inch

   D. 1 inch

   E. 2 inches

10. You work as a materials inspector for a precision parts manufacturer. One of your tasks is to examine each part for flaws. Today's record shows that 480 parts were made. Of that total, 24 parts were rejected. What is the ratio of total parts to rejected parts?

   F. 1:100

   G. 1:50

   H. 1:20

   J. 1:5

   K. 20:1

11. You are a formulation technician in a chemical manufacturing plant. You record the weight when you transfer materials from large drums to the reaction vessel. You emptied 8 drums and recorded a total of 1,624 kilograms of material. What is the average amount of chemical in a drum?

   A. 23 kilograms

   B. 203 kilograms

   C. 230 kilograms

   D. 812 kilograms

   E. 1,624 kilograms

12. As a clinic nurse, you are setting the flow rate on a patient's oxygen cylinder. The patient needs a flow rate of 0.5 liter per minute. The cylinder can deliver 160 liters of oxygen. How long can the patient use the cylinder before it must be replaced?

   F. 80 minutes

   G. 120 minutes

   H. 160 minutes

   J. 320 minutes

   K. 1,600 minutes

13. As an administrative service manager, one of your tasks is to keep a call log of product problems. You recorded the number of calls each day for one week. There were 12 calls on Monday, 14 on Tuesday, 20 on Wednesday, 4 on Thursday, and 15 on Friday. What is the average number of calls per day?

    A. 4

    B. 13

    C. 15

    D. 18

    E. 65

14. In your work as an architectural intern, you make a scale model of an office building. The drawing shows that the building foundation is 90 feet long and 40 feet wide. Your model is 20 inches wide. How long is the model?

    F. 30 inches

    G. 40 inches

    H. 45 inches

    J. 55 inches

    K. 90 inches

15. You are a studio photographer. You are printing a photo as a large poster. The photo measures 8 inches high by 10 inches wide. The poster must be 2 meters high. How wide will it be?

    A. 1.6 meters

    B. 2.5 meters

    C. 4 meters

    D. 16 meters

    E. 40 meters

16. You are an assistant admissions director at a community college. You want to find the ratio of students to faculty members. There are 6,000 students enrolled in the school. There are 400 faculty members. What is the ratio of students to faculty at your school?

    F. 1 to 15

    G. 1 to 25

    H. 15 to 1

    J. 60 to 1

    K. 400 to 6,000

Answers are on page 237.

In the last lesson, you had a number of instances where you used two operations to solve problems.

Proportions

Multiple operations are used when solving proportions. After the proportion statement is set up, multiply to find cross products. Then divide each side of the equation by the factor being multiplied by the unknown variable to solve for the unknown variable.

$$\frac{n}{8} \times \frac{16}{40}$$

$$40 \times n = 16 \times 8$$

$$40\,n = 128;$$

$$n = \frac{128}{40} = 3\frac{1}{5}$$

Averages

Finding the average of a set of numbers also requires two operations. First, add the numbers in the set together. Then, divide that sum by the number of numbers that were added to find the average.

Find the average of this set of data: 24, 15, 12, 29.

$$24 + 15 + 12 + 29 = 80$$

Since four numbers were added to reach this sum, divide the sum by 4.

$$80 \div 4 = 20$$

Lesson 9 ▪ ▪ ▪
Solve Problems Using One or Two Operations

Skill: Solve problems that require one or two operations

When you solve mathematics problems in the workplace, you must first decide whether to add, subtract, multiply, or divide. Sometimes, one of these math operations will be enough to solve the problems. Many problems, however, require two steps to solve. For instance, you might need to calculate how much work can be done in 1 hour, and then use that amount to determine how much work can be finished in an 8-hour workday. You might need to find out how many items are needed for a construction job, where each part of the job requires a certain number of items.

Skill Examples

Example 1
Solve problems that involve addition and subtraction.

$$\$12.99 - \$3.00 + \$6.99 + \$4.79$$

Since this example requires only addition and subtraction, there is more than one way to solve. One approach is to work left to right and add or subtract each number in order. Another approach is to add the positive numbers together (items purchased) then add each negative number (discounts). Both approaches will lead to the same answer.

```
  12.99              12.99
-  3.00               6.99
 ──────            +  4.79
   9.99      OR      24.77
+  6.99            -  3.00
 ──────             21.77
  16.98
+  4.79
 ──────
  21.77
```

Example 2
Solve problems that involve multiplication and division.

$$315 \div 3 \times 11$$

Solving this example requires division and multiplication. Unlike problems that involve only addition and subtraction, this problem must be solved by working from left to right. Divide 315 by 3. Then multiply the answer by 11.

$$315 \div 3 = 105$$

$$105 \times 11 = 1,155$$

For all calculations that involve more than one operation, you must be certain to follow the correct order of operations. You will learn about the order of operations in the next lesson.

Skill Practice

A. Multiply two whole numbers, then add another whole number.

$$42 \times 178 + 3 \ = \ \underline{\hspace{2cm}}$$

B. Divide by a whole number, then subtract another whole number.

$$801 \div 9 - 11 \ = \ \underline{\hspace{2cm}}$$

Try It Out! ▪ ▪ ▪

As a banquet manager, you are in charge of ordering food. There will be 112 guests at a party next week. You need enough beans to give each person a 5-ounce serving. There are 160 ounces of beans in a can. How many cans of beans do you need?

A. 3   B. 4   C. 30   D. 40   E. 480

 Step 1 ## Understand the Problem ▪ ▪ ▪

Complete the *Plan for Successful Solving*.

Plan for Successful Solving

What am I asked to do?	What are the facts?	How do I find the answer?	Is there any unnecessary information?	What prior knowledge will help me?
Find the number of cans of beans that are needed.	There are 112 guests. Each guest needs 5 ounces of beans. Each can has 160 ounces of beans.	Multiply the number of serving ounces by the number of guests. Then divide by the number of ounces in a can.	No.	If my answer (number of cans) results in a decimal, I will need to round up to the next number.

 Step 2 ## Find and Check Your Answer ▪ ▪ ▪

▪ Confirm your understanding of the problem and revise your plan as needed.

▪ Based on your plan, determine your solution approach: *I am going to use multiplication and division to find the total number of ounces of beans needed.*

    5 ounces per serving × 112 people = 560 ounces ◂····· Multiply ounces in each serving by the number of guests.

    560 ounces ÷ 160 ounces in a can = 3.5 cans ◂····· Divide total number of ounces needed by the number of ounces in 1 can to find the number of cans needed.

    3.5 cans → 4 cans ◂····· Round up to the next whole number to solve.

▪ Check your answer. Check multiplication and division by using the opposite operations to find the original number of ounces per serving.

▪ **Select the correct answer:** B. 4
By multiplying the ounces per serving by the number of guests, you find that you need 560 ounces of beans. You must divide 560 by the number of ounces in a can to find how many cans you need. Since you cannot buy a half can, you round up to the nearest whole number.

Problem Solving Tip

By working backward and using opposite operations, you can check to see if your answer is correct. In the *Try It Out!* example, you multiplied 112 by 5 to find the total number of ounces needed, then divided by 160 to find how many cans would provide the correct amount.

$$112 \times 5 \div 160 = 3.5$$

To check your answer, start with the answer and work backward by using the opposite operations that were used to arrive at the answer.

$$3.5 \times 160 \div 5 = 112$$

The answer will be the number of people attending.

Remember!

When calculating how many items to buy, you must think about what the answer means. In most cases, if your answer includes a decimal, you must actually buy more, not less, of the item than needed. You must round up the number to the next whole number. For example, if you needed 12.1 cans of food to feed a group of people, even though 12 cans is closer to 12.1 than 13 cans is, you still must buy 13 cans to have enough to feed the group.

On Your Own ■ ■ ■

1. As an orthodontic assistant, you make 4 bottles of solution to clean dental instruments. The solution contains water and disinfectant in a ratio of 2:3. How many parts water will you need for 9 parts disinfectant?

    A. 2

    B. 3

    C. 6

    D. 8

    E. 9

2. You are a pipe fitter. You have a pipe measuring 36 inches in length. You cut a 14–inch piece from the pipe. How much pipe is left?

    F. 12 inches

    G. 18 inches

    H. 22 inches

    J. 32 inches

    K. 50 inches

3. As an assembler, you are attaching fixtures to each cabinet door in a new home. There are 12 cabinet doors in the kitchen. The kitchen fixtures are bars that each require 2 screws. There are 4 cabinet doors in the master bathroom and 2 cabinet doors in another bathroom. All of the bathroom fixtures are knobs that each require 1 screw. How many screws will you need to attach fixtures to all of the cabinets in the home?

    A. 8

    B. 10

    C. 18

    D. 22

    E. 30

4. You work as a customer service supervisor for a restaurant chain. This month you gathered survey data from each of the restaurants in your region. You visited three restaurants week 1, four restaurants week 2, two restaurants week 3, and three restaurants week 4. How many restaurants did you visit on average per week this month?

    F. 2

    G. 3

    H. 4

    J. 9

    K. 12

5. You are a collections manager for a hospital. One patient has an overdue balance of $550. If the bill is paid within 1 year, no interest fees will be charged. The patient has agreed to pay 11 monthly payments of $50. How much will the patient owe after she makes 2 monthly payments?

    A. $50

    B. $100

    C. $400

    D. $450

    E. $500

6. As a flight attendant, you must stock an airplane with food for an upcoming flight. The flight will have 96 passengers on board. Of the food being stocked, $\frac{1}{4}$ of the snacks need to be bags of pretzels, $\frac{1}{2}$ of the snacks need to be bags of peanuts, and $\frac{1}{4}$ of the snacks need to be bags of potato chips. If you stock just enough to allow for one snack per passenger, how many bags of pretzels will you need for the flight?

    F. 4

    G. 12

    H. 24

    J. 48

    K. 96

7. In your job at a dog kennel, you must build a fence around a new outdoor exercise yard. The yard is 50 feet long and 35 feet wide. On one side of the yard, you will not need fencing for the 20 feet that is bordered by the building. How much fencing do you need?

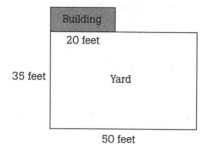

    A. 70 feet

    B. 85 feet

    C. 150 feet

    D. 170 feet

    E. 190 feet

8. You work as a data analyst for an insurance company. In March, you collected 340 surveys. You collected 408 surveys in April. You can enter 68 surveys into the database per day. How many days will you need to enter all of the surveys collected in March and April?

    F. 4

    G. 5

    H. 6

    J. 8

    K. 11

9. You are a travel agent booking a weeklong vacation for a couple. Total roundtrip airfare for 2 adults costs $1,332. The hotel room costs $1,500 for 6 nights. The couple will rent a car for 7 days at $60 per day. All prices include taxes and fees. How much will the couple's trip cost?

A. $2,226

B. $2,586

C. $2,892

D. $3,252

E. $4,584

10. As an instructional assistant, you are in charge of handing out materials for an art project. To create this project, each student needs 3 sheets of red paper, 2 sheets of green paper, 2 sheets of blue paper, and 1 sheet of yellow paper. There are 24 students in the class. How many total sheets of paper will you hand out?

F. 16

G. 32

H. 48

J. 168

K. 192

11. You are an accounting technician. You receive the following weekly timesheet.

Employee Name: M. O'Donnell				
Date	Hours Worked [Regular Time]	Hourly Rate	Hours Worked [Overtime/ Holiday]	Hourly Rate
8/6	8	$15		
8/7	8	$15		
8/8	8	$15		
8/9	8	$15		
8/10	8	$15	2	$22.50
8/11			4	$22.50
8/12				

How much money did this employee earn in overtime/holiday pay during this week?

A. $22.50

B. $45.00

C. $90.00

D. $135.00

E. $600.00

12. As a banquet chef at a resort, you need to create a dessert display. You have 13 apple pies, 14 coconut cream pies, 108 cookies, and 54 fruit tarts. How many pies and tarts are in the display?

F. 27

G. 54

H. 81

J. 180

K. 261

13. You are a delivery driver. You are hauling a load of watermelons. The trip is 1,820 miles. The trip will take 36 hours. You are paid $0.60 per mile. How much will you be paid for this trip?

    A. $21.60

    B. $1,092.00

    C. $2,092.00

    D. $10,920.00

    E. $65,520.00

14. You work as a server at a small diner. You must calculate the bill for each table. One table orders a ham sandwich for $4.89, a meatball hoagie for $5.79, and two orders of curly fries for $4.25 each. They also order an iced tea for $1.25 and a lemonade for $1. Sales tax is already included in the prices. How much should you charge the table?

    F. $16.18

    G. $17.18

    H. $20.43

    J. $21.43

    K. $23.43

15. As a sheriff, you wrote 30 tickets last month. You wrote 3 tickets for disorderly conduct, 26 for speeding, and 1 for defacing property. This month you wrote twice as many tickets for defacing property. You wrote 20 tickets in all this month. What fraction of this month's tickets was for defacing property?

    A. $\frac{1}{30}$

    B. $\frac{1}{20}$

    C. $\frac{1}{10}$

    D. $\frac{1}{5}$

    E. $\frac{2}{5}$

16. In your work as a personnel recruiter for a marketing company, you give skill tests to prospective proofreaders. Candidates must score an average of 90 or higher on their tests to be considered for hiring. One candidate's scores for the four skill tests he was given were 87, 96, 83, and 98. What was his average test score?

    F. 83

    G. 87

    H. 90

    J. 91

    K. 93

Answers are on page 237.

Lesson 10 ▪ ▪ ▪
Put Information in the Right Order

Skill: Put the information in the right order before performing calculations

In performing workplace calculations, you may need to put the information in the right order before solving the problem. For example, you may need to determine a monthly insurance premium for a customer who wants to have multiple types of insurance. Each insurance type will require a separate calculation to determine the premium. These premiums will then need to be added together to determine the total cost.

Remember!

When a calculation requires you to use more than one operation, you must follow the order of operations. Any operation contained in parentheses must be calculated first. Exponents come next in the order of operations, followed by multiplication and division. Addition and subtraction come last.

Exponents

An exponent is an expression that shows a number is multiplied by itself. The base is the number to be multiplied. The exponent tells how many times the base is multiplied by itself.

$$2^3$$

The base is 2. The exponent is 3.

$$2 \times 2 \times 2 = 8$$

Skill Examples

Example 1
Solve a problem using the correct order of operations.

You order 8 tickets at $5 apiece. There is a $3 handling fee added to the total. What is the total cost of your ticket order?

In the order of operations, multiplication comes before addition.

8 × $5 + $3	◂······ Number of tickets × price per ticket + handling fee
$40 + $3 = $43	◂······ Multiply to find the total ticket cost, and add the handling fee.

Example 2
Solve a problem containing parentheses using the correct order of operations.

You order 8 tickets at $5 apiece. There is a $1.50 surcharge for each ticket, plus a $3 handling fee added to the total. What is the total cost of your ticket order?

In the order of operations, calculate anything in parentheses first.

8 × ($5 + $1.50) + $3	◂······ Number of tickets × (price per ticket + surcharge) + handling fee
8 × $6.50 + $3	◂······ Add what is in parentheses to first find the total cost per ticket.
$52 + $3 = $55	◂······ Multiply to find the total ticket cost, and then add the handling fee to find the total cost of the order.

Skill Practice

A. Use addition and division in the correct order.

$$23 + 112 \div 8 \quad = \quad \underline{\hspace{1cm}}$$

B. Solve a problem involving all operations.

$$(54 - 23) \times 3 + 81 \div 27 \quad = \quad \underline{\hspace{1cm}}$$

Applied Mathematics

Try It Out! ■ ■ ■

As the office clerk at an advertising agency, you are responsible for ordering supplies each week. You need four packs of pens at $4.29 each. You also need one case of copy paper, which usually costs $35.99. Copy paper is on sale this week for $5 off. How much will you spend on supplies this week?

A. $13.83   **B.** $17.16   **C.** $30.99   **D.** $35.28   **E.** $48.15

 Step 1 ## Understand the Problem ■ ■ ■

Complete the *Plan for Successful Solving.*

Plan for Successful Solving

What am I asked to do?	What are the facts?	How do I find the answer?	Is there any unnecessary information?	What prior knowledge will help me?
Calculate the amount of money to be spent on supplies.	You buy 4 packs of pens at $4.29 each and 1 case of paper. Paper is usually $35.99, but is on sale for $5 off.	Multiply the number of packs of pens by $4.29. Subtract $5 from the cost of paper. Add the costs together.	No.	Operations within parentheses must be performed first.

 Step 2 ## Find and Check Your Answer ■ ■ ■

■ Confirm your understanding of the problem and revise your plan as needed.

■ Based on your plan, determine your solution approach: *First, I am going to write expressions to help me determine the total cost of each set of items. I will then combine (add) these expressions together to find the total supply order cost.*

4 × $4.29   ◄······ Write the cost of 4 packs of pens as an expression.

$35.99 − $5   ◄······ Write the cost of the sale price of paper as an expression.

(4 × $4.29) + ($35.99 − $5)   ◄······ Add the two expressions to find the total cost of supplies.

$17.16 + $30.99   ◄······ Calculate items in parentheses first.

$48.15   ◄······ Solve by adding to find the total cost.

■ Check your answer. Estimate the costs to see if your answer makes sense. Answer option E. $48.15 is the answer that makes the most sense.

■ **Select the correct answer:**   E. $48.15
By multiplying the number of packs of pens by the cost for each, you find the cost of the pens. By subtracting the sale from the regular price of the paper, you find the cost of the paper. Adding the costs together shows the total.

Problem Solving Tip

PEMDAS, or *Please Excuse My Dear Aunt Sally,* is an easy way to remember the order of operations.

Parentheses
Exponents
Multiplication
Division
Addition
Subtraction

Remember!

Multiplication and division are related operations. These calculations must be completed first, in order from left to right.

Addition and subtraction are also related operations and can be completed only after all multiplication and division has been done, except when a different order is determined by parentheses. Like multiplication and division, these calculations should be completed in order from left to right.

On Your Own ▪ ▪ ▪

1. You work as a salesperson for a pharmaceutical company. Each week you receive 300 drug samples to give away. You discover that 37 samples were damaged and could not be given to patients. How many drug samples did you give away during the month, assuming there were four weeks this month?

   A. 900

   B. 1,052

   C. 1,163

   D. 1,200

   E. 9,900

2. You are a school social worker. You are hosting a training program on school violence this week. You will hold 3 sessions of the program. There is room for 163 teachers in each session. You will hold an additional training session on Friday for the district's 97 substitute teachers. How many teachers and substitute teachers will you be able to train this week?

   F. 260

   G. 291

   H. 489

   J. 586

   K. 780

3. One of your jobs as a paramedic is to keep a trip log for the ambulance. This week you logged 112.34 miles on Monday. You logged 84.27 miles each day for Tuesday, Thursday, and Friday. On Wednesday you logged the same number of miles as Monday. How many miles did you enter on this week's trip log?

   A. 252.81 miles

   B. 337.08 miles

   C. 377.79 miles

   D. 476.79 miles

   E. 477.49 miles

4. In your job with a construction crew, you are calculating how much time was spent on a job. There are 5 workers in your construction crew. Each worker spent 10 hours on the job. Your foreman spent 4 hours on the job. Which expression shows the number of hours spent on the job?

   F. $10 \times (4 + 5)$

   G. $(4 \times 10) + 5$

   H. $10 + 5 + 4$

   J. 5×10

   K. $(5 \times 10) + 4$

5. In your job as a zookeeper, you exercise the camels by walking them around an outdoor arena twice a day. The arena is 50 yards long and 35 yards wide. How many yards do you walk each camel every day?

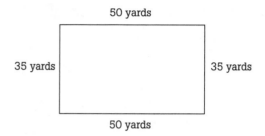

50 yards

35 yards   35 yards

50 yards

    A.   70 yards

    B.   140 yards

    C.   170 yards

    D.   340 yards

    E.   3,570 yards

6. You work as a food server at a local diner. You work for 9 hours. You make $5.50 an hour. You make a total of $124 in tips. How much did you make in all during your shift?

    F. $49.50

    G. $129.50

    H. $173.50

    J. $455.00

    K. $1,165.50

7. As a surgical dental assistant, you take X-rays of patients' teeth. Monday you took 2 sets of X-rays. Wednesday you took 1 more set than you did on Monday. On Friday, you took twice as many X-rays as you did on Wednesday. Which expression shows the total number of X-rays you took?

    A. $2 + (2 + 1)$

    B. $(2 + 1) + 2 \times (2 + 1)$

    C. $2 + (2 + 1) + 1 \times (2 + 1)$

    D. $2 + (2 + 1) + 2 + (2 + 1)$

    E. $2 + (2 + 1) + 2 \times (2 + 1)$

8. You are a bakery chef. You have ordered 14 pounds of green apples and 9 pounds of red apples. You have also ordered twice as many yellow apples as red. You used 26 pounds of apples for pies. How many pounds of apples do you have left?

    F.   5 pounds

    G.   15 pounds

    H.   18 pounds

    J.   23 pounds

    K.   41 pounds

9. As an office nurse, you have drawn 48 vials of blood. You sent 12 vials to the clinic's in-house lab. You packed the remaining vials in crates of 4 to send to an outside lab. Which expression shows the number of crates you packed?

    A. $48 - 12 \div 4$

    B. $(48 - 12) \div 4$

    C. $48 - (12 \div 4)$

    D. $48 + 12 \div 4$

    E. $(48 + 12) \div 4$

10. As an X-ray technician, you have seen 352 male patients this month. You have seen three times as many female patients. How many patients have you seen in all this month?

    F.   704

    G.   956

    H.   1,056

    J.   1,308

    K.   1,408

11. You are a school library clerk. The library has received a shipment of 12 boxes of dictionaries. There are 5 dictionaries in each box. Two boxes were sent to the English department. How many dictionaries are left?

    A.   10

    B.   40

    C.   50

    D.   60

    E.   90

12. You work as a personnel recruiter for a healthcare company. You are in the process of hiring a physician's assistant. You reviewed 12 résumés Monday and 11 on Tuesday. Today you reviewed twice as many as you did Tuesday. You decide to call 9 candidates for an interview. How many candidates will not get an interview?

    F.   22

    G.   32

    H.   36

    J.   45

    K.   68

13. As an insurance broker, you have put together an insurance package for a client. The client's homeowner's insurance will be $4,527 a year. The client wants a rider on the policy to cover some artwork. The rider will cost $358 more per year. The client also needs auto insurance that will cost $1,298 a year. How much is the client's monthly premium?

  A. $138.00

  B. $407.08

  C. $515.25

  D. $5,152.50

  E. $6,183.00

14. You are a box spring upholsterer for a mattress company. On Monday you secured material onto 136 box springs. On Tuesday you finished 165, and today you finished 149. Based on your average number of completed box springs for these three days, about how many box springs will you upholster in 5 days?

  F. 90

  G. 150

  H. 450

  J. 750

  K. 1,050

15. You are a warehouse manager for a cloth diaper company. You have just received 20 crates of new diapers. There are 200 diapers in each crate. 40 diapers were sewn backward and must be returned. The remaining diapers will be packed into boxes of 40 each for distribution to local retail outlets. How many boxes of diapers are going to local retail outlets?

  A. 99

  B. 200

  C. 220

  D. 240

  E. 300

16. One of your responsibilities as a treasurer for a non-profit organization is to send out copies of the annual report to board members and employees. There are 8 board members and 20 employees. Each board member needs 2 copies of the report. Each employee needs 1 copy of the report. Which expression shows the number of reports you need to send out?

  F. $8 + 20$

  G. $8 + 20 + 2 + 1$

  H. $(8 + 2) \times (20 + 1)$

  J. $(8 \times 2) + (20 \times 1)$

  K. $(20 \times 8) + (2 \times 1)$

Answers are on page 237.

Lesson 11 ■ ■ ■
Multiply Negative Numbers

Skill: Multiply negative numbers

In performing workplace calculations, you may need to multiply negative numbers. For example, you may need to find the monthly net profit gain or loss for a business. Or, you may need to calculate a fine or penalty for late payment from a client over a period of time.

When multiplying an expression in which one or more of the factors is a negative number, there are specific rules that must be followed. Knowing how to apply these rules correctly is important when calculating with negative numbers.

Remember!

Multiplying negative numbers is similar to multiplying positive numbers except for these two rules.

1. When multiplying a positive number and a negative number, the answer is always negative.

    $8 \times (-6) = -48$

2. When multiplying two negative numbers, the answer is always positive.

    $-2 \times (-7) = 14$

Skill Examples

Example 1
Multiply two numbers with opposite signs.

Multiply: -5×3

You know that 5 x 3 is the expression used to find 3 equal sets of 5. Since multiplication is like repeated addition, $5 + 5 + 5 = 15$. In this example, although one of the numbers is negative, the same rule applies.

$$-5 \times 3 = (-5) + (-5) + (-5)$$

$$-5 \times 3 = -15$$

Example 2
Multiply two numbers with the same sign.

Multiply: $-12 \times (-3)$

$-12 \times (-3) = 36$ ◄····· The product of two negative numbers is a positive number.

Multiply: 6×5

$6 \times 5 = 30$ ◄····· The product of two positive numbers is a positive number.

Skill Practice

A. Multiply a positive and a negative number.

$9 \times (-8)$ = _____

-9×8 = _____

$4 \times (-7)$ = _____

-2×10 = _____

B. Multiply two numbers with the same sign.

$-5 \times (-15)$ = _____

5×15 = _____

$-6 \times (-10)$ = _____

6×10 = _____

Applied Mathematics

Try It Out! ▪ ▪ ▪

You are a bookkeeper for a retail toy company. Since the beginning of this year, the company has operated at a loss of $16,000 each month for the last 4 months. What is the net loss of the company for the year so far?

A. −$64,000   D. $40,000

B. −$40,000   E. $64,000

C. −$4,000

Step 1 Understand the Problem ▪ ▪ ▪

Complete the *Plan for Successful Solving*.

Plan for Successful Solving				
What am I asked to do?	**What are the facts?**	**How do I find the answer?**	**Is there any unnecessary information?**	**What prior knowledge will help me?**
Find the net loss of the company.	The company lost $16,000 each month for 4 months.	Multiply the amount lost per month (negative number) by the number of months (positive number).	No.	The product of two numbers with opposite signs is always a negative number.

Step 2 Find and Check Your Answer ▪ ▪ ▪

- Confirm your understanding of the problem and revise your plan as needed.

- Based on your plan, determine your solution approach: *I am going to multiply the amount the company lost each month by the number of months.*

    −$16,000 × 4   ◄······ Write a multiplication expression.

    −16,000 × 4 = −64,000   ◄······ Solve.

    The company's net loss so far this year is −$64,000.

- Check your answer. Since the company has lost money every month so far this year, the answer must be a negative number. The rule for multiplying two numbers with opposite signs confirms this fact.

- **Select the correct answer:** A. −$64,000
    Since the company had a loss for 4 months, the answer is the loss times the number of months. A loss indicates a negative amount, so the answer is negative.

Remember!

Look for these words to describe a negative number: *loss; net loss;* or an amount *off, short,* or *under.*

Problem Solving Tip

By knowing the rules of multiplying positive and negative numbers, you can rule out incorrect answers before performing any calculations. In the *Try It Out!* example, the expression for finding the total net loss involves multiplying a negative number by a positive number. Since the product of two numbers with opposite signs is always a negative number, you can rule out answers D and E immediately.

On Your Own ■ ■ ■

1. In your role as an administrative assistant for a plastics manufacturing company, you are preparing the profit and loss statement. In the last quarter, the company had a $15,000 loss each month for 3 months. What is the net loss for the quarter?

    A. −$45,000

    B. −$35,000

    C. −$5,000

    D. $5,000

    E. $45,000

2. One of your responsibilities as a clinical assistant is to check patients' weights. A patient lost 5 pounds a month for 15 months. What is the patient's net change in weight?

    F. −85 pounds

    G. −75 pounds

    H. 3 pounds

    J. 20 pounds

    K. 75 pounds

3. You work as a hairstylist. Your client asks you to trim twice the length off her hair as you did six months ago. Last time you trimmed 3 inches. What is the net loss of her hair's length after this trim?

    A. −6 inches

    B. −3 inches

    C. 1 inch

    D. 3 inches

    E. 6 inches

4. As an auditor, you are checking the golf scores after a major tournament. A golfer shoots 2 strokes under par each round for 3 rounds. At the end of the three rounds, how many strokes under par is the golfer's score?

    F. −6 strokes

    G. −5 strokes

    H. 1 stroke

    J. 5 strokes

    K. 6 strokes

5. As an analyst, you monitor the price of the company's stock. The value of a share of stock went down $2.25 each day for three days. What is the net loss of the share's value?

    A.   −$8.25

    B.   −$7.75

    C.   −$6.75

    D. $6.50

    E. $6.75

6. As a heat treat operator, you are responsible for a machine that applies heat to metal to make it ready for use in products. You adjust controls on the machine to change the length of time and temperature required for the heat treating process. One project requires that the temperature drop by 1.5°F each hour for 8 hours. The temperature of the machine starts at 150°F. What is the temperature after 8 hours?

    F.   134°F

    G.   138°F

    H.   142°F

    J.   146°F

    K.   158°F

7. As a supervisor of automotive mechanics at a car dealership, you supervise eight full-time mechanics. On Tuesday, one mechanic takes a scheduled vacation, one mechanic takes a personal leave day, and another mechanic calls in sick for the day. Each mechanic on your staff works an 8-hour shift. How many hours can you schedule for auto repairs on Tuesday?

    A.   8 hours

    B.   24 hours

    C.   30 hours

    D.   36 hours

    E.   40 hours

8. You are employed as a dog groomer. You need to trim the coat of a dog. Your client wants you to trim 3 times as much hair off the dog's coat as you did last time. You cut off 2.5 centimeters of hair last time. What is the net loss of dog hair after this trim?

    F.   −10 centimeters

    G.   −9 centimeters

    H.   −7.5 centimeters

    J.   6 centimeters

    K.   7.5 centimeters

9. As a polishing machine setter, you remove excess material from metal surfaces. You polish off 3 millimeters from both sides of a sheet of metal. What is the change in the dimensions of the sheet of metal?

    A. 6 millimeters smaller

    B. 3 millimeters smaller

    C. 3 millimeters larger

    D. 6 millimeters larger

    E. 9 millimeters larger

10. You work as a room service waiter. A customer orders a meal that costs $10. She presents you with a coupon for $1.25. Today you are offering double the value of the coupon. What is the total change in price?

    F. −$5.00

    G. −$2.50

    H. −$2.00

    J. $2.50

    K. $250

11. You are a chemical equipment tender. You adjust controls to regulate temperature and flow of liquids. You must drop the temperature 0.07°F per hour for 7 hours. What is the total drop in temperature?

    A. −4.9°F

    B. −0.49°F

    C. 4.09°F

    D. 4.9°F

    E. 49°F

12. As part of your job as a farm laborer, you are in charge of prepping fertilizer for crop dusting. You prepare 600 gallons of fertilizer. The plane can drop 3 gallons of fertilizer each minute. What is the net change in the load after the plane flies for 90 minutes?

    F. −5,400 pounds

    G. −270 gallons

    H. −270 bags

    J. 600 bags

    K. 5,400 gallons

13. You work in a school library. A patron returns 3 books that are each overdue by 2 weeks. The overdue fine rate is $1 per week for each book. The patron gives you $3. You input the amount in your computer. What amount does the computer show as the patron's balance?

    A.   −$6

    B.   −$3

    C. $1

    D. $3

    E. $6

14. You review credit histories. One client has reduced her balance by making payments of $133.45 for 5 months. She originally owed $6,356.17. What is her balance after making the payments, assuming that her balance is at a 0.0% Annual Percentage Rate (APR)?

    F.   −$5,688.92

    G.   −$646.25

    H.   −$546.25

    J. $5,688.92

    K. $7,002.45

15. You are an engineering technician who has the task of preparing work-time estimates for projects. You estimate that it will take 12 hours of labor for each of 5 workers. 3 workers take 12 hours each to finish the project. But the other 2 workers only take 10 hours each to finish the project. Did you meet your project estimate?

    A.   Yes, 4 hours less than estimated

    B.   Yes, 2 hours less than estimated

    C.   Yes, 0 hours less than estimated

    D.   No, 2 hours more than estimated

    E.   No, 4 hours more than estimated

16. You are working with a marine biologist to monitor beach erosion. You see a trend that the beach is eroding about 2 feet each year. You make a prediction for how much beach will be lost within 4 years. What is the amount of net beach loss due to erosion that you predict?

    F.   −8 feet

    G.   −6 feet

    H.   2 feet

    J.   6 feet

    K.   8 feet

Answers are on page 237.

Level 4 Performance Assessment

The following problems will test your ability to answer questions at a Level 4 rating of difficulty. These problems are similar to those that appear on a Career Readiness Certificate test. For each question, you can refer to the answer key for answer justifications. The answer justifications provide an explanation of why each answer option is either correct or incorrect and indicate the skill lesson that should be referred to if further review of a particular skill is needed.

1. As a construction laborer, you are building a fence around a yard. The sides of the yard measure 10.25 meters, 3.75 meters, 15.5 meters, 4 meters, and 8.5 meters. The side of the yard that is 15.5 meters borders the house. How much fencing do you need to enclose the yard?

   A.   7.75 meters

   B.   18 meters

   C.   26.5 meters

   D.   29.5 meters

   E.   42 meters

2. You work as a prepress technician for a company that prints business forms. The spec sheet for a form calls for a $\frac{3}{8}$-inch page margin on each side. It also calls for another $\frac{1}{8}$-inch margin on each side within one section of print. What is the total margin that you should set for that section?

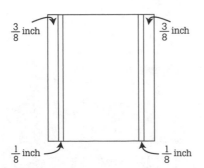

   F. $\frac{3}{64}$ inch

   G. $\frac{1}{8}$ inch

   H. $\frac{2}{8}$ inch

   J. $\frac{4}{8}$ inch

   K.   1 inch

3. You are a dental assistant helping to install a crown. You record the curing time for an adhesive. The recommended time is $2\frac{1}{2}$ minutes for each crown. The dentist is installing 3 crowns on the patient. How much total curing time should you allow?

   A. $2\frac{1}{2}$ minutes

   B. $5\frac{1}{2}$ minutes

   C. $6\frac{1}{2}$ minutes

   D. $7\frac{1}{2}$ minutes

   E. $8\frac{1}{2}$ minutes

4. You are a stone sawyer. A customer shows you a drawing of paving stones for a driveway. The scale drawing shows stones that measure 2 inches wide by 4.5 inches long. The customer wants the actual stones to be cut to measure 18 inches long. How wide will you cut the stones?

   F.   2 inches

   G.   8 inches

   H.   22.5 inches

   J.   40.5 inches

   K.   162 inches

5. As a sales manager for an organic food company, you do $\frac{1}{3}$ of your business with grocery stores and $\frac{2}{3}$ of your business with specialty markets. You sold 2,130 cases of product in June. You sold 1,932 cases in July and 2,352 cases in August. How many cases did you sell in grocery stores in August?

    A. 644

    B. 710

    C. 784

    D. 1,420

    E. 1,568

6. You are a sewing machine operator. You sew curtains together. Each panel has a length of 18 inches. You need to sew 2 panels together to make a curtain. The seam allowance is $\frac{1}{4}$ inch. How long is the finished curtain?

    F. $34\frac{1}{2}$ inches

    G. 35 inches

    H. $35\frac{1}{2}$ inches

    J. 36 inches

    K. $36\frac{1}{2}$ inches

7. As a construction estimator, you estimate the cost of bathroom remodels for a general contractor. One client asks for an estimate for 2 bathroom remodels. You estimate it will cost $20,000 for both remodels. When the project is finished, all the supplies came in at the estimated budget except for 2 vanities, which were each $100 less than the budgeted amount. What was the difference between the actual cost and the estimated cost for the 2 bathroom remodels?

    A. $200 less than estimated

    B. $100 less than estimated

    C. $0 less than estimated

    D. $100 more than estimated

    E. $200 more than estimated

8. As a farm operations manager, you are inspecting tomato crops in your fields. You find that 25% of the crops failed because of too much rainfall and 10% of the crops failed due to insect infestations. 65% of the crops are ready to be harvested. What percent of the crops failed inspection?

    F. 30%

    G. 35%

    H. 75%

    J. 90%

    K. 100%

9. You work at a bicycle shop repairing bicycles. A cycling team, which consists of 24 bikers, has an account at your shop. The team pays a monthly fee of $100 so that they will not incur a huge cost in any one month. The team had a balance of $500 in its account at the beginning of June. During the month, 24 bikes were inspected and 3 were repaired. If you do not charge for inspections and charge $50 for each repair, what is the team's account balance at the end of June?

    A. −$700

    B. −$150

    C. $350

    D. $450

    E. $500

10. As an e-learning developer, you must write 5 training modules for a new software product. In addition, you must write 4 separate training modules for each of 13 revised software products. How many training modules must you write in all?

    F. 9

    G. 20

    H. 52

    J. 57

    K. 117

11. In your job at the electric company, you dispatch work crews to fix downed power lines. There are 3 people on each crew. There is a severe storm, and you dispatch a crew once every 15 minutes. After two hours, how many people will you have dispatched?

    A. 4

    B. 12

    C. 20

    D. 24

    E. 90

12. As a teacher's assistant, you are calculating student grades. One student had the following test scores: 85, 93, 91, 81, and 89. What is the student's average score?

    F. 73.2

    G. 87.8

    H. 89

    J. 109.8

    K. 439

13. As a metal precision layout worker making parts from sheets of metal, you measure and mark the sheets for cutting. You need to leave a $2\frac{3}{8}$-inch border on each side of the sheet for the next step. What is the total extra width that you should measure?

A. $2\frac{3}{8}$ inches

B.   4 inches

C. $4\frac{3}{8}$ inches

D. $4\frac{1}{2}$ inches

E. $4\frac{3}{4}$ inches

14. You are a physical therapist working with a patient in a clinic. The patient's training plan calls for $\frac{1}{4}$ hour stretching, $\frac{1}{4}$ hour active therapy, and $\frac{1}{4}$ hour cool-down period. What is the total length of the patient's therapy session?

F. $\frac{1}{2}$ hour

G. $\frac{3}{4}$ hour

H.   1 hour

J. $1\frac{1}{4}$ hours

K. $1\frac{1}{2}$ hours

15. You are working as a window cutter. The installation guide states that you must cut the window opening $\frac{1}{8}$ inch larger than the window on each side. The window is 48 inches × $28\frac{3}{8}$ inches. What are the dimensions of the opening?

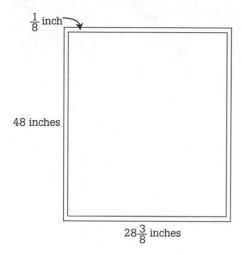

A.   48 inches × $28\frac{5}{8}$ inches

B. $48\frac{1}{8}$ inches × $28\frac{1}{2}$ inches

C. $48\frac{1}{4}$ inches × $28\frac{3}{8}$ inches

D. $48\frac{1}{4}$ inches × $28\frac{1}{2}$ inches

E. $48\frac{1}{4}$ inches × $28\frac{5}{8}$ inches

16. You work as a production inspector at a plant that manufactures fuel from waste products. You prepare a sample by blending $\frac{2}{5}$ gallon from the early part of the run and $\frac{4}{5}$ gallon from the middle of the run. You blend in $\frac{1}{5}$ gallon from the last part of the run. What is the total volume of your sample?

F. $\frac{1}{15}$ gallon

G. $\frac{7}{15}$ gallon

H.   1 gallon

J. $1\frac{1}{5}$ gallons

K. $1\frac{2}{5}$ gallons

17. You are a prep cook in a restaurant. A particular recipe uses $4\frac{1}{2}$ cups sugar. You only need to make $\frac{1}{3}$ of the normal amount. How many cups of sugar should you measure?

A. $\frac{5}{6}$ cup

B. $1\frac{1}{2}$ cups

C. $2\frac{1}{4}$ cups

D. $2\frac{1}{2}$ cups

E. $13\frac{1}{2}$ cups

18. You work as a mine cutting machine operator at a marble quarry. You cut soft marble at a rate of 3.5 square meters per hour. How much cutting can you do in an 8-hour shift?

F. 2.3 square meters

G. 4.5 square meters

H. 11.5 square meters

J. 24 square meters

K. 28 square meters

19. You are a project manager for a waterproofing company. A homeowner needs a new drainage system in the basement. A pump will cost $680. The job will require drain pipes that cost $450. Other materials, such as concrete and gravel, will cost $1,200. The cost of labor will be $2,400. Which estimate will you give the homeowner?

A. $1,630

B. $2,330

C. $3,530

D. $4,050

E. $4,730

20. One of your jobs as an office manager at a textbook company warehouse is to track the cost of shipping packages. How much money did it cost you to ship packages this week?

Monday	Tuesday	Wednesday	Thursday	Friday
$3,504.50	$2,497.75	$5,000.25	$2,389.75	$4,731.00

F. $6,002.25

G. $11,002.50

H. $12,229.00

J. $13,392.25

K. $18,123.25

21. As a rigging foreman, you are responsible for selecting the appropriate gear. You have 5 containers to move during your shift. The containers weigh 40 tons, 52 tons, 46 tons, 39 tons, and 63 tons. You need 2 pulleys for every 6 tons. Which expression shows how many pulleys you need to move all the containers?

A. $(40 + 52 + 46 + 39 + 63) \div 6 \times 2$

B. $(40 + 52 + 46 + 39 + 63) \div 6 + 2$

C. $(40 + 52 + 46 + 39 + 63) \div 6$

D. $(40 + 52 + 46 + 39 + 63) \div 2$

E. $(40 \times 52 \times 46 \times 39 \times 63) \div 6 \times 2$

22. You manage a department at a university. The university's president has given you a new annual budget, which is $5,000 less than last year's budget. You have eliminated $1,000 worth of purchases in 6 spending categories. Did you meet the new annual budget?

F. Yes, you are $6,000 under budget.

G. Yes, you are $5,000 under budget.

H. Yes, you are $1,000 under budget.

J. No, you are $1,000 over budget.

K. No, you are $11,000 over budget.

23. You are an engineering technician, drawing a layout of transfer pipes in a factory that handles liquid materials. The pipes on both sides extend $\frac{3}{8}$ inch into one pipe fitting. There should be a gap of $\frac{1}{8}$ inch between the two pipes. What is the fitting length that you should show on your drawing?

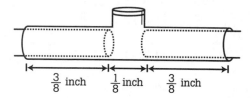

$\frac{3}{8}$ inch $\frac{1}{8}$ inch $\frac{3}{8}$ inch

A. $\frac{1}{2}$ inch

B. $\frac{5}{8}$ inch

C. $\frac{3}{4}$ inch

D. $\frac{7}{8}$ inch

E. 1 inch

24. You are a family counselor scheduling your appointments. Each session lasts 1 hour. You use the 15 minutes that follow each session to update your files, meaning you spend a total of $1\frac{1}{4}$ hours per appointment. Next week you need to schedule 30 sessions. How many hours will you need for appointments and filing?

F. $1\frac{1}{4}$ hours

G. 30 hours

H. 35 hours

J. $37\frac{1}{2}$ hours

K. 75 hours

25. You are a construction estimator for a company that installs energy-efficient windows. You must calculate the labor charge. A typical job of this size takes 5 hours for installation. The estimated total cost of labor for this installation is $185. What is the rate that you use in your estimate for installation time?

    A. $37 per installer

    B. $37 per hour

    C. $185 per day

    D. $185 per hour

    E. $925 per installation

26. One of your duties as a research associate is to order lab supplies. Last week you ordered 20 liters of hydrochloric acid and 200 pH testing strips. You also ordered 54 new test tubes and 3 new microscopes. This week you used 12 liters of hydrochloric acid and 83 testing strips. How many testing strips are left?

    F. 117

    G. 146

    H. 188

    J. 197

    K. 217

27. You are a hairdresser in a salon. Your first client today gets a haircut for $60 and a coloring that costs twice as much as the haircut. She pays by credit card, and would like to add a $36 tip to the total charge. What total do you enter into the system?

    A. $96

    B. $156

    C. $180

    D. $192

    E. $216

28. You work in a lab that records barometric pressure. One day the pressure was 30.95 inches of mercury. The pressure drops steadily by 0.06 inch of mercury per hour for 24 hours. What is the barometric pressure at the end of the 24 hours?

    F. −29.51 inches of mercury

    G. 1.44 inches of mercury

    H. 29.51 inches of mercury

    J. 32.39 inches of mercury

    K. 44.57 inches of mercury

Answers are on page 237.

Level 5 Introduction ....

The lesson and practice pages that follow will give you the opportunity to develop and practice the mathematical skills needed to solve work-related problems at a Level 5 rating of difficulty. The *On Your Own* practice problems provide a review of math skills and instruction for specific problem-solving strategies. The *Performance Assessment* provides problems similar to those you will encounter on a Career Readiness Certificate test. By completing the Level 5 *On Your Own* and *Performance Assessment* problems, you will gain the ability to confidently approach workplace scenarios that require understanding and application of the skills featured in the following lessons:

Lesson 12: Calculate with Mixed Units

Lesson 13: Calculate Perimeter and Area

Lesson 14: Choose the Right Information

Lesson 15: Convert Measurements

Lesson 16: Find the Best Deal

Lesson 17: Calculate Prices with Discounts or Markups

Lesson 18: Divide Negative Numbers

These skills are intended to help you successfully understand and solve problems requiring mathematics in the workplace that involve more complex calculations, including those that use mixed units, percentages, different units of measurement, and negative numbers. Solving these types of problems often requires the ability to:

- understand the numbers you deal with and what they quantify,
- reason through multiple steps of logic,
- perform multiple calculations within a single problem.

Through solving problems at this level, you will continue to develop problem-solving approaches and strategies that will help you determine the correct answer in real-world and test-taking situations.

For a complete list of measurement conversions, including those used in this lesson, refer to the *Applied Mathematics Formula Sheet* on page 266 of this book.

Remember!

Before converting measurements, you should first determine in what unit of measurement the answer should be written. If you are working with feet and inches and the answer is expected to be in inches, you will want to convert any measurements that are in feet to inches.

Using Proportions to Convert Measurements

You can also use your understanding of proportions to convert measurements. Using the measurements in *Skill Example 1*, you can write the following proportion to convert 5,820 milligrams to grams:

$$\frac{1 \text{ gram}}{1{,}000 \text{ milligrams}} = \frac{x}{5{,}820 \text{ milligrams}}$$

Find cross products

$$1{,}000x = 5{,}820$$

Divide by 1,000 to solve for x

$$\frac{1{,}000x}{1{,}000} = \frac{5{,}820}{1{,}000}$$

$$x = 5.82 \text{ grams}$$

Lesson 12 ■ ■ ■
Calculate with Mixed Units

Skill: Calculate using mixed units

When calculating or comparing measurements, you will sometimes need to convert one of the measurements so that all of the amounts being worked with are in the same unit of measurement. Pharmacists convert units of measure when working with medication. Carpenters and auto mechanics must add or subtract measurements, which often requires converting at least one of the measurements involved. Knowing when measurements need to be converted, and how to do so, is an important skill in many careers.

Skill Examples

Example 1
Compare measurements using mixed units.

Compare 4.8 grams and 5,820 milligrams

Use the formula 1 milligram = 0.001 grams. To convert 5,820 milligrams to grams, multiply both sides of the formula by 5,820.

1 milligram = 0.001 grams

1 milligram × 5,820 = 0.001 grams × 5,820

5,820 milligrams = 5.82 grams

The two measurements can now be compared.

4.8 grams < 5.82 grams, so

4.8 grams < 5,820 milligrams.

Example 2
Add measurements using mixed units.

Add: 6 quarts + 2 gallons

Use the formula 1 gallon = 4 quarts. To find out how many quarts are in 2 gallons, multiply both sides of the formula by 2.

4 quarts = 1 gallon

4 quarts × 2 = 1 gallon × 2

8 quarts = 2 gallons

The two measurements can now be added to find the total volume.

6 quarts + 2 gallons = 14 quarts

Skill Practice

A. Calculate using mixed units of length. 15 meters − 314 centimeters = _____

B. Calculate using mixed units of volume. 5 quarts ÷ 2 cups = _____

C. Calculate using mixed units of weight. 12 pounds − 10 ounces = _____

D. Calculate using mixed units of time. 6 hours ÷ 20 minutes = _____

Try It Out! ■ ■ ■

There are 12 students in the business education class you teach. Each student must make a 15-minute presentation. You are only able to use $2\frac{1}{2}$ hours of class time for presentations this week. You want all the presentations done by the end of next week. If you use all of the available time this week for student presentations, how much time do you need to schedule for presentations next week?

A. 15 minutes   B. 30 minutes   C. 60 minutes   D. 12 hours   E. 30 hours

 Step 1 Understand the Problem ■ ■ ■

Complete the *Plan for Successful Solving.*

Plan for Successful Solving

What am I asked to do?	What are the facts?	How do I find the answer?	Is there any unnecessary information?	What prior knowledge will help me?
Find how much time is needed for presentations next week.	12 students will do 15-minute presentations. $2\frac{1}{2}$ hours are scheduled.	Find the time needed for all presentations, then subtract $2\frac{1}{2}$ hours.	No.	To convert hours to minutes, multiply by 60.

 Step 2 Find and Check Your Answer ■ ■ ■

- Confirm your understanding of the problem and revise your plan as needed.

- Based on your plan, determine your solution approach: *I am going to multiply to calculate how much time (in minutes) is needed for all 12 presentations. I will then subtract $2\frac{1}{2}$ hours to calculate how much time is needed next week. To do so, I first will need to convert $2\frac{1}{2}$ hours to minutes.*

  $15 \times 12 = 180$ ◄------ Multiply to calculate how many minutes are needed for all presentations.

  $2\frac{1}{2} \times 60 = 150$ ◄------ Convert the time available this week into minutes. Multiply to convert hours to minutes.

  $180 - 150 = 30$ ◄------ Subtract to find how many minutes are needed next week.

- Check your answer. Divide the number of minutes scheduled for each week by 15 to see if there is enough time scheduled for all twelve student presentations.

  Week 1: $150 \div 15 = 10$ presentations

  Week 2: $30 \div 15 = 2$ presentations

  $10 + 2 = 12$. Enough time is scheduled for 12 presentations.

- **Select the correct answer:**   B. 30 minutes
  By converting the total time available this week to minutes, you are able to subtract this amount from the total amount of time needed to determine how much time is needed next week.

Problem Solving Tip

Visualizing or drawing pictures can sometimes help you determine the correct answer. In the *Try It Out!* example, you can imagine an hour broken into four 15-minute segments with the following drawing:

1 hour = 4 presentations

Using this, you can see how many 15-minute segments (the amount of time needed for each presentation) are in $2\frac{1}{2}$ hours.

$2\frac{1}{2}$ hours = 10 presentations

Remember!

Always be careful to check that the units you are using when calculating make sense. There is a big difference between 30 minutes and 30 hours!

1. As a surveyor, you are a member of a team working to correct errors on a property map. According to the map, the northwest corner of the property is located 96.5 feet from the road. You measure the northwest corner of the property as 97 feet, 3 inches from the road. What is the difference in the measurements?

   A. 2 inches

   B. 3 inches

   C. 8 inches

   D. 9 inches

   E. 10 inches

2. As a stable manager on a farm, you are deciding between two different feeders. One brand of feeder has a capacity of 30 quarts and the second brand rates its capacity as 6 gallons. What is the difference in the volumes of the two feeders?

   F. $1\frac{1}{2}$ quarts

   G. 5 quarts

   H. 6 quarts

   J. $7\frac{1}{2}$ quarts

   K. 24 quarts

3. As part of your job as a veterinary assistant, you are weighing a 1-year-old cat. The cat weighed $3\frac{1}{2}$ ounces at birth and 3 pounds, 4 ounces at 12 weeks of age. Now, it weighs 8 pounds, 12 ounces. How many times greater is the cat's current weight than its birth weight?

   A. 15

   B. 35

   C. 40

   D. 48

   E. 96

4. You work as a pharmacy assistant. You often compound medications. You need to mix 400 milligrams of one powder with 5 grams of another. You will then use 270 milligrams of the mixture in each dose of a prescription medication. How many doses of the final medication can you make using the powder that you mixed?

   F. 15

   G. 20

   H. 40

   J. 100

   K. 200

5. You are the manager of a specialty coffee shop that sells coffee in 14-ounce bags. Your roaster can prepare small batches of 42 pounds of coffee beans at one time. How many bags of beans can be packaged from one batch?

    A. 3

    B. 28

    C. 42

    D. 48

    E. 56

6. As an engineer, you are preparing a proposal to pave a 2-mile section of a rural lane. The cost of materials for each linear foot of the 20-foot-wide road is $23.35. What is the total cost of the materials needed to pave the road?

    F. $934

    G. $12,329

    H. $246,576

    J. $2,465,760

    K. $4,931,520

7. You are a contractor specializing in small commercial projects. You have been contracted to refinish the restrooms in an office building. In order to lay out a tile pattern for the floor, you need to know how many tiles you will use in each row. The width of the room is 16 feet, 8 inches and the client has chosen a square tile that measures 4 inches on each side. Assuming there is no spacing allotment needed, how many tiles will you use for each row across the room?

    A. 44

    B. 50

    C. 66

    D. 100

    E. 200

8. You work as a medical laboratory technician. You are preparing a glucose solution that is 5% glucose by weight. To make 1,000 grams of the solution, you dissolve 50 grams of glucose in 950 grams of distilled water. How much glucose will you need to measure if you are preparing 2 kilograms of 5% solution?

    F. 25 grams

    G. 50 grams

    H. 75 grams

    J. 100 grams

    K. 200 grams

9. You work as a kitchen supervisor at a day care center. You have a standing order for 10 quarts of apple juice per week for the day care center. This week, your supplier shipped 10 one-gallon bottles of juice. How much more juice did you receive than you ordered?

    A. 20 quarts

    B. 25 quarts

    C. 30 quarts

    D. 36 quarts

    E. 40 quarts

10. As a transportation manager for a distribution warehouse, you need to determine the time to allow for delivery of a truck load of equipment. The truck has one driver, so the maximum legal driving time is 11 hours per day. In order to calculate the total driving time for the delivery, you use average times in your records for the four segments of the route: 13 hours, 45 minutes; 8 hours, 30 minutes; 10 hours, 45 minutes; 2 hours, 15 minutes. How many days should you allow for the delivery?

    F. 2

    G. 3

    H. 4

    J. 5

    K. 6

11. As a nursing manager at a hospital, you are looking for ways to improve the quality of patient care. You have found that, among other tasks, the nurses on your staff spend an average of $2\frac{1}{2}$ hours during each 8-hour shift filling out paperwork. If a nurse cares for 6 patients during a shift, how many minutes are spent on paperwork for each patient?

    A. 15

    B. 25

    C. 80

    D. 150

    E. 900

12. You are the office manager in a sales office. To prepare coffee for a meeting, you make enough coffee to fill a 1.5-gallon carafe. The mugs hold up to 12 fluid ounces of coffee. About how many mugs can be filled with coffee from the carafe?

    F. 2

    G. 12

    H. 15

    J. 16

    K. 24

13. As a parks department administrator, you are putting together the budget for the care and maintenance of a city park. You have decided to use an organic protein fertilizer on the park lawn. One bag of fertilizer is needed for each 3,600 square feet of the 3-acre lawn. What is the minimum number of bags needed for one application of fertilizer to the entire lawn?

    A. 12

    B. 18

    C. 30

    D. 37

    E. 1,200

14. You work as an environmental engineering assistant. You need 8 tons of straw for a reclamation project. Each large bale of straw weighs about 800 pounds. How many bales should you order?

    F. 10

    G. 20

    H. 100

    J. 200

    K. 1,600

15. As a lab technician, you are assisting in the study of the effects of a chemical on the growth of mice. In four weeks, the mice that were exposed to the chemical grew an average of 5,600 milligrams. In the same four weeks, the mice that were not exposed to the chemical grew an average of 6.7 grams. What is the difference in the average growth of the two groups of mice?

    A. 1.1 grams

    B. 11 grams

    C. 900 grams

    D. 1,100 grams

    E. 5,593 grams

16. You are a medical assistant purchasing rolls of surgical tape for the clinic where you work. Each roll is 5 yards long. A roll of Sticky brand tape costs $2.25. A roll of Tacky brand tape costs $3.90. What is the difference in cost per linear foot of tape?

    F. $0.11

    G. $0.30

    H. $0.55

    J. $1.65

    K. $5.55

Answers are on page 242.

Remember!

Perimeter measures the length of the outer edge of a shape. The space enclosed within this edge is measured by area. Area is a two-dimensional measurement that measures the number of square units of a surface.

Formulas for Perimeter and Area of Rectangles

To understand the formulas for finding perimeter and area, consider the figure below, which is 3 units wide and 5 units long.

Perimeter By counting the number of units on each side of the rectangle, you find that the perimeter is 16 units.

Area By counting the total number of squares that make up the rectangle, you find that its area is 15 square units. So, the formula is area = length × width.

Lesson 13 ■ ■ ■
Calculate Perimeter and Area

Skill: Calculate perimeters and areas of basic shapes (rectangles and circles)

In a variety of workplace situations, you may need to find the perimeter or area of an object. An industrial engineer may be required to calculate the perimeter and area of a canister and the label that will cover the face of the canister. A surveyor may need to find the area, using property lines, in order to prepare a map of a property.

Skill Examples

Example 1
Find the perimeter and area of a rectangle.

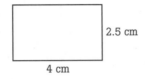

2.5 cm

4 cm

Find the formulas for perimeter and area of a rectangle and calculate.

$$perimeter = 2 \times (length + width)$$
$$= 2 \times (4 + 2.5)$$
$$= 2 \times 6.5$$
$$= 13 \text{ centimeters}$$

$$area = length \times width$$
$$= 4 \times 2.5$$
$$= 10 \text{ square centimeters (cm}^2)$$

Example 2
Find the circumference and area of a circle.

diameter = 6 inches

Find the formulas for circumference and area of a circle and calculate.

$$circumference \approx 3.14 \times diameter$$
$$\approx 3.14 \times 6$$
$$\approx 18.84 \text{ inches}$$

To calculate area, you need to know the radius. The radius is the length from the center of the circle to its edge, which is half the diameter. Divide the diameter by 2 to find the radius (3 inches).

$$area \approx 3.14 \times (radius)^2$$
$$\approx 3.14 \times (3)^2$$
$$\approx 3.14 \times 9$$
$$\approx 28.26 \text{ square inches (in}^2)$$

Skill Practice

A. Find the area of a triangle.

What is the area of a triangle that has a base of 5 inches and height of 8 inches? _____

B. Find the area of a circle.

What is the area, rounded to the nearest square meter, of a circle that has a diameter of 12 meters? _____

Applied Mathematics

Try It Out! ■ ■ ■

You are installing crown molding around the perimeter of a living room. The room is 12 feet long and $10\frac{1}{2}$ feet wide. Crown molding is sold in 78-inch segments. How many segments of crown molding should be bought to complete the job?

A. 3   **B.** 6   **C.** 7   **D.** 22   **E.** 45

Step 1   Understand the Problem ■ ■ ■

Complete the *Plan for Successful Solving.*

Plan for Successful Solving				
What am I asked to do?	**What are the facts?**	**How do I find the answer?**	**Is there any unnecessary information?**	**What prior knowledge will help me?**
Find how many segments of crown molding are needed.	Room = 12 feet × $10\frac{1}{2}$ feet Each molding segment = 78 inches	Find the room perimeter and convert to inches. Divide by 78 inches.	No.	To convert feet to inches, multiply by 12.

Step 2   Find and Check Your Answer ■ ■ ■

- Confirm your understanding of the problem and revise your plan as needed.

- Based on your plan, determine your solution approach: *I am going to find the perimeter of the room, then convert the result from feet to inches. I will then divide by 78 to find out how many segments of crown molding are needed.*

  $2 \times (length + width) = 2 \times (12 + 10\frac{1}{2}) = 45$ feet ◄····· Use the formula to find the perimeter of the room.

  $45 \times 12 = 540$ inches ◄····· Multiply to convert feet to inches.

  $540 \div 78 = 6$ r 72 ◄····· Divide the total amount of crown molding needed by the length of each segment to find the number of segments needed.

  7 segments needed ◄····· Interpret the remainder. If you divide on paper, the remainder of 72 identifies the number of leftover inches not covered by the 6 segments. Therefore, one additional 78-inch segment will be needed.

- Check your answer. Use opposite operations.
  7×78 inches = 546 inches. By purchasing seven 78-inch segments, I will have enough crown molding to cover the 540-inch perimeter of the room.

- **Select the correct answer:**   C. 7
  By finding the perimeter of the room and then dividing by the length of one segment of crown molding, you find that you need 7 segments.

Problem Solving Tip

When solving problems, it is important that you interpret the remainder correctly. Sometimes, the remainder can be ignored. Many times, however, the remainder affects the answer. In the *Try It Out!* example, the remainder represents 72 additional inches of crown molding that is needed. You will need one segment of crown molding for those 72 inches, so 1 (segment) must be added to the whole number part of the quotient. If you were to use a calculator for this example, your answer would be 6.923. Similar to answers with remainders, this decimal answer represents 6 whole segments and 0.923 additional segments, meaning you must round up to the next whole number for the correct answer.

Remember!

To check division when there is a remainder, first multiply the whole number part of the quotient by the divisor. Then, add the remainder.

$(6 \times 78) + 72 = 540$

You need 540 inches to have enough molding for the entire room.

On Your Own ■ ■ ■

1. At the farm where you work as a manager, you need to replace the fence that encloses a small rectangular pasture. The pasture is 60 yards long and 30 yards wide. How many feet of fencing do you need to buy?

   A. 60 feet

   B. 90 feet

   C. 180 feet

   D. 270 feet

   E. 540 feet

2. As a general contractor, you will be replacing the hardwood floors of a loft office space. The client has selected flooring that costs $2.79 per square foot. The rectangular office space is 16 feet long and 30 feet wide. What is the cost of the flooring?

   F. $48.79

   G. $128.34

   H. $256.68

   J. $1,339.20

   K. $2,678.40

3. As a surveyor, you are preparing a map of a property with the dimensions shown below. The western property line and southern property line are perpendicular. What is the area of the property?

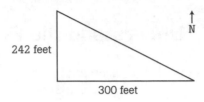

   A. 542 square feet

   B. 24,200 square feet

   C. 36,300 square feet

   D. 72,600 square feet

   E. 145,200 square feet

4. You are an electrical apprentice working for a business that installs solar panels. You are preparing a 5-solar-panel array for a home. Each panel in the array is 1.6 meters long and 0.9 meter wide. What is the total area of the array?

   F. 1.44 square meters

   G. 5.95 square meters

   H. 7.2 square meters

   J. 8.0 square meters

   K. 25 square meters

5. As an interior designer, you are planning the retiling of an apartment building lobby. The rectangular lobby is 36 feet long and 12 feet wide. The tiles are triangular, with the dimensions shown below. How many tiles will you need to order to cover the lobby floor?

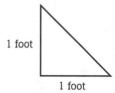

1 foot

1 foot

A. 144

B. 216

C. 432

D. 864

E. 1,296

6. You are a mechanical engineer developing blueprints for a specialized water meter. On your blueprints, which are 5 times as large as the actual meter, the face of the meter has a radius of 15 centimeters. For readability, your client has specified a minimum area for the face of the meter. What is the approximate area of the meter face?

F. 9.0 square centimeters

G. 9.4 square centimeters

H. 18.8 square centimeters

J. 27.0 square centimeters

K. 28.3 square centimeters

7. You are a finish carpenter who designs and builds frames for art galleries and museums. You are determining the cost to make wooden frames for 3 large paintings. Each frame will be 4 feet long and 7 feet wide. What is the total length of the wood needed to make the frames?

A. 22 feet

B. 28 feet

C. 33 feet

D. 63 feet

E. 66 feet

8. In your work as an industrial engineer, you are designing the packaging for a new product. The product will be sold in a cylindrical canister with a radius of 3 inches and a height of 10 inches. What are the dimensions of a label that will cover the face of the canisters?

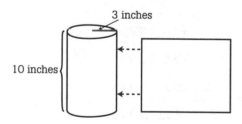

3 inches

10 inches

F. 10 inches × 3 inches

G. 10 inches × 6 inches

H. 10 inches × 18.8 inches

J. 10 inches × 28.3 inches

K. 10 inches × 30 inches

9. You are a marketing assistant writing a product description for a new rug to be provided to retailers. The rug will be made in two different rectangular sizes. The smaller rug is 5 feet long and 8 feet wide. The larger rug is 9 feet long and 12 feet wide. What is the difference in the area of the two rugs?

A. 8 square feet

B. 40 square feet

C. 64 square feet

D. 68 square feet

E. 108 square feet

10. As a civil engineer, you are drafting the plans for a new water treatment plant. The water mains for this plant measure 48 inches in diameter. At each joint between pipes in the main, a strip of rubber will be bonded to the outside of the pipe joint to improve the seal. About how long will the rubber seal be when it is trimmed to fit around the pipe?

F. 48.0 inches

G. 75.4 inches

H. 150.7 inches

J. 244.9 inches

K. 1,808.0 inches

11. You work as the distribution manager for a company that processes maple products. You ship syrup in 55-gallon cylindrical drums. Each has a radius of 12 inches. The drums need to be shipped on pallets that measure 48 inches long and 72 inches wide. How many drums can fit on each pallet?

A. 6

B. 10

C. 12

D. 18

E. 24

12. You are an athletic trainer and have been hired to put together an after-school fitness program. You want to use the track at a local high school for some of the activities. What is the approximate distance around the track shown in the diagram below?

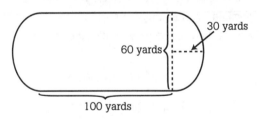

F. 294 yards

G. 320 yards

H. 388 yards

J. 577 yards

K. 6,000 yards

13. As an employee of a landscape maintenance company, you are drafting a proposal for your business to care for the lawn at a small park. At one end of the park is a large circular fountain. The diameter of the basin of the fountain is 14 feet. A 3-foot-wide stone path encircles the fountain. What is the approximate area covered by the fountain and the path?

    A.   154 square feet

    B.   314 square feet

    C.   804 square feet

    D.   908 square feet

    E.   1,256 square feet

14. You are a commercial designer for a furniture accessories manufacturer. For a new cushion design, your company will use fabric made of recycled materials. For each cushion, 2 circular pieces of fabric are needed. The radius of each piece of fabric is $1\frac{3}{4}$ feet. What is the approximate area of fabric needed to make one cushion?

    F.   9.6 square feet

    G.   11.0 square feet

    H.   22.0 square feet

    J.   19.2 square feet

    K.   60.4 square feet

15. You work for a transportation engineer redesigning the parking lot at a small shopping center. The dimensions of the lot are shown below. What is the area of the parking lot?

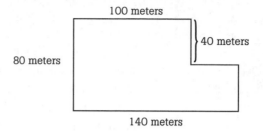

    A.   8,000 square meters

    B.   9,600 square meters

    C.   11,200 square meters

    D.   13,600 square meters

    E.   14,000 square meters

16. As a manager in the municipal parks department, you run an urban composting program. At one community garden, the area set aside for composting bins is 12 feet long and 3 feet wide. The bins are cylindrical: 45 inches high and 36 inches in diameter. How many bins will fit in the area for composting?

    F.   1

    G.   4

    H.   9

    J.   12

    K.   18

Answers are on page 242.

Remember!

If you have been using the *Plan for Successful Solving* throughout this book, you already have the tools you need to solve the types of problems you will see in this lesson. To solve any problem, first identify what the problem asks you to do. Identify the facts and sort out any unnecessary information. Plan the calculations you will do and identify the knowledge you need, including any formulas. Then confirm and execute your plan. Finally, don't forget to check your calculations to confirm that your answer makes sense.

Lesson 14 ■■■
Choose the Right Information

Skill: Decide what information, calculations, or unit conversions to use to solve the problem

In any job, it is important to be able to identify the information needed to solve a problem. It is also important to know how to use that information which is needed. For example, a contractor must know how to take the measurements for a tiling job. With this information, she must consider both the sizes of the tiles being used and the quantities in which they are packaged if she is to order the correct amount. Understanding what calculations and unit conversions need to be used will help her order correctly. Knowing how to correctly choose and use the information when solving problems is an important workplace skill.

Skill Examples

You are covering a 50-square-foot bathroom floor with custom tile. Each tile is 4 square inches. Each box of one hundred 4-square-inch tiles costs $22.

Example 1
Decide what unit conversions to use.

How many tiles will cover the floor?

To determine how many 4-square-inch tiles will cover a 50-square-foot floor, you first need to convert square feet to square inches. The formula is 1 square foot = 144 square inches.

50 × 144 = 7,200 square inches

Divide to find the number of tiles that will cover the floor.

7,200 ÷ 4 = 1,800 tiles

Example 2
Decide what information you need.

What is the cost of 18 boxes of tiles?

You need to know the cost of 18 boxes of tiles. To solve this problem, you do not need to know there are 100 tiles in the box or that each tile is 4 square inches. Determine what information is needed to find the answer, then calculate.

$22 × 18 = $396

You are determining the retail price for a new brand of cereal at the store that you manage. The cereal is sold in 18-ounce boxes. The retail price for a new product is normally determined by increasing the wholesale cost by 70%. The wholesale cost of a case of 12 boxes is $30. What retail price should you use?

Skill Practice

Use the scenario to the left to:

A. Decide what information is not needed.

B. Decide what calculations to perform.

Which figure from the problem will not be needed to find the answer? _____

Once you have determined the retail price per case, how will you calculate the retail price per box? _____

Try It Out! ▪ ▪ ▪

You are a sales representative for an electronics equipment company. You are driving to a sales meeting 150 miles away, and you want to be sure you will be on time. You drive at an average speed of 50 miles per hour, and your car gets about 35 miles per gallon of gas. At the rate you are driving, about how long will it take you to get to the meeting?

A. 1 hour, 20 minutes   D. 3 hours

B. 1 hour, 50 minutes   E. 5 hours

C. 2 hours

 Step 1 ## Understand the Problem ▪ ▪ ▪

Complete the *Plan for Successful Solving*.

Plan for Successful Solving				
What am I asked to do?	**What are the facts?**	**How do I find the answer?**	**Is there any unnecessary information?**	**What prior knowledge will help me?**
Determine how long it will take to drive to a meeting.	The meeting is 150 miles away. You drive 50 miles per hour.	Divide the distance to the meeting by the rate of travel.	The car gets 35 miles per gallon of gas.	Distance equals rate times time, so distance divided by rate equals time.

 Step 2 ## Find and Check Your Answer ▪ ▪ ▪

- Confirm your understanding of the problem and revise your plan as needed.

- Based on your plan, determine your solution approach: *Since I know the rate of speed in miles per hour, I can divide the total distance I will travel by the rate. This will help me calculate the time it will take to get to the meeting.*

  150 miles at 50 mph   ◄····· Identify what information is needed to solve the problem.

  150 miles ÷ 50 mph = 3 hours   ◄····· Choose the operation needed to solve the problem.

- Check your answer. Does your answer make sense?
  50 miles per hour in 3 hours = 50 + 50 + 50 = 150. The distance to the meeting is 150 miles.

- **Select the correct answer:**   D. 3 hours
  Speed is an average measure of rate that is found by dividing the distance traveled by the time it takes to travel this distance (speed = distance ÷ time). Since you know the speed at which you will be traveling and the distance that you will travel, you can rearrange this basic formula to help you find the time it will take to make the trip (time = distance ÷ speed).

1. As a general contractor on a construction site, you need 4 tons of gravel and $\frac{1}{2}$ ton of sand for a project. Gravel costs $24 per ton, and sand costs $12 per ton. How much will you pay for the gravel?

   A. $12

   B. $48

   C. $54

   D. $96

   E. $108

2. As a legal assistant at a law firm, one of your tasks is monitoring and ordering office supplies. Your office printer uses one toner cartridge in about 6 weeks. This month, you place an order for 4 toner cartridges at a cost of $15.95 each. Your supplier gives a $5 discount for orders that total at least $100. How much will the toner cartridges cost altogether?

   F. $43.80

   G. $58.80

   H. $63.80

   J. $95.70

   K. $382.80

3. You are a Geographic Information System (GIS) specialist preparing a zoning map for a county agency. The area that you are mapping is a square measuring 4 miles on each side, and it includes all or part of 998 separate lots ranging from $\frac{1}{4}$ acre to 987 acres. The map scale is 1 inch = 500 feet. About how long is each side of the map that you will print?

   A. 2 inches

   B. 4 inches

   C. 10 inches

   D. 24 inches

   E. 42 inches

4. You work as an occupational therapist. You are setting up your schedule for next Wednesday. During the morning, you work with patients who need your full attention, so you schedule them one at a time for an hour each. In the afternoon, however, you schedule patients who can work out on their own once you have started their therapy. You can schedule as many as 3 overlapping appointments during this time. You have 40-minute appointments scheduled at 2:00, 2:40, and 3:20 P.M. If all your remaining patients need one-hour appointments, how many appointments do you have room to schedule between 2:00 and 4:00 P.M.?

   F. 2

   G. 3

   H. 4

   J. 6

   K. 7

5. As a personal trainer, you work with clients to improve their fitness. You have determined that a particular client's maximum heart rate should be 150 beats per minute. Exercise with the heart rate at 70–85% of the maximum is recommended to achieve aerobic fitness. You direct your client to measure her heart rate for 10 seconds just after she stops running. She counts 25 heartbeats in that time. What is her heart rate?

    A.   133 beats per minute

    B.   150 beats per minute

    C.   161 beats per minute

    D.   195 beats per minute

    E.   250 beats per minute

6. In your work as a traveling registered nurse, you spend part of every day driving to and from patients' homes. You are scheduled to work with 3 patients on Tuesday. The distance from the first to the second patient's home is 15 miles, and the distance from the second to the last patient's home is 12 miles. It takes you about 20 minutes to drive from each home to the next. You will spend 2 hours with each of the first 2 patients. If you plan to arrive at the first patient's home at 7:30 A.M., at about what time will you reach the last patient's home?

    F.   8:10 A.M.

    G.   9:30 A.M.

    H.   9:50 A.M.

    J.   11:30 A.M.

    K.   12:10 P.M.

7. As a public works director for a small city, you are working on a campaign to promote recycling. In your city, about 65% of recyclable materials are generally discarded as trash. Flyers illustrating how to recycle will be sent to each of the 22,500 households in the city. An additional 1,200 flyers will be distributed to schools, health clinics, and other public organizations. The flyers will cost $0.16 each to create. What is the total cost of the flyers?

    A. $192

    B. $3,600

    C. $3,792

    D. $14,625

    E. $15,405

8. A master plan for a city park calls for 12 acres of the park to be plowed for use as a community garden. In 5 years, the park trustees may add an additional 8 acres of garden area, depending on the success of the first stage of the project. As a park designer, you will prepare the layout of the first stage of the project. The garden area will be rectangular with a length of 1,089 feet. A fence will be required along the width at one end of the plot. How much fencing will you need to have installed?

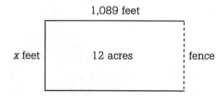

    F.   40 feet

    G.   480 feet

    H.   960 feet

    J.   1,080 feet

    K.   3,138 feet

9. You work as a travel coordinator in a corporate travel office. You are planning a business trip from New York to Washington DC for an executive. You have found first-class, round-trip train fare for $278. The travel time is 3 hours, 25 minutes. The hotel cost for the one-night stay is $285. If $900 is budgeted for the trip, how much will be available for meals, local transportation, and other expenses?

    A. $132

    B. $337

    C. $563

    D. $615

    E. $622

10. As the purchasing manager for a large animal shelter, you need to place an order for a particular brand of dog food. You order the food in pallets of 36 cases. Each case contains 24 cans of dog food. Your cost for each pallet is $895. What is the minimum number of pallets that you can order to receive at least 10,000 cans of dog food?

    F.   10

    G.   11

    H.   12

    J.   558

    K.   864

11. As a human resources representative, you are scheduling interviews for job candidates. The vice president of the group seeking candidates wants to interview the top candidates on Thursday. She asks you to schedule 40 minutes for each interview and 10 minutes between interviews. She can begin seeing candidates at 9:00 A.M. and does not want to conduct any interviews after 1:00 P.M. What is the greatest number of interviews you can schedule on Thursday?

    A.   5

    B.   6

    C.   8

    D.   9

    E.   10

12. You are a customer service manager in charge of a call center for a large utility company. Each customer service representative working at the center handles an average of 18 calls per hour. The volume of calls is up 20% from last year, so you need to plan to handle 2,520 calls per day. The call center is open 10 hours per day. How many customer service representatives should you have staffing the phones at any given time?

    F.   14

    G.   16

    H.   140

    J.   280

    K.   252

13. As a clinical dietician, you are working with a child with iron-deficiency anemia. You help the child select iron-rich snacks to eat. You want the child to eat a total of 8 milligrams of iron from snacks every day. Most people absorb only 5–10% of the iron they eat. Which combination of snacks includes exactly 8 milligrams of iron?

Snack	Milligrams of Iron per $\frac{1}{2}$ cup
Prune juice	5.2
Walnuts	3.75
Chick peas	3.0
Bran flakes	2.8
Cashews	2.65
Raisins	2.55
Peanuts	1.5

    A. chick peas, raisins, and peanuts

    B. walnuts and peanuts

    C. cashews and raisins

    D. walnuts and chick peas

    E. prune juice and bran flakes

14. You are the facility director of an 84-room hotel. All department supervisors have been asked to find ways to reduce the environmental impact of the hotel. You propose replacing 4 incandescent light bulbs in each room of the hotel with compact fluorescent light bulbs. You point out that each compact fluorescent light bulb uses 75% less energy and costs $30 less over its lifetime than an incandescent light bulb. How much money will the hotel save if your proposal is accepted?

    F. $336

    G. $2,520

    H. $10,080

    J. $25,200

    K. $756,000

15. You are the project manager overseeing the design and construction of a 5-acre sports field facility. The facility will have 2 soccer fields, a baseball field, and a 12,000-square-foot play area with jungle gyms and swings. Each soccer field will be 58,000 square feet. Once the soccer fields and play area have been laid out, how much field area will remain?

    A. 26,440 square feet

    B. 89,800 square feet

    C. 101,800 square feet

    D. 147,800 square feet

    E. 159,800 square feet

16. You work as a shipping supervisor for a company that produces hand-crafted hardwood furniture. You are loading a truck with a delivery to a local retail outlet that handles your products. The 400-cubic-foot truck can handle a 1-ton load, and you have already loaded 1,200 pounds of furniture onto it. You have 25-pound chairs that you would like to load onto the truck. How many of these chairs can you load onto the truck?

    F. 16

    G. 32

    H. 48

    J. 64

    K. 80

Answers are on page 242.

Remember!

In the United States, we use two systems of measurement, the customary (standard) system and the metric system. For example, milk is usually sold by the gallon (customary), while soda is sold by the liter (metric).

The Metric System

The metric system of measurement is used by most of the world. Units of length in the metric system include centimeters, meters, and kilometers. Units of volume (capacity) include liters and milliliters. Units of weight include milligrams, grams, and kilograms. The metric system follows the base-10 system of numeration. This system is commonly used in the sciences and medicine.

The Customary System

The customary, or standard, system of measurement is the system most commonly used in everyday life in the United States. Units of length in this system include inches, feet, and miles. Units of volume include cups, quarts, and gallons. Units of weight include ounces, pounds, and tons. Unlike the metric system, the customary system of measurement does not follow a base-10 pattern.

Lesson 15 ■■■
Convert Measurements

Skill: Look up a formula and perform single-step conversions within or between systems of measurement

For some careers, you will sometimes need to convert measurements. You may need to convert measurements in order to compare them or in order to perform calculations. A registered nurse may be required to convert kilograms to pounds in order to determine the weight of a patient. A chemical technician needs to know the relationship between grams and milligrams when preparing solutions.

The formulas you have used so far in this book have helped you convert within the same system of measurement. However, knowing how to use formulas to convert between different systems of measurement is an equally important workplace skill.

Skill Examples

Example 1
Convert within a system of measurement.

Convert 114 inches to feet

Use the formula 1 foot = 12 inches. To convert from a smaller unit of measurement to a larger unit of measurement, you need to divide.

$$114 \div 12 = 9 \text{ r } 6$$

You can express the remainder as the number of inches that remain, convert it to a fraction of 1 foot, or convert it to a decimal. So 114 inches equals

9 feet, 6 inches

or

$9\frac{1}{2}$ feet ($9\frac{6}{12}$ feet)

or

9.5 feet

Example 2
Convert between systems of measurement.

Convert 5 miles to kilometers

Use the formula 1 mile ≈ 1.61 kilometers. To perform this conversion, multiply both sides of the formula by 5.

1 mile ≈ 1.61 kilometers

1 mile × 5 ≈ 1.61 kilometers × 5

5 miles ≈ 8.05 kilometers

Skill Practice

A. Convert within a system of measurement.

Convert 5 gallons to quarts. _____

B. Convert between systems of measurement.

Convert 3 liters to gallons. _____

C. Convert between systems of measurement.

Convert 15 inches to centimeters. _____

Try It Out! ■ ■ ■

As the dietician at a nursing care facility, you have determined that some patients should drink 1 cup of vegetable juice every day. The facility needs 3 gallons of juice for these patients every day. The juice is sold in 2-liter containers. How many containers does the facility need to provide enough juice for one week?

| A. 3 | B. 6 | C. 12 | D. 40 | E. 80 |

 Step 1 **Understand the Problem** ■ ■ ■

Complete the *Plan for Successful Solving.*

Plan for Successful Solving

What am I asked to do?	What are the facts?	How do I find the answer?	Is there any unnecessary information?	What prior knowledge will help me?
Find how many containers of vegetable juice the facility needs for one week.	3 gallons are needed per day. Containers hold 2 liters.	Find how many gallons are needed for one week. Convert to liters, then divide by 2.	Some patients should drink 1 cup each day.	To convert gallons to liters, use the formula 1 liter ≈ 0.264 gallons. (See the Formula Sheet on page 266 of this book.)

 Step 2 **Find and Check Your Answer** ■ ■ ■

- Confirm your understanding of the problem and revise your plan as needed.

- Based on your plan, determine your solution approach: *I am going to multiply to determine how many gallons of juice are needed for one week. Then I will divide to convert to liters. Finally, I will divide by 2 to find the number of containers.*

  $3 \times 7 = 21$ gallons ◁····· Multiply to find how many gallons of juice are needed for seven days, or one week.

  $21 \div 0.264 \approx 79.5 \rightarrow 80$ ◁····· Divide to convert to liters, then round up to the nearest whole number.

  $80 \div 2 = 40$ containers ◁····· Divide the amount of juice needed by the amount per container to find the number of containers.

- Check your answer. Use opposite operations.
  $40 \times 2 = 80$; $80 \times 0.264 \approx 21$; $21 \div 7 = 3$
  The facility needs 3 gallons of juice each day.

- **Select the correct answer:** D. 40
  By converting the amount of juice needed to liters, then dividing by the number of liters in each container, you find that the facility needs 40 containers of juice for one week.

Problem Solving Tip

You can estimate to eliminate answer choices. For example, if 1 liter ≈ 0.264 gallons, then there are about 4 liters in 1 gallon. If 3 gallons are needed every day, then about 12 liters, or 6 containers, are needed each day. If you multiply this by 7 days, you get an estimate of 42 containers. Using this estimate, you can eliminate choices A, B, and C.

You can also use estimates to check that your answer makes sense. If about 6 containers are needed each day, then about 42 are needed each week. This estimate shows that choice D is reasonable.

Remember!

If you are unsure of whether to multiply or divide to convert from one unit of measurement to another, you can set the problem up as a proportion. To solve the *Try It Out!* example, you could write a proportion where:

$$\frac{1 \text{ liter}}{0.264 \text{ gallons}} = \frac{x \text{ liters}}{21 \text{ gallons}}$$

By finding cross products, you see that:

$$0.264\,x = 21$$

The final step needed to solve is to divide both sides of the equation by 0.264, giving you the answer of $x = 79.5$ liters. From here, you would follow the same steps as shown to the left.

1. You are a registered nurse at a community health clinic. In your initial assessment of a new patient who recently arrived in the United States, she tells you that she weighed 70 kilograms last year. According to your scale, she now weighs 165 pounds. About how much weight has she gained?

    A. 9 pounds

    B. 11 pounds

    C. 95 pounds

    D. 118 pounds

    E. 165 pounds

2. As a purchasing agent, you are writing a proposal to supply a public office space with furniture. The request asks for storage shelves that are 3 feet, 9 inches wide and 2 feet deep. Your company makes shelves that are 1 meter wide and 65 centimeters deep. What is the approximate difference in the width of the requested shelves and the shelves your company makes?

    F. 0.10 meter

    G. 0.14 meter

    H. 0.19 meter

    J. 2.9 meters

    K. 4.25 meters

3. As a manufacturing engineer, you are replacing the temperature gauges on dryers used to make a starting material for a particular type of plastic. The material remains in a dryer for at least 4 hours, during which the dryer should not be heated above 318°F. The only temperature gauges available that can be attached to the fitting display degrees in Celsius. What approximate Celsius temperature should be labeled as the maximum drying temperature?

    A. 27°C

    B. 146°C

    C. 160°C

    D. 604°C

    E. 694°C

4. You are the events coordinator for a running club that is sponsoring a road race to celebrate its twenty-fifth anniversary. The race course is 25 kilometers long. The club plans to set up water stations at the end of every 1-mile interval, except the first mile of the race. There will be an additional water station at the finish line. How many water stations need to be prepared?

    F. 15

    G. 16

    H. 24

    J. 39

    K. 40

Use this table for questions 5 and 6.

Storage Bins	
Size	width × depth × height (in centimeters)
Small	33 × 38 × 22
Medium	35 × 55 × 27
Large	43 × 55 × 30

5. You work as the administrative coordinator for an energy consulting firm. You need to purchase storage bins for the office. These bins will be placed in a unit with 10 inches between shelves. What height will remain between the top of the tallest storage bin that will fit on a shelf and the shelf above it?

   A.   1.4 centimeters

   B.   1.6 centimeters

   C.   3.4 centimeters

   D.   4.6 centimeters

   E.   12 centimeters

6. You also plan to buy medium-sized bins to use with a unit that has shelves that are 33 inches wide. How many bins should you order for each shelf?

   F.   2

   G.   3

   H.   4

   J.   5

   K.   6

7. As a chemical technician, you need to measure 3 grams of a substance to prepare a solution. You have weighed 1,800 milligrams of the substance. How much more do you need?

   A.   0.6 gram

   B.   1.2 grams

   C.   1.5 grams

   D.   1.8 grams

   E.   5.4 grams

8. As a home health aide, you are helping a client prepare a shopping list. The client needs to drink 2 cups of juice every day. You calculate that 1 gallon will be enough juice for about a week. The best brand of juice is sold in 1-liter bottles for $1.96 per bottle. If you plan to buy about a gallon of juice, how much will it cost?

   F. $0.49

   G. $0.52

   H. $1.96

   J. $5.88

   K. $7.84

9. You are an environmental health specialist. You check conditions in different kinds of workplaces. In one laboratory, which has equipment that intermittently produces a large amount of heat, you find a wide temperature variation. You record temperatures, ranging from 19°C to 30°C. What is the approximate difference between these temperatures in degrees Fahrenheit?

    A.   10°

    B.   18°

    C.   20°

    D.   68°

    E.   86°

10. As a veterinarian, you find that a cat weighs 13 pounds, 6 ounces. You tell the cat's owner that the cat should weigh closer to $10\frac{1}{2}$ pounds. About how much weight does the cat need to lose?

    F.   2 pounds, 6 ounces

    G.   2 pounds, 10 ounces

    H.   2 pounds, 14 ounces

    J.   3 pounds, 2 ounces

    K.   3 pounds, 8 ounces

11. As a GIS cartographer, you are analyzing a map to make sure that the route of a new pipeline is correctly designated. A map provided by the company planning the pipeline indicates that the length of one segment is $\frac{1}{2}$ mile. Your data indicates that the distance is 0.85 kilometer. What difference between the two measurements needs to be resolved?

    A.   0.045 kilometer

    B.   0.09 kilometer

    C.   0.35 kilometer

    D.   0.425 kilometer

    E.   1.7 kilometers

12. You are a quality control supervisor in a packaging plant. You check the net weight of product in a shipping canister. Specifications call for a product weight of 12.6 kilograms per canister. When you check a randomly selected canister, you find that it contains 12.57 kilograms of material. How much more material should be in the canister?

    F.   3 grams

    G.   30 grams

    H.   51 grams

    J.   300 grams

    K.   510 grams

13. You are a physical therapist planning a fitness program for a patient. You want the patient to walk about 1 mile each day. The patient plans to walk laps around a 400-meter track. About how many laps should the patient walk each day?

    A. $1\frac{1}{2}$

    B. $2\frac{1}{2}$

    C. 4

    D. $13\frac{1}{4}$

    E. 40

14. As a marketing associate, you are preparing a catalog to be used to sell your company's most popular clothing and shoe styles to customers abroad. You need to convert the weight of some items to the metric system. Each pair of Featherweight Slippers weighs 12.2 ounces. About how many grams does a pair of these slippers weigh?

    F. 2 grams

    G. 28 grams

    H. 173 grams

    J. 346 grams

    K. 692 grams

15. Part of your responsibilities as a distribution manager is to calculate available weights on one of your delivery trucks. The truck can carry loads up to 1,200 pounds. You have already loaded 250 pounds onto the truck. In addition, you will be delivering a shipment of 30-kilogram containers. How many containers can you load onto your truck?

    A. 14

    B. 18

    C. 21

    D. 31

    E. 40

16. As the assistant to an industrial engineer, you are reviewing plans to replace 30-gallon water tanks with 110-liter tanks. What is the approximate difference between the capacities of these tanks?

    F. 1 gallon

    G. 59 gallons

    H. 80 gallons

    J. 102 gallons

    K. 387 gallons

Answers are on page 242.

Lesson 16 ■ ■ ■
Find the Best Deal

Skill: Find the best deal using one- and two-step calculations and then comparing results

Many jobs require you to make decisions that involve purchasing equipment, supplies, and services. Among the considerations in making such purchasing decisions is the price. Sometimes you may need to choose between two or more vendors for the same item or service. In order to compare the prices offered by each vendor, you need to make sure that you are comparing the cost of like items. In order to do so, you may need to perform certain calculations. Knowing what calculations to use in order to find the best deal is an important skill for making smart financial decisions both in the workplace and at home.

Skill Examples

> You are a marketing manager who needs to have a 90-page book copyedited. One copyeditor estimates the job will take 15 hours at $32 per hour. Another copyeditor charges $6 per page. Which copyeditor offers the lower estimate?

Example 1

Calculate the total cost based on an hourly rate.

15 hours at $32 per hour

To find the total cost based on an hourly rate, multiply the number of hours worked by the hourly rate.

$$15 \times 32 = \$480$$

Example 2

Calculate the total cost based on a per unit rate.

90 pages at $6 per page

To find the total cost based on a per unit rate, multiply the number of pages by the per unit (page) rate.

$$90 \times 6 = \$540$$

At $480, the first copyeditor's estimate is lower.

Skill Practice

To design a 90-page book, one graphic designer charges $250 per day and estimates that the job will take 5 workdays. Another graphic designer charges $15 per page.

Use the information to the left to:

A. Calculate the total cost based on an hourly rate.

What is the cost at $250 per day for 5 days? _____

B. Calculate the total cost based on a per unit rate.

What is the cost at $15 per page for 90 pages? _____

C. Compare costs.

Which costs less? _____

Try It Out! ■ ■ ■

As a facilities manager, you must select a vendor to install 4 workstations. Vendor A will charge $45 per hour of labor, plus the cost of materials. The vendor estimates that the job will take 6 hours and the materials will cost $1,000. Vendor B will charge $300 per workstation, plus a flat fee of $400 for labor. If you select the vendor that offers the lower estimate, what will be the total cost of installing the workstations?

   A. $1,270   B. $1,600   C. $1,800   D. $2,200   E. $6,000

Step 1   Understand the Problem ■ ■ ■

Complete the *Plan for Successful Solving*.

Plan for Successful Solving				
What am I asked to do?	**What are the facts?**	**How do I find the answer?**	**Is there any unnecessary information?**	**What prior knowledge will help me?**
Find the estimate for installing workstations that is lowest.	Vendor A: $45 per hour (6 hours), plus $1,000 Vendor B: $300 per workstation (4 workstations), plus $400	Determine the price offered by each vendor, and then compare.	No.	Use the order of operations when writing and evaluating expressions.

Step 2   Find and Check Your Answer ■ ■ ■

- Confirm your understanding of the problem and revise your plan as needed.

- Based on your plan, determine your solution approach: *I am going to write expressions to determine the price offered by each vendor, then compare.*

   $(45 \times 6) + 1{,}000 = (270) + 1{,}000 = 1{,}270$ ◄······ Write an expression and evaluate it to find the price offered by Vendor A.

   $(300 \times 4) + 400 = (1{,}200) + 400 = 1{,}600$ ◄······ Write an expression and evaluate it to find the price offered by Vendor B.

   $1{,}270 < 1{,}600$ ◄······ Compare the total costs of the two vendors.

- Check your answer. Use opposite operations to check your answer.

   $1{,}270 - 1{,}000 = 270$; $270 \div 6 = 45$; Vendor A charges $45 per hour.

   $1{,}600 - 400 = 1{,}200$; $1{,}200 \div 4 = 300$; Vendor B charges $300 per workstation.

- **Select the correct answer:** A. $1,270
  By using per unit rates to calculate the total estimate for both vendors, you find that vendor A offers the lower estimate.

Problem Solving Tip

Selecting a vendor often involves considerations besides price. There may be good reasons to choose the vendor whose price is higher, such as positive past experiences and quality of work. However, the *Try It Out!* question does not ask you about these considerations. It only asks for the cost of the job at the lower estimate. Be sure you understand what the question is asking before you begin planning an approach for solving it.

Remember!

If you use the order of operations to evaluate an expression, be sure to use the opposite operations in the opposite order to check your answer.

On Your Own ■ ■ ■

1. As a retail buyer, you are purchasing T-shirts for a small oceanfront gift shop. One supplier offers T-shirts in cases of 36 at a total cost of $153.28. Another supplier offers T-shirts in cases of 24 at a cost of $137.20. If you use the supplier with the lower price, how much will you pay per T-shirt?

A. $1.46

B. $4.26

C. $5.72

D. $8.52

E. $9.98

2. You are the catering manager for a hotel. You are comparing suppliers of lemonade and fruit juices. One supplier sells lemonade and juice by the gallon, at $2.95 per gallon. Another supplier sells lemonade and juice by the quart, at $0.80 per quart. If you use the supplier with the lower price, how much will you pay per gallon?

F. $0.74

G. $0.80

H. $2.15

J. $2.95

K. $3.20

3. As the director of operations for a small insurance company, you are hiring a cleaning service to clean your office. One vendor offers a $750 monthly rate. Another vendor charges $22 per hour. What is the greatest number of hours per month the second vendor could work for you and still cost less than the first vendor?

A. 12 hours

B. 22 hours

C. 34 hours

D. 35 hours

E. 728 hours

4. As a sales representative for an electrical supply company, you need to rent a car for one day. Wheels for Rent charges $89.95 per day, plus $0.12 per mile after 100 miles. Go with Us charges a flat rate of $108.95 per day, with unlimited free miles. You estimate that you will drive the car 150 miles. Based on this estimate, what is the total of the lowest-cost rental car?

F. $18.00

G. $19.00

H. $95.95

J. $107.95

K. $108.95

5. As part of your work as a human resources specialist, you are reviewing bids to staff an on-site day-care center. One bidder will charge $42 per child per day. Another bidder will charge $5.50 per child per hour. Your company will pay half the cost of the child care. The employee will pay the rest. A survey of employees shows that most children will be in day care 8 hours each day, 5 days per week. If you choose the bidder offering the lower price for a child in this situation, how much will the company pay per week for each child?

   A. $91.25

   B. $105.00

   C. $110.00

   D. $210.00

   E. $220.00

6. You work as the director of materials for a school district. You are buying pencils for an elementary school. The School Store offers pencils in packages of 72 for $4.98. For orders of 3 or more packages, the price goes down to $4.80 per package. Write It Now offers similar pencils in packages of 144 for $9.65. You need to order 2,160 pencils. If you use the supplier with the lower price, how much will you pay?

   F. $72.00

   G. $144.00

   H. $144.75

   J. $149.40

   K. $345.60

7. You are the director of purchasing for a medical clinic. The cost of a list of supplies from one vendor is $5,045, plus $125 for shipping. The cost of the same supply list from another vendor is $4,998, plus $150 for shipping. If you use the vendor with the lower price, what is your total cost?

   A. $125

   B. $4,848

   C. $4,998

   D. $5,148

   E. $5,170

8. You are a clinical laboratory manager. Your office needs to purchase a new refrigerator for the testing laboratory. A 24-cubic-foot refrigerator costs $3,552. A 32-cubic-foot refrigerator costs $4,160. Which refrigerator has the lower cost per cubic foot?

   F. $111.00

   G. $130.00

   H. $148.00

   J. $173.34

   K. $608.00

9. As a certified kitchen designer, you are helping a client choose tile for a kitchen. The client has narrowed the choice to two different tiles. The first is a 6-inch tile that costs $128 per box of 100 tiles that will cover 25 square feet. The second is an 8-inch tile that costs $185 per box of 100 tiles that will cover 44.4 square feet. What is the cost per square foot of the less expensive tile?

    A. $1.28

    B. $1.85

    C. $4.17

    D. $5.12

    E. $6.72

10. As a procurement clerk for a non-profit organization, you are comparing the cost of copy paper. The store brand paper costs $40.98 per case. The name brand paper costs $42.98 per case. If you purchase 10 cases of the name brand paper, you pay half price for the tenth case. If you buy 10 cases of the paper that is less expensive, how much will you pay altogether?

    F. $214.90

    G. $389.31

    H. $408.31

    J. $409.80

    K. $429.80

11. You are the regional sales manager for a chain of bakeries. One supplier offers wheat at $5.41 per bushel. You estimate that transportation from this supplier will add $1.03 to the cost per bushel. Another supplier offers wheat at $5.62 per bushel. You estimate that transportation from this supplier will add $0.94 to the cost per bushel. What is the total cost per bushel from the supplier with the lower estimated price?

    A. $0.94

    B. $5.41

    C. $5.57

    D. $6.44

    E. $6.56

12. As a farm manager, you need to buy hay. One supplier offers an alfalfa mix at $120 per ton. Another supplier offers a similar alfalfa mix at $5.60 per 80-pound bale. What is the cost per pound from the supplier with the lower price?

    F. $0.06

    G. $0.07

    H. $0.12

    J. $1.50

    K. $14.29

13. You work as a food service manager for a hotel. You are buying peanut butter for the breakfast buffet. A 9-pound tub of Nutty Nuts costs $19.89. A 15-pound tub of Goin' Nuts costs $28.05. What is the cost per pound of the brand with the lower price?

    A. $0.45

    B. $1.33

    C. $1.43

    D. $1.87

    E. $2.21

14. As the general manager of a hardware store, you are evaluating the cost of mobile phone service for your staff. You currently pay $139 per phone per month for unlimited calling, text messaging, and data services. A competitor is offering a similar package for $119 per phone per month. If you switch to the competitor, you will need to buy new phones for your staff. The new phones will cost $79 each. What is the total cost per phone for the first year for the less expensive plan?

    F. $948

    G. $1,428

    H. $1,507

    J. $1,668

    K. $2,376

15. You are the promotions manager for an electronics outlet. For an upcoming advertising campaign, one designer offers to provide creative services for a flat fee of $1,350. A competitor offers to provide the same services for $65 per hour. You estimate that the job will take 25 hours to complete. Based on your estimate, what would be the cost of working with the designer who will charge less for the job?

    A. $1,300.00

    B. $1,350.00

    C. $1,500.00

    D. $1,625.00

    E. $1,687.50

16. You are a medical technologist assisting in the hiring of a medical equipment repairer to do a repair job. One candidate charges $24 per hour. This candidate estimates that the work will take 15 hours. Another candidate will charge a $380 flat fee for the work. The candidate who charges an hourly rate is hired, and takes 18 hours to complete the work. How much would have been saved if the candidate who charges a flat fee had been hired?

    F. $20

    G. $52

    H. $360

    J. $380

    K. $412

Answers are on page 242.

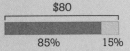
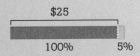
Lesson 17 ■ ■ ■
Calculate Prices with Discounts or Markups

Skill: Calculate percent discounts or markups

When purchasing equipment, supplies, or services in the workplace, you may need to use percents to calculate the price after a discount or markup. When purchasing items for which there is a sales tax, you use the tax rate, written as a percent, to determine what amount is added to the total cost. When purchasing mass quantities of items, such as supplies specific to your industry, you may be offered a percentage discount if you buy a specific amount. You can use this percentage to determine what amount will be taken off the total cost. Knowing how to use percents to calculate the total cost of goods and services after a discount or markup is an important workplace skill.

Skill Examples

Example 1
Calculate the price after a discount.

Find the price after 15% is taken off the regular price of $80.

To find 15% of $80, multiply $80 by the decimal equivalent of 15%, which is 0.15. The product represents the amount of the discount. Subtract the discount from the original price.

$80 − ($80 × 0.15) =

$80 − $12 = $68

Example 2
Calculate the price with a markup.

Find the price after taxes when the original price is $25 and the sales tax is 5%.

To find 5% of $25, multiply $25 by the decimal equivalent of 5%, which is 0.05. The product represents the amount of the markup. Add the markup to the original price.

$25 + ($25 × 0.05) =

$25 + $1.25 = $26.25

Skill Practice

A. Calculate the price after a discount.

$65 at 20% off _____

5 items that cost $8 each at 10% off _____

B. Calculate the price after a markup.

$400 marked up 3% _____

2 items that cost $10.50 each marked up 8% _____

Try It Out! ■ ■ ■

In your role as office manager at a mortgage firm, you have chosen a vendor to provide coffee service. The vendor offers the coffee service at a flat rate of $250 per month. If you sign a 12-month contract with the vendor, you will get a 25% discount on the first 3 months of the contract. What will be the cost of the coffee service for a year if you decide to sign the 12-month contract?

   A. $2,250.00   **B.** $2,437.50   **C.** $2,812.50   **D.** $3,000.00   **E.** $3,187.50

Step 1   Understand the Problem ■ ■ ■

Complete the *Plan for Successful Solving.*

Plan for Successful Solving

What am I asked to do?	What are the facts?	How do I find the answer?	Is there any unnecessary information?	What prior knowledge will help me?
Find the cost of the coffee service based on a 12-month contract.	Cost = $250 per month. 25% discount on the first 3 months	Calculate the cost for the year, then calculate and subtract the discount.	No.	The decimal equivalent of 25% is 0.25.

Step 2   Find and Check Your Answer ■ ■ ■

- Confirm your understanding of the problem and revise your plan as needed.
- Based on your plan, determine your solution approach: *I am going to calculate the cost for the year before the discount. Next, I will calculate the amount of the discount and subtract it from the total.*

  ($250 × 12) = $3,000   ◄······ Multiply to calculate the cost for the year before the discount.

  ($250 × 0.25) × 3 = $62.50 × 3 = $187.50 ◄······ Calculate the amount of the discount. (price per month × percent discount) × 3 months

  $3,000 − $187.50 = $2,812.50   ◄······ Subtract the discount from the total price to find the discount price.

- Check your answer. Solve the problem in a different way, and see if your answers match.
  $250 − ($250 × 0.25) = $250 − $62.50 = $187.50
  (3 × $187.50) + (9 × $250) = $562.50 + $2,250 = $2,812.50
- **Select the correct answer:** C. $2,812.50
  By subtracting the amount of the discount, $187.50, from the cost before the discount, $3,000, you find the total cost for a 12-month contract is $2,812.50.

Problem
Solving Tip
Breaking a problem down into smaller problems is a helpful step as you determine your solution approach. In the *Try It Out!* example, to find the cost of the coffee service for one year, you need to solve a number of smaller problems. You need to find the cost for one year before the discount. You need to find the discount for one month. You then need to find the discount for three months. Finally, you need to subtract to find the solution.

Remember!
Using opposite operations is not the only way to check your solution. Solving the problem in a different way and seeing if both solutions are equal is another way to check to see if your solution is correct.

On Your Own ▪ ▪ ▪

1. You are the associate sales manager for a children's clothing store. For one week, your store offered a 25% discount on all back-to-school items. A backpack that cost $12 during the sale was very popular. After the sale was over, you decided to mark up the backpack only 10% from its sale price. How much does the backpack cost now?

   A. $9.00

   B. $10.80

   C. $13.20

   D. $15.00

   E. $17.60

2. You are the administrative supervisor for a large consulting firm. You have decided that some support staff needs additional training. A three-day professional development seminar costs $1,200 per person. You will receive a 20% discount if 5 or more people attend. You decide to send 6 staff members. How much will you pay for the staff members to attend?

   F. $960

   G. $2,880

   H. $4,800

   J. $5,760

   K. $7,200

3. As an executive secretary, you are helping to prepare budgets for trips during the coming year. For one particular route, which people in your office travel frequently, the round-trip airfare has been $240. Your travel office expects fares to rise 12% next year, so you are adjusting your budget calculations. What cost should you use for the airfare?

   A. $28.80

   B. $248.80

   C. $252.00

   D. $260.00

   E. $268.80

4. As a self-employed commercial designer, you base your fee on a $44 hourly rate. On projects that you estimate will take 120 or more hours, you offer a discount of 10% off the total price. What fee will you charge for a project that you estimate will take 150 hours?

   F. $4,752

   G. $5,280

   H. $5,940

   J. $6,600

   K. $7,260

5. You work as an IT director for a large corporation. Upper management wants your advice about whether or not to lease some computers. One vendor leases computers for $35 per month. If you agree to a 3-year lease, the vendor offers a 15% discount for the first year of the lease. How much would be paid for a computer over the period of a 3-year lease?

    A. $357

    B. $420

    C. $1,071

    D. $1,197

    E. $1,260

6. You are the buyer for a grocery store. Conventional apples cost $32 per 40-pound case. Organic apples cost 10% more per 40-pound case. You decide to buy 100 cases of conventional apples and 100 cases of organic apples. What is the total cost?

    F. $168

    G. $2,688

    H. $3,200

    J. $3,520

    K. $6,720

7. As a plant manager in an industrial metal shop, you need to replace two lathes. The two models you need cost $1,150 and $980. The vendor offers a 12% discount if you buy both models. How much will you pay if you buy both models?

    A. $1,724.80

    B. $1,874.40

    C. $2,024.00

    D. $2,130.00

    E. $2,385.60

8. You are the manager of an appliance store. Every August, you offer air conditioners at a 15% discount. There are 12 units in your inventory that you need to sell. You will offer a discount of an additional 10% off the original price. If their original price is $139 and you sell all 12, how much will the store receive in payment for the units?

    F. $1,251.00

    G. $1,417.80

    H. $1,501.20

    J. $1,584.60

    K. $1,668.00

9. As a medical secretary for a pediatric practice, you are putting together a 48-page report. The printer charges $0.12 per page. The printer also offers a 5% discount for orders of 5,000 pages or more and an 8% discount for orders of 10,000 pages or more. You need to print 150 copies of the report. How much will it cost to print the reports altogether?

A. $18.00

B. $570.00

C. $794.88

D. $820.80

E. $864.00

10. You are a buyer for a retail fashion chain and recently ordered 40 cases of jeans at $280 per case. The supplier is going to be late in filling the order. You ask for a 15% discount on the order, and the supplier agrees. How much will be paid for the order?

F. $59

G. $70

H. $9,520

J. $11,200

K. $12,880

11. As a Web site designer, you based your $1,760 bid for a project on a $22 hourly rate. The client has changed the plan several times. Because of this, you have spent more time on the project than you estimated. Based on the terms of the contract, you now will charge 18% more than your original bid because of the increased time you have had to spend on the project. How much will you charge?

A. $1,778.00

B. $2,076.80

C. $2,147.20

D. $2,464.00

E. $3,200.00

12. As a purchasing manager, you are responsible for buying supplies for a community health clinic. Your supplier has raised the shipping fee by 10% for orders under $100. The fee was $4.50. You place an order for $85 of supplies. How much will the order cost with shipping?

F. $80.05

G. $80.50

H. $89.50

J. $89.95

K. $93.50

13. You are an occupational safety specialist. You are putting together a training video on workplace safety. To create the video, you need to rent video equipment for 10 days. The charge per day for the equipment is $159. Because you are renting the equipment for more than 5 days, you will receive a 10% discount on the total cost of the rental. How much will you pay?

    A. $159.00

    B. $715.50

    C. $1,431.00

    D. $1,510.50

    E. $1,590.00

14. As an assistant principal you are responsible for the business operations of your school, including purchasing food for the kitchen and cafeteria. Your distributor informs you to expect the cost of flour to go up next month. The supplier expects the cost to go up 5% but says that it could go up as much as 8%. The cost of 50 pounds of flour is now $16. If the cost goes up the highest possible amount, what will be the new price for 50 pounds of flour?

    F. $16.05

    G. $16.08

    H. $16.80

    J. $17.28

    K. $24.00

15. As a conference planner, you are organizing a welcome dinner for the speakers at the conference. You expect 270 guests to attend. The caterer charges $55 per person and offers an 8% discount per person for meals with 100 or more guests. How much will the catering for the dinner cost?

    A. $1,188

    B. $13,662

    C. $14,850

    D. $16,038

    E. $17,226

16. You are the operations manager for a non-profit business. You need to hire a company to offer information technology (IT) support. One company offers support for $890 per month. If you sign a 1-year contract with this company, there will be a 20% discount on the first 3 months. If you accept this offer, what is the total amount you will pay over the term of the contract?

    F. $2,136

    G. $8,544

    H. $10,146

    J. $10,680

    K. $11,214

Answers are on page 242.

Lesson 18 ■ ■ ■
Divide Negative Numbers

Skill: Divide negative numbers

To perform calculations in the workplace, you sometimes may need to divide negative numbers. Remember, negative numbers are less than zero. In business, for example, debts may be represented using negative numbers. Negative numbers can also be used to represent movement in a certain direction. For example, working in a museum, you may have to track the decline in membership over a period of years. In many industries, it is necessary to divide negative numbers when working with budgets or inventory.

As is the case when multiplying numbers, there are two rules to remember regarding signs when dividing negative numbers. When the signs of both numbers are the same, the quotient is positive. When the signs of the two numbers are different, the quotient is negative.

Skill Examples

Example 1
Divide a negative number by a positive number.

Divide: $-15 \div 3$

To divide when one of the numbers is negative, consider the numbers without their signs and divide. Then add the sign to the quotient. Because the numbers' signs are different, the quotient is negative.

$$-15 \div 3 = -5$$

To see why the answer is negative, consider the following number line:

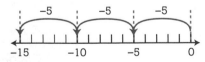

Example 2
Divide two negative numbers.

Divide: $-96 \div -12$

Again, consider the numbers without their signs, and divide. Then add the sign to the quotient. Because the signs of the dividend and divisor are the same, the quotient is positive.

$$-96 \div -12 = 8$$

Skill Practice

A. Divide a positive number by a negative number.

$55 \div -5$ = _____

B. Divide a negative number by a positive number.

$-18 \div 3$ = _____

C. Divide two negative numbers.

$-24 \div -6$ = _____

Try It Out! ■ ■ ■

You are arranging to repay a loan that you took out to purchase a table saw for your business. You plan to pay a total of $4,500, including interest, in 12 equal payments over one year. If you make $2,880 in the first month of that year and have no other costs besides the monthly loan payment, what is your net profit for the month?

A. $240   B. $375   C. $1,620   D. $2,505   E. $4,125

Step 1   Understand the Problem ■ ■ ■

Complete the *Plan for Successful Solving.*

Plan for Successful Solving

What am I asked to do?	What are the facts?	How do I find the answer?	Is there any unnecessary information?	What prior knowledge will help me?
Find the profit for the first month of the year.	$4,500 will be paid in 12 equal payments over one year. First month's income is $2,880.	Find amount paid for the loan in one month. Add that amount to the first month's income.	No.	When calculating profit, amounts paid out can be represented as negative numbers.

Step 2   Find and Check Your Answer ■ ■ ■

- Confirm your understanding of the problem and revise your plan as needed.

- Based on your plan, determine your solution approach: *I will divide –$4,500 by 12 to find my monthly payment. The result of this expression can be added to the amount I make in the first month of the year to find my net profit for that month.*

     (–4,500 ÷ 12) + 2,880 ◄······ Set up an expression that represents the monthly loan payment (–$4,500 ÷ 12) plus the income for the first month of the year ($2,880).

     (–375) + 2,880 ◄······ Calculate what is in parentheses first to find the monthly loan payment.

     $2,505 ◄······ Add the monthly loan payment—a negative number—to the income made in the first month to determine the net profit for the month.

- Check your answer. Use opposite operations.
  2,505 – 2,880 = –375; –375 × 12 = –4,500
  The loan amount is $4,500.

- **Select the correct answer:** D. $2,505
  By dividing $4,500 by 12, you find the monthly payment: $375. After $375 is paid for the loan, the profit for the first month of the year is $2,505.

Remember!

Adding a negative number is the same as subtracting a positive number.

Problem Solving Tip

After you select an answer, review the problem to be sure that your answer makes sense. In the *Try It Out!* example, answer choice E does not make sense. The profit for the month cannot be greater than the amount earned in the month.

On Your Own ▪ ▪ ▪

1. You are a curator for an earth science museum. As part of your job, you plan and conduct climate research projects. You collect data for a study on climate change. For the study, you record the temperature at the same location at 4 A.M. every morning for one week. The table shows your data. What was the average temperature at 4 A.M. that week?

Temperature at 4 A.M.						
MON	TUE	WED	THU	FRI	SAT	SUN
2°C	−7°C	−3°C	−2°C	−3°C	−2°F	1°C

    A. −20°C

    B. −14°C

    C. −2°C

    D. 2°C

    E. 3°C

2. As a brokerage clerk, you are discussing the price of a stock with a client. The stock closed at $45.72 per share 4 months ago. Today the stock closed at $34.28 per share. What is the average change in the price of the stock per month?

    F. −$45.76

    G. −$2.86

    H. $8.57

    J. $11.43

    K. $11.44

3. You are an office manager for a small dental practice. The practice will owe $14,400 to rent office equipment and furniture for the year. The practice will pay this amount in 12 equal monthly payments. The vendor renting the equipment and furniture to the practice has offered a $250 discount on the first monthly payment. What amount should you write in the ledger for the first monthly payment?

    A. −$14,150

    B. −$1,450

    C. −$1,200

    D. −$950

    E. −$250

4. As a dietician, you work with adults trying to lose or maintain weight. One of your clients weighed 189 pounds 12 months ago. Now the client weighs 135 pounds. What is the average change in the client's weight per month?

    F. −54 pounds

    G. −4.5 pounds

    H. 11 pounds

    J. 15.5 pounds

    K. 54 pounds

5. In your work as a refinery operator, you are monitoring the transfer of heating oil from a storage tank into a barge. Your computer monitor constantly updates the level of oil in the tank, showing a negative change as the level decreases. If the initial level was 15.8 meters and 30 minutes into the transfer the level is 11.3 meters, what is the transfer rate?

    A.   −1,500 centimeters/minute

    B.   −150 centimeters/minute

    C.   −120 centimeters/minute

    D.   −15 centimeters/minute

    E.   150 centimeters/minute

6. One of your responsibilities as a sales manager for a local sporting goods store is to review reports to determine your company's profitability. For the past year, the total cost of goods sold was $180,000. The net sales for the year were $330,000. Gross profit is the difference between net sales and the cost of goods sold. What was the average monthly gross profit for the year?

    F.   −$15,000

    G.   −$12,500

    H. $12,500

    J. $15,000

    K. $27,500

7. You work as a chemical engineer consultant. You are helping a manufacturing plant design a system to decrease its carbon emissions. Last year the plant released 24,500 metric tons of carbon dioxide into the atmosphere. In each of the next 5 years, the plant will decrease its yearly emissions by the same amount. Its emissions will be 20,000 metric tons of carbon dioxide in the fifth year. What will be the change in the carbon emissions in each of the 5 years?

    A.   −8,900 metric tons

    B.   −4,900 metric tons

    C.   −4,000 metric tons

    D.   −900 metric tons

    E.   4,500 metric tons

8. You are a technician working for a company that manufactures medical supplies. One of your tasks involves testing the properties of plastic formulations to be used for medical applications. You monitor the plastic as it cools from 148°C to room temperature, 18°C. It takes the plastic 26 minutes to cool. What is the average change in temperature per minute?

    F.   −18°C

    G.   −8°C

    H.   −5°C

    J.   130°C

    K.   166°C

9. As the executive secretary to a zoo administrator, you keep track of zoo membership and direct the annual membership drive. Three years ago, the zoo membership was 8,370. The zoo now has 7,920 members. What was the average change in membership per year?

    A. −450

    B. −150

    C. 1,350

    D. 2,640

    E. 2,790

10. You are a store manager at an outlet store for a large retail chain. A burst pipe at a distribution center damaged inventory valued at $11,250. The distribution center serves 8 shopping outlets, including the one you manage. Each outlet will share equally in the loss. You had expected to report a profit of $283,400. Accounting for the loss, what profit will you report?

    F. −$11,250.00

    G. −$9,843.75

    H. −$1,406.25

    J. $272,150.00

    K. $281,993.75

11. As an environmental restoration planner, you track changes to an eroding shoreline. You compare current measurements to historical surveying data. A certain point was 72 yards from the shore 4 years ago. That point is now 64 yards from the shore. What was the average change per year in the distance between the point and the shore?

    A. −18 yards

    B. −16 yards

    C. −2 yards

    D. 8 yards

    E. 32 yards

12. As a fitness instructor, you train people who have never run before to compete in 5-kilometer races. One of your clients completes her first 5-kilometer race in 36 minutes, 15 seconds. She completes her next 5-kilometer race, 10 weeks later, in 31 minutes, 55 seconds. What is the change in rate?

    F. −52 seconds per kilometer

    G. −40 seconds per kilometer

    H. −26 seconds per kilometer

    J. 260 seconds per kilometer

    K. 520 seconds per kilometer

13. You are an environmental scientist, monitoring the oxygen levels in a lake and the effect of changing levels on the population of invertebrates. During a 3-week period, rainfall was substantially below normal and several of the feeder streams stopped flowing into the lake. At a particular sampling site, your records show a change in oxygen concentration from 10.3 milligrams per liter to 8.8 milligrams per liter. What is the rate of change in oxygen concentration during this period?

    A.   −1.5 milligrams/Liter per week

    B.   −0.5 milligram/Liter per week

    C.   −0.1 milligram/Liter per week

    D.   0.5 milligram/Liter per week

    E.   1.0 milligram/Liter per week

14. As a public relations specialist for a private university, you are trying to reduce costs for supplies used during promotional campaigns. Your office has been purchasing printer ink cartridges in bulk for $46.35 per box. You now plan to buy another brand of printer ink cartridge that costs $39.95 per box. Each box contains 10 cartridges. What is the change in the cost of printer ink per cartridge for your office?

    F.   −$6.40

    G.   −$0.64

    H. $33.55

    J. $45.71

    K. $64.00

15. You are an aquarium maintenance technician making repairs to a 1,350-gallon sea life exhibit tank. In order to make the repairs, you need to empty the exhibit tank water into a secondary holding tank. You are using a pump that can remove water from the tank at a rate of 25 gallons per minute. How long will it take to empty the tank?

    A.   25 minutes

    B.   54 minutes

    C.   1,296 minutes

    D.   1,325 minutes

    E.   33,750 minutes

16. As a financial planner, you help clients reduce their debt. After paying for fixed expenses, one client has $1,850 in net income each month. Over the next 12 months, the client wants to pay a total of $9,000 toward his debt in equal monthly payments. How much income will the client have left each month after the monthly debt payment?

    F.   −$7,150

    G.   −$750

    H. $1,100

    J. $2,600

    K. $108,000

Answers are on page 242.

Level 5 Performance Assessment

The following problems will test your ability to answer questions at a Level 5 rating of difficulty. These problems are similar to those that appear on a Career Readiness Certificate test. For each question, you can refer to the answer key for answer justifications. The answer justifications provide an explanation of why each answer option is either correct or incorrect and indicate the skill lesson that should be referred to if further review of a particular skill is needed.

1. As a nurse-midwife, you deliver babies. A newborn baby weighs 3.4 kilograms. The parents are unfamiliar with the metric system of measurement. What is the baby's weight in pounds and ounces, to the nearest ounce?

   A. 1 pound, 2 ounces

   B. 1 pound, 5 ounces

   C. 5 pounds, 6 ounces

   D. 7 pounds, 5 ounces

   E. 7 pounds, 8 ounces

2. You work as an industrial designer. You are creating specifications for workstations. Each station will have a work surface that is $2\frac{1}{2}$ feet from the floor, 2 feet deep, and 4 feet wide. How many square feet is the area of the work surface?

   F. 2

   G. 5

   H. 8

   J. 10

   K. 20

3. As a financial manager, you discuss the price of a fund with a client. The fund cost $64.20 per share 6 months ago. Today it costs $54.90 per share. What is the average change per month in the cost of one share of this fund?

   A. −$9.30

   B. −$1.55

   C. $9.15

   D. $10.70

   E. $19.85

4. You are the information systems manager for a small publishing company that is planning a move to a new building. The new building will provide Internet service to the company for an additional $425 per month in rent. A different vendor will provide Internet service to the company for $399 per month, plus a one-time $250 installation fee. If you select the vendor that offers the lower price, what will be the total cost of Internet service in the first year?

   F. $3,000

   G. $4,788

   H. $5,038

   J. $5,100

   K. $7,788

5. You work as a quality control auditor for a company that makes commercial shelving and furniture. The specification sheet shows that a shelving unit measures 1.2 meters tall, 0.8 meter wide, and 36 centimeters deep. You find that it is 1.197 meters tall. What is the difference between the actual height of the unit and the specified height?

    A. 0.003 millimeter

    B. 3 millimeters

    C. 195 millimeters

    D. 397 millimeters

    E. 2,397 millimeters

6. As a shift supervisor for a packaging and distribution center, you learn that production in your unit has fallen by 15%. The unit of 8 workers is filling 720 orders per 9-hour shift. Over the next 4 weeks, management wants to see the number of orders filled in one shift increase to 792. How many more orders per shift will each worker need to fill?

    F. 8

    G. 9

    H. 10

    J. 18

    K. 72

7. You are the shipping coordinator for a business that sells children's books and toys through the Internet. You have learned that the company's shipping carrier is raising its prices. The cost to ship a 1-pound package was $2.50, and the cost per additional pound up to 9 additional pounds was $0.40. The company is raising the cost to $2.85 for the first pound and $0.50 for each additional pound. If you generally ship packages that weigh 5 pounds, what is a good estimate of the percentage increase in your annual shipping costs?

    A. 0.18%

    B. 1.8%

    C. 14%

    D. 15%

    E. 18%

8. You are the facility maintenance supervisor of a health clinic. A staff member needs your help ordering supplies. There are 9 gallons of bleach in stock, but 40 gallons are needed. The bleach is now sold in 4-liter containers. How many of these containers should be ordered?

    F. 3

    G. 10

    H. 29

    J. 30

    K. 118

9. You work as a display specialist. You are designing a display for the front window of a shop. You plan to install light bulbs every 3 inches around the perimeter of the window. The window is 6 feet long and 3 feet wide. How many light bulbs will you need?

    A. 6

    B. 9

    C. 18

    D. 54

    E. 72

10. As a truck driver, you are transporting goods to a city in Canada. You are driving 55 miles per hour. A sign indicates that you are 178 kilometers from your destination. About how long will it take for you to reach your destination?

    F. 1 hour, 16 minutes

    G. 1 hour, 50 minutes

    H. 2 hours

    J. 3 hours, 14 minutes

    K. 5 hours, 12 minutes

11. You are an account manager. You offer a client a discount on the training manuals that accompany the professional development services the client bought. The charge for the manuals is usually $12, and you are offering a 60% discount. How much will the client pay for 55 manuals?

    A. $264

    B. $396

    C. $627

    D. $660

    E. $3,300

12. As a veterinarian, you find that a dog weighs 38.8 pounds. The dog weighed 40 pounds 6 months ago, and its owner was told then that the dog should lose 4 pounds. How many more pounds does the dog need to lose?

    F. 1.2

    G. 2.8

    H. 4.8

    J. 5.2

    K. 36

13. In your work as a program director for a youth organization, you are helping a group of teens design a course for skateboarding. Your team has designed a ramp that has three sections, measuring 7 feet, 10 inches; 15 feet, 8 inches; and 12 feet, 8 inches. What is the total length of the ramp?

    A.   34 feet

    B.   35 feet, 6 inches

    C.   36 feet, 2 inches

    D.   36 feet, 6 inches

    E.   37 feet

14. As the property manager of several apartment buildings, you will be hiring painters to repaint an apartment for new tenants. The apartment includes 2 bedrooms, 1 living room, a small kitchen, and a bathroom. One company estimates a charge of $450 for each of the 3 larger rooms and $200 for each of the 2 smaller rooms. Another company will charge $85 per hour for the job and estimates that the job will take 20 hours. If you select the vendor that offers the lower estimate, what will be the total cost of the paint job?

    F. $650

    G. $1,550

    H. $1,700

    J. $1,750

    K. $3,250

15. As a graphic designer, you charge $38 per hour for your work. For a recent job, you worked 18 hours to design and produce 5 mock-ups of a proposed advertisement for a client. How much do you charge for this job?

    A. $56

    B. $90

    C. $190

    D. $684

    E. $3,420

16. You are the manager of member services at a botanical garden. You notice a decline in the number of members. The garden had 24,360 members 12 months ago. It now has 20,040 members. What is the average change per month in the number of members?

    F.   −4,320

    G.   −360

    H.   1,670

    J.   2,030

    K.   3,700

17. You are a stonemason who has been hired to lay a stone path around the perimeter of a rectangular garden. The garden is 5 meters long and 3.5 meters wide. The stone path will be 1 meter wide.

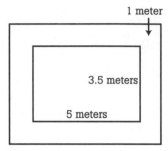

1 meter

3.5 meters

5 meters

What is the total area of the garden and the path around it?

A.   9.5 square meters

B.   17.5 square meters

C.   21 square meters

D.   27 square meters

E.   38.5 square meters

18. As a research technician, you are preparing a solution. You need 450 grams of a chemical. You have a 12-ounce bottle of the chemical. How much more of the chemical do you need?

F.   15.4 grams

G.   37.5 grams

H.   109.8 grams

J.   438.0 grams

K.   12,417.3 grams

19. As part of your work as a physician's assistant, you measure patients' blood pressure, height, and weight. A patient weighed 186 pounds 12 months ago and now weighs 138 pounds. What is the average change per month in the patient's weight?

A.   −48 pounds

B.   −12 pounds

C.   −4 pounds

D.   11.5 pounds

E.   15.5 pounds

20. As the buyer for a grocery store, you are comparing the cost of produce from two different vendors. One vendor offers a mixed pallet of thirty-six 40-pound boxes of fruit for $1,224. Another vendor offers a mixed pallet of twenty-four 40-pound boxes of a similar variety of fruit for $840. What is the lower price per 40-pound box?

F. $21.00

G. $23.33

H. $30.60

J. $34.00

K. $35.00

21. As the purchasing manager for a medical facility, you are comparing prices for latex exam gloves. One vendor charges $73.90 for a case that includes 10 boxes, each with 100 gloves. Another vendor charges $87 for a case that includes 12 boxes, each with 100 gloves. What is the cost per box at the lower price?

    A. $0.74

    B. $0.87

    C. $7.25

    D. $7.39

    E. $73.90

22. As a building contractor, you are working with a hotel to build a concrete wading pool. The pool will be circular, with a diameter of 10 feet. You need to estimate the amount of concrete needed for the pool floor. What is the approximate area of the pool floor?

    F. 15 square feet

    G. 15.7 square feet

    H. 31.4 square feet

    J. 78.5 square feet

    K. 314 square feet

23. You are a self-employed medical transcriber. You have decided to raise your hourly rate of $14 by 8%. At the new rate, how much more will you make in a week when you work 25 hours?

    A. $2.00

    B. $15.12

    C. $28.00

    D. $200.00

    E. $378.00

24. You work as a market researcher. You are conducting interviews to follow up a written survey. You will interview 20 consumers one-on-one. You have a 4-hour, 30-minute block for interviews, and you need to schedule 18 minutes for each interview. If you do the maximum number of interviews possible in this block of time, how many interviews will you have left to do afterward?

    F. 5

    G. 15

    H. 25

    J. 35

    K. 250

25. As a commercial interior designer, you order fabric for a project. You order 25 yards of blue fabric for $75, 32 yards of green fabric for $120, and 28 yards of gray fabric for $109. The company offers a 10% discount on orders of $150 or more and charges $12 for shipping. How much will your order cost?

    A. $154.00

    B. $273.60

    C. $285.60

    D. $304.00

    E. $316.00

26. In your work as a research associate, you check the freezer in which specimens are stored 4 times each day. One day, you record temperatures of −20°C, −18°C, −17°C, and −17°C. Based on these measurements, what is the average temperature of the freezer on that day?

    F. −288°C

    G. −72°C

    H. −18°C

    J. 18°C

    K. 72°C

27. You are an industrial engineering technician. You measure a wheel on a machine to be sure that it meets specifications. The width of the wheel is 2 inches and its diameter is 9 inches. What is its approximate circumference?

    A. 9.42 inches

    B. 12.14 inches

    C. 14.13 inches

    D. 28.26 inches

    E. 56.52 inches

28. As an event manager, you learn that 40 quarts of milk have been delivered instead of the 40 gallons that were ordered. The kitchen staff tells you that they need at least 36 gallons of milk to make the desserts for an upcoming event. How much more milk is needed?

    F. 1 gallon

    G. 26 gallons

    H. 30 gallons

    J. 120 gallons

    K. 124 gallons

Answers are on page 242.

Level 6 Introduction ...

The lesson and practice pages that follow will give you the opportunity to develop and practice the mathematical skills needed to solve work-related problems at a Level 6 rating of difficulty. The *On Your Own* practice problems provide a review of math skills and instruction for specific problem-solving strategies. The *Performance Assessment* provides problems similar to those you will encounter on a Career Readiness Certificate test. By completing the Level 6 *On Your Own* and *Performance Assessment* problems, you will gain the ability to confidently approach workplace scenarios that require understanding and application of the skills featured in the following lessons:

Lesson 19: Find the Best Deal and Use the Result

Lesson 20: Calculate with Numbers in Various Forms

Lesson 21: Find Volume of Rectangular Solids

Lesson 22: Rearrange a Formula

Lesson 23: Change from One Unit to Another in the Same Measurement System

Lesson 24: Convert from One System of Measurement to Another

Lesson 25: Calculate Multiple Rates

Lesson 26: Apply Formula Rearrangements and Unit Conversions to Calculate Area

These skills are intended to help you successfully understand and solve problems requiring mathematics in the workplace that involve numbers in various forms and calculating and working within and between systems of measurement using formulas. Solving these types of problems often requires the ability to:

- translate calculations from verbal form to mathematical expressions
- set up extensive problems that involve multiple-step calculations.

Through solving problems at this level, you will continue to develop problem-solving approaches and strategies that will help you determine the correct answer in real-world and test-taking situations.

Lesson 19 ■ ■ ■
Find the Best Deal and Use the Result

Skill: Find the best deal and use the result in another calculation

Many workplace decisions require you to use mathematics to determine the best deal for goods and services. To determine the best company from which to order supplies, you may need to calculate and compare the prices of both supplies and shipping costs for various suppliers. Sometimes you may have to calculate the cost per unit for items offered in different quantities to find the best deal.

Skill Examples

Example 1
Find the total cost for goods and shipping.
There are two options for ordering a printer.

Option A:

Subtotal = $125.50

Shipping = $19.25

Option B:

Subtotal = $140.27

Shipping = Free for all orders of $100 or more

To calculate the total cost for Option A, add the shipping amount to the subtotal.

$125.50 + $19.25 = $144.75

Compare Option A to Option B

$144.75 > $140.27

Although the cost of the printer is higher for Option 2, with no shipping fee, it is the better deal.

Example 2
Find the cost per unit.
There are two options for ordering boxes of staples.

Option A:

$25.99 for 12 boxes of 500 staples

Option B:

$50 for 25 boxes of 500 staples

Compare Option A to Option B by finding the cost per unit (box). To calculate, divide the cost by the number of boxes.

Option A: $25.99 ÷ 12 = $2.17 per box

Option B: $50.00 ÷ 25 = $2.00 per box

The cost per unit for option B is cheaper.

Skill Practice

A. Add dollar amounts. $39.95 + $4.95   = _____

B. Subtract a smaller dollar amount from a larger dollar amount. $1034 − $995   = _____

C. Multiply a dollar amount by a whole number. $4.15 × 12   = _____

D. Divide a dollar amount by a whole number. $72.40 ÷ 20   = _____

Try It Out! ■ ■ ■

As a caterer, you are following a new recipe at the request of your client. The recipe calls for 75 ounces of an artisan cheese that you do not use in any other recipes. The cheese can be purchased in two sizes—$16 for a 25-ounce block or $18 for 30-ounce block. What is the least amount of money you can pay to have enough cheese for the recipe?

A. $18   B. $32   C. $36   D. $48   E. $54

Step 1 Understand the Problem ■ ■ ■

Complete the *Plan for Successful Solving.*

Plan for Successful Solving

What am I asked to do?	What are the facts?	How do I find the answer?	Is there any unnecessary information?	What prior knowledge will help me?
Determine the lowest cost for buying enough cheese for the recipe.	A 25-oz. block is $16. A 30-oz. block is $18. You need 75 ounces total.	Use division to determine how many blocks will be needed, depending on the size purchased.	No.	If ingredients are not sold in the exact amount needed, you may have extra when finished.

Step 2 Find and Check Your Answer ■ ■ ■

- Confirm your understanding of the problem and revise your plan as needed.

- Based on your plan, determine your solution approach: *I am going to divide to determine how many blocks of cheese I will need for both options. I will then multiply this by the cost per block for each size to determine what the total cost will be for each.*

  75 ounces ÷ 25 oz./block = 3 blocks   ◄---- Divide the amount needed by the amount in each block to determine how many blocks will be needed.
  75 ounces ÷ 30 oz./block = 2.5 → 3 blocks

  3 × $16 per block = $48   ◄---- Multiply to determine how much it will cost to purchase the amount needed for each block.
  3 × $18 per block = $54

- Check your answer. 3 × 25 ounces = 75 ounces; 3 × 30 ounces = 90 ounces. Regardless of which size is chosen, 3 blocks are needed to make the recipe. This means that the cheapest option is to buy three, 25-ounce blocks of cheese.

- **Select the correct answer:**   D. $48
  Although the cheese that is sold in 30-ounce blocks has a lower unit cost (per ounce), three blocks are needed in order to have enough to make the recipe. Because of this, purchasing 25-ounce blocks is actually the cheapest option.

Problem Solving Tip

When finding the best deal, consider all aspects of the situation before making your decision. In situations where you need a particular item and it is sold in different sizes or amounts, it is often an appropriate first step to determine which option has the lowest per unit cost. This makes sense if you don't mind purchasing more of the item than is needed and are certain you will use up the entire supply. In the *Try It Out!* example, however, this is not the case. While the 30-ounce block of cheese is less expensive per ounce, purchasing it means that you will have to spend more in order to have the amount needed and there will be extra cheese when the recipe is complete. Because of this, it is actually cheaper to purchase the cheese that is more expensive per ounce but will give you the exact amount.

Remember!

When dividing to find the amount needed, a remainder or decimal amount can often indicate that you need to round up to the next highest whole number. In the *Try It Out!* example, when you divide you find that you need 2.5 blocks of the 30-ounce block. Since you cannot purchase 0.5 blocks, you must round up, meaning that 3 blocks are needed.

On Your Own ■ ■ ■

1. As an accountant, you are going over your client's expenses and making recommendations. You notice that your client spends $24.39 on shipping for each overnight package she sends. She shipped one overnight package per week for 50 weeks of the year. You know of a shipping company that offers a deal for shipping one overnight package per week for a yearly flat rate of $1,000. Assuming she will again send 50 packages in the upcoming year, is the flat rate a better deal and what is the price difference?

   A. Yes, she would spend $119.50 less per year.

   B. No, she would spend $219.50 more per year.

   C. Yes, she would spend $219.50 less per year.

   D. No, she would spend $878.05 more per year.

   E. Yes, she would spend $878.05 less per year.

2. You are an occupational safety and health technician. You must order 100 respiratory masks to use while testing air quality. One company sells a pack of 20 masks for $10.77, and another company sells a pack of 50 masks for $14.99. What is the least amount of money you can spend on 100 masks?

   F. $21.54

   G. $29.98

   H. $43.08

   J. $53.85

   K. $74.95

3. You are a biological technician in a lab and you need to order 800 Petri dishes. A pack of 100 Petri dishes costs $45. A pack of 300 Petri dishes costs $95. What is the lowest cost you could spend on the order?

   A. $280

   B. $285

   C. $320

   D. $360

   E. $450

4. As an electrician, you need 450 feet of electrical wire for a job. A 500-foot roll of the wire costs $39.95, a 100-foot roll costs $9.95, and a 50-foot roll costs $5.95. What is the least amount of money you can spend on the electrical wire for this job?

   F. $34.00

   G. $39.80

   H. $39.95

   J. $45.75

   K. $53.55

5. As a nurse practioner, one of your responsibilities is ordering blood collection tubes for the entire lab. You go through about 2 boxes of tubes a week. The shelf life of the tubes is one year (52 weeks) and unused tubes must be destroyed when they expire. There are two suppliers who offer the type of tube your lab needs. What is the lowest price you could pay for a year's supply if you can only use one supplier?

Supplier A: 10 boxes for $109; 25 boxes for $265

Supplier B: 20 boxes for $214; 50 boxes for $525; 150 boxes for $1,530

    A. $1,050

    B. $1,159

    C. $1,169

    D. $1,199

    E. $1,284

6. As a business analyst going over a client's books, you notice your client spends $29.95 per month to have printer ink delivered. He uses 3 printer ink cartridges per month. You know that a local store charges $8.95 per cartridge for a box of 9 cartridges. Would your client get a better deal if he bought boxes of cartridges at the store?

    F. Yes, he would save $3.10 per month.

    G. No, he would lose $3.10 per month.

    H. Yes, he would save $12.02 per month.

    J. No, he would lose $12.02 per month.

    K. Yes, he would save $21 per month.

7. You are working as a solar panel technician. You need 60 solar panel connecting kits for a job. One company sells boxes of 8 kits for $155.45. Another company sells boxes of 10 kits for $190.00. What is the lowest price you could pay to get at least 60 kits?

    A. $777.25

    B. $932.70

    C. $950.00

    D. $1,140.00

    E. $1,243.60

8. As a clinical lab technician, one of your instruments has broken and must be replaced immediately. Company A sells the instrument for $695.00 and will charge $39.95 for overnight shipping. Company B sells the instrument for $619.95 and will charge $45.00 for shipping. Who has the better deal and by how much?

    F. Company B by $30.00

    G. Company B by $70.00

    H. Company B by $74.95

    J. Company A by $75.05

    K. Company A by $115.00

9. In order to conduct your work as a computer specialist for a geologic consulting firm, you need a special software program. You can get the program by subscription for $19.95 per month, or you can buy the program for $210.00. Which is the better deal over the course of one year and how much will you save?

A. The subscription is a better deal. You will save $10.50.

B. Buying the program is a better deal. You will save $12.05.

C. The subscription is a better deal. You will save $24.00.

D. Buying the program is a better deal. You will save $29.40.

E. The subscription is a better deal. You will save $190.05.

10. You are a sales representative for a company that makes specialty alloys. You have received two offers for some of your recovered metal scrap. Company X will pay $12.49 per pound, and it will cost you $140.00 to package 100 pounds in the 1-pound containers that they need. Company Y will pay $12.18 per pound, and it will cost you $100.00 to package the material in 5-pound containers. Which is the most profit you can make on 100 pounds?

F. Sell to Company X for a profit of $1,109

G. Sell to Company Y for a profit of $1,118

H. Sell to Company X for a profit of $1,249

J. Sell to Company Y for a profit of $1,318

K. Sell to Company X for a profit of $1,389

11. You are a health and safety manager. You need a supply of 1,000 disposable rubber gloves for your job. A box of 500 gloves costs $19.95, and a box of 250 gloves costs $10.95. Which is the better deal and how much do you save on 1,000 gloves?

A. The box of 500; $0.10

B. The box of 500; $1.00

C. The box of 500; $3.90

D. The box of 250; $6.10

E. The box of 250; $9.00

12. You are a plant manager at a biofuels plant. You need to order a new pump. Pump A costs $4,400 with $350 shipping, while pump B costs $4,100 with $380 shipping. Which is the better deal and by how much?

F. Pump A by $30

G. Pump A by $80

H. Pump B by $80

J. Pump B by $270

K. Pump B by $300

13. You are a certified public accountant. When looking over a client's records, you see that she is paying $500/month for a 1,000–square foot office. You know that market value for office space in the area is $0.35 per square foot. Which best describes whether you should advise your client to move offices?

    A. Yes, because she is paying $150 per month over market value.

    B. Yes, because she is paying $250 per month over market value.

    C. Yes, because she is paying $350 per month over market value.

    D. No, because she is saving $150 per month compared to market value.

    E. No, because she is saving $350 per month compared to market value.

14. As a stonemason, your job is to cut slabs of granite rock. You need to order rock-cutting blades for your saw. You have tried two different kinds of blades. Blade A costs $130 and lasts 10 days, and blade B costs $100 and lasts 6 days. What is the least amount you can pay for a 30-day supply?

    F. $300

    G. $390

    H. $500

    J. $600

    K. $1,300

15. Part of your job as an air pollution control engineer is to periodically test for acid rain. You need a supply of pH strips for the study you are conducting this month. You go through about 150 pH strips per week. A box of 100 pH strips costs $15. A box of 200 pH strips costs $25. Which is the better deal, and how much will a 4-week supply cost?

    A. Box of 100, $45

    B. Box of 100, $60

    C. Box of 200, $75

    D. Box of 100, $90

    E. Box of 200, $100

16. You are a surveyor and you need a mapping program for your laptop. The program is updated every year. You can either buy the software update for $177 or subscribe for $12 per month. Which option is the better deal for one year, and by how much?

    F. the subscription, by $12

    G. the subscription, by $33

    H. buying it, by $36

    J. the subscription, by $144

    K. buying it, by $183

Answers are on page 248.

For a complete list of measurement conversions, including those used in this lesson, refer to the *Applied Mathematics Formula Sheet* on page 266 of this book.

Remember!

You may need to convert among fractions, decimals, and percentages.

Converting from a Percentage to Another Number

A percentage tells the amount that you have out of a total of 100. Because of this, it is easy to convert percentages to fractions and decimals, as both of these number forms can easily be stated as "hundredths."

$$35\% = \frac{35}{100} = 0.35$$

Converting from a Fraction to Another Number

A fraction tells the amount of something you have (numerator) in comparison to the total amount (denominator). Since the total may not always be the same, you cannot always convert directly from a fraction to a percentage. Instead, you may first need to calculate the decimal equivalent. To do this, simply divide the numerator by the denominator.

$$\frac{24}{40} = 24 \div 40 = 0.6$$

Then, to find the percentage, multiply the decimal by 100.

$$0.6 \times 100 = 60\%$$

Lesson 20 ■ ■ ■
Calculate with Numbers in Various Forms

Skill: Use fractions, negative numbers, ratios, percentages, or mixed numbers

Most workers use numbers in some form or another to perform everyday job functions. Filling in time sheets requires an understanding of the relationship between fractions and decimals. Counting change requires an understanding of adding and subtracting decimals. If you are charging for a service, you need to understand how ratios are used to calculate a per hour or per unit rate. When calculating discounts or markups, you need to understand how to calculate percentages of whole numbers and decimals. The ability to know how and when to use different forms of numbers is a key workplace skill.

Skill Examples

Example 1
Add a fraction and a mixed number.

Add: $\frac{5}{8} + 2\frac{1}{4}$

Convert the mixed number to a whole number plus a fraction.

$$\frac{5}{8} + 2\frac{1}{4} = \frac{5}{8} + 2 + \frac{1}{4}$$

Rearrange the order of the addends.

$$\frac{5}{8} + 2 + \frac{1}{4} = \frac{5}{8} + \frac{1}{4} + 2$$

Convert fractions into equal terms.

$$\frac{1}{4} = \frac{2}{8}$$

Add and solve.

$$\frac{5}{8} + \frac{2}{8} + 2 = \frac{7}{8} + 2 = 2\frac{7}{8}$$

Example 2
Find the percentage of a number

Calculate: 35% of $12,000

Convert the percentage into a fraction, then to a decimal:

$$35\% = \frac{35}{100} = 0.35$$

Multiply the number for which you are finding the percentage by the decimal.

$$\$12,000 \times 0.35 = \$4,200$$

Skill Practice

A. Find a percentage of a number.

5% of $10,000 = _____

B. Multiply by a mixed number.

$25,000 × $1\frac{1}{4}$ = _____

C. Add a negative number to a positive number.

145 + (−191) = _____

Try It Out! ■ ■ ■

As a credit analyst, you are trying to determine if a customer spends the recommended 20% or less of monthly income on housing. The customer's annual income is $47,000, and her monthly rent is $1,100. What is the approximate percentage of monthly income the customer spends on housing?

A. 9.4%   **B.** 22%   **C.** 23%   **D.** 28%   **E.** 43%

Step 1 Understand the Problem ■ ■ ■

Complete the *Plan for Successful Solving.*

Plan for Successful Solving

What am I asked to do?	What are the facts?	How do I find the answer?	Is there any unnecessary information?	What prior knowledge will help me?
Find the percentage of monthly income spent on housing.	Yearly income is $47,000 Monthly rent is $1,100	Calculate the monthly income. Then, divide monthly rent by monthly income to calculate the percentage.	You do not need to know that the customer should spend less than 20% of her income on housing.	To find a percentage, divide the partial amount by the total amount and multiply by 100.

Step 2 Find and Check Your Answer ■ ■ ■

- Confirm your understanding of the problem and revise your plan as needed.

- Based on your plan, determine your solution approach: *I am going to calculate monthly income by dividing the annual income by 12 (months). To find the percentage of the monthly income the customer spends on rent, I will divide the cost of rent by the monthly income and multiply by 100.*

    $47,000 ÷ 12 = $3,917   ◄····· Divide the annual income by 12 months.
    $1,100 ÷ $3,917 = 0.281   ◄····· Divide the monthly rent by the monthly income.
    0.281 × 100 = 28%   ◄····· Multiply by 100 to convert the decimal to a percentage.

- Check your answer. Check division by multiplying.
    1,100 ÷ 3,917 = 0.281; 0.281 × 3,917 = 1,100

- **Select the correct answer:** **D.** 28%
    By dividing the customer's annual income by the number of months in the year, you determine her monthly income. You then divide her monthly rent by her monthly income and multiply by 100 to find the percentage of monthly income that is spent on rent.

Problem Solving Tip

Be sure to think about how numbers relate to one another before calculating. In the *Try It Out!* example, you are given two numbers with which to calculate— annual, or yearly, income and monthly rent. Before you can calculate the percentage of income spent on rent, you must first be sure that the numbers relate to the same period of time. In this case, you have two options:

1. Divide the annual income by 12 months to calculate the monthly income.

2. Multiply the monthly rent by 12 months to calculate the annual amount spent on rent.

Remember!

When calculating with money, decimals that go beyond the hundredths place should be rounded to the nearest cent. In the *Try It Out!* example, when you divide the customer's annual income by 12 months to find the monthly income, the result is $3,916.667 (actually $3,916.6̄). Since physical money only goes so far as the hundredth place, you should round this number to the nearest hundredth—$3,916.67— before performing any further calculations.

On Your Own ■ ■ ■

1. You are an accountant helping a client prepare a monthly budget. The client can spend $3,500 per month on expenses. Currently, he spends $900 per month to rent office space. You recommend that rent should be no more than 20% of total monthly expenses. How much do you recommend that the client spend per month on rent?

   A. $320 or less

   B. $350 or less

   C. $600 or less

   D. $700 or less

   E. $1,400 or less

2. You are a credit manager explaining balance transfer fees to a customer who wishes to transfer money to a lower interest credit card. The balance transfer fee is 3%, and the customer wants to transfer $5,000. What is the balance transfer fee for this customer?

   F. $15

   G. $25

   H. $50

   J. $150

   K. $250

3. As an architect, you are drafting floor plans of a room at a scale of 1:10. If a wall in the room is to be 3 meters long, what is the length of the line that should represent the wall in the plans?

   A. 0.3 centimeter

   B. 1 centimeter

   C. 3 centimeters

   D. 10 centimeters

   E. 30 centimeters

4. As a lab assistant, you are preparing Petri dishes for an experiment. You split 2,440 dishes into two equal groups for two trials. You will inoculate $\frac{1}{4}$ of one group of the Petri dishes for the first trial. How many Petri dishes do you need to inoculate?

   F. 300

   G. 305

   H. 405

   J. 488

   K. 610

5. As a credit representative for a mortgage agency, you need to determine the percentage of monthly income spent on housing in order to evaluate a customer's credit line. One customer makes $4,000 a month. His mortgage is $1,200 a month, and his personal expenses are $1,000 a month. What percent of his monthly income is spent on housing?

   A.   12%

   B.   15%

   C.   28%

   D.   30%

   E.   61%

6. You are an electrician and have taken on a job to repair an electric motor. The motor should spin at 2,500 rotations per minute (rpm); instead, it is spinning at 2,000 rpm. By how much does the rpm need to increase?

   F.   12.5%

   G.   25%

   H.   125%

   J.   250%

   K.   500%

7. You are an interior designer and you want to add wallpaper to one wall section of a client's living room. The wall section is $12\frac{1}{2}$ feet long and $3\frac{1}{4}$ feet tall. The wallpaper comes in rolls of 150 square feet. How much wallpaper do you need to cover the wall section?

   A. $28\frac{3}{4}$ square feet

   B. $36\frac{3}{16}$ square feet

   C. $36\frac{3}{4}$ square feet

   D. $40\frac{1}{8}$ square feet

   E. $40\frac{5}{8}$ square feet

8. As a social scientist working for a polling agency, you need to survey at least 10% of the voting population in a town. The town you are surveying has a population of 12,534, with 7,533 registered voters. What is the minimum number of people you need to survey?

   F.   75

   G.   126

   H.   754

   J.   1,254

   K.   2,007

9. You are a mechanical engineering intern creating a set of drawings for machine parts at a scale of 3 times their actual size. If a certain machine part has an actual height of 55 millimeters, what should the height dimension be on your drawing?

A. 19 millimeters

B. 58 millimeters

C. 85 millimeters

D. 155 millimeters

E. 165 millimeters

10. You are a land surveyor establishing the boundaries of a lot. The northern boundary is $153\frac{1}{2}$ feet long. The western boundary is $64\frac{1}{4}$ feet long. The southern boundary is $144\frac{1}{2}$ feet long. The eastern boundary is $70\frac{3}{4}$ feet long. What is the perimeter of the property?

F. 431 feet

G. $431\frac{2}{3}$ feet

H. $432\frac{1}{2}$ feet

J. 433 feet

K. $433\frac{1}{4}$ feet

11. As a hydrologist, you supervise the drilling of wells for a geothermal heating and cooling system. Your team drills to a depth of 3.2 meters then stops to assess the water flow. You determine that so far the team has drilled $\frac{4}{5}$ of the required depth. How much farther does your team need to drill?

A. 0.4 meter

B. 0.8 meter

C. 2.4 meters

D. 2.6 meters

E. 4.0 meters

12. You are a credit counselor for a small bank. You are examining a loan application for a $30,000 home equity loan. According to the bank policy, a customer's annual income-to-debt ratio for all credit other than the primary mortgage must be at least 4:1 to issue this type of loan. If the client's debt is $8,000, what is the minimum income for which you can approve his loan?

F. $12,000

G. $32,000

H. $40,000

J. $48,000

K. $120,000

13. You are a construction supervisor whose crew is digging a foundation for a five-story building. When you return to the work site to check the progress of the foundation pit, you notice the crew has excavated to 1.45 times the depth they should have. If the excavated hole is 12 meters deep, to what depth should they have dug?

    A.   0.125 meter

    B.   8.3 meters

    C.   10.5 meters

    D.   13.5 meters

    E.   18 meters

14. You are a business analyst who reviews a client's monthly income and expenses on a balance sheet as shown below:

income	$4,200
rent	−$800
office supplies	−$250
communications	−$350
shipping	−$210

What is your client's balance for this month?

    F.   −$1,610

    G.   −$1,510

    H. $1,610

    J. $2,590

    K. $3,400

15. As a project manager for a publishing company, you have been asked to present an update for the status of a current series of books. Each book is 272 pages. There are 142 pages completed for Book A, 198 pages completed for Book B, and Book C is complete. Based on these numbers, what percentage of the total pages have been completed?

    A.   52%

    B.   72%

    C.   73%

    D.   75%

    E.   100%

16. You are a financial analyst calculating trends in quarterly income. Sales from the current quarter totaled $43,569, and sales from the previous quarter totaled $50,963. The average quarterly sales for the past 2 years is $49,500. What is the difference in quarterly sales from the previous quarter to the current quarter?

    F.   −$7,394

    G.   −$5,931

    H. $1,463

    J. $5,931

    K. $7,394

Answers are on page 248.

For a complete list of
measurement conversions
and geometric formulas,
including those used in
this lesson, refer to the
Applied Mathematics
Formula Sheet on
page 266 of this book.

Remember!

Area is a 2-dimensional
(2-D) measurement that
measures a surface. To
calculate area, you need
to know the length and
width of the surface being
measured. Area is
measured in *square units*.

Volume is a 3-dimensional
(3-D) measurement that
measures the amount of
space taken up by an
object. Like area, you
need to know the length
and width of an object in
order to calculate volume.
In addition to this, you
need to know the object's
height. Volume is
measured in *cubic units*.

Lesson 21 ■ ■ ■
Find Volume of Rectangular Solids

Skill: Find the volume of rectangular solids

A rectangular solid is a three-dimensional shape in which each face is a rectangle.
In the workplace, you may need to find the volume of rectangular solids. Volume is
the measure of the space inside a three-dimensional (3-D) figure. For example,
when shipping items to a customer, you may need to choose what box size should
be used for shipping these items. Understanding how the volume of the boxes
compares to the total volume of the items being shipped can help you make the
right choice. The ability to calculate volume can help you determine what amount
of an object can fit within rectangular 3-D spaces such as shipping boxes, storage
bins or shelves.

Skill Examples

Example 1
Find the volume of the rectangular solid.

A shipping box is 8 inches long,
11 inches wide, and 4 inches high.

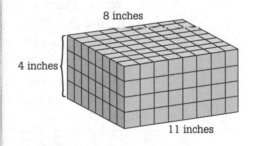

Use the formula for calculating volume.

$V = l \times w \times h$

$V = 8 \text{ inches} \times 11 \text{ inches} \times 4 \text{ inches}$

$V = 352 \text{ cubic inches}$

The volume of the box is 352 inches³.

Example 2
Find the volume of a rectangular solid for
which different units of measurements
are known.

A shipping box is 1 foot, 3 inches
long, 1 foot wide, and 4 inches high.

Convert from feet to inches so that you
are calculating using the same units
of measurement.

1 foot, 3 inches = 15 inches

1 foot = 12 inches

Use the formula for calculating volume.

$V = l \times w \times h$

$V = 15 \text{ inches} \times 12 \text{ inches} \times 4 \text{ inches}$

$V = 720 \text{ cubic inches}$

The volume of the box is 720 inches³.

Skill Practice

A. Find volume (metric units)

A box is 7 centimeters × 3 centimeters
× 4 centimeters. What is the volume
of the box? _____ centimeters³

B. Find volume (customary units)

A box is 6 inches × 6 inches ×
6 inches. What is the volume of
the box? _____ feet³

Try It Out! ▪ ▪ ▪

You work as a manufacturing engineer for a company that produces boxes. You need to write production specifications for a box to ship an object that is 2 feet long, 1 foot wide, and 8 inches high. The box must include room for 1 inch of packing material on all sides of the object. What is the volume of the box?

A. 50 cubic inches   D. 364 cubic inches

B. 140 cubic inches   E. 3,640 cubic inches

C. 260 cubic inches

 Step 1 **Understand the Problem** ▪ ▪ ▪

Complete the *Plan for Successful Solving.*

Plan for Successful Solving				
What am I asked to do?	**What are the facts?**	**How do I find the answer?**	**Is there any unnecessary information?**	**What prior knowledge will help me?**
Find the volume of a box.	Object is 2 feet × 1 foot × 8 inches. 1 inch of padding is needed around the object.	Convert all measurements to like units. Find dimensions of object plus packing and multiply.	No.	The formula for finding volume is $V = l \times w \times h$ The formula for converting length is 12 in. = 1 ft.

 Step 2 **Find and Check Your Answer** ▪ ▪ ▪

▪ Confirm your understanding of the problem and revise your plan as needed.

▪ Based on your plan, determine your solution approach: *I will first convert length and width to inches. Then, I will add 2 inches to each dimension to account for the packing material. I will then apply the volume formula.*

2 feet × 12 = 24 inches   ◄······ Multiply length and width by
1 foot × 12 = 12 inches   12 to convert feet to inches.

length = 24 inches + 2 inches = 26 inches   ◄······ Find the dimensions with
width = 12 inches + 2 inches = 14 inches   packing material.
height = 8 inches + 2 inches = 10 inches

V = 26 inches × 14 inches × 8 inches   ◄······ Write the volume formula.

V = 3,640 cubic inches   ◄······ Multiply.

▪ Check your answer. Adding the inch of packing around all the sides of the object adds 2 inches to the dimensions of the object.

▪ **Select the correct answer:** E. 3,640 cubic inches
By converting all measurements into the same unit of measurement, the formula for volume can be applied.

Problem Solving Tip

When performing calculations that involve measurements, it is important to pay close attention to the units of measurement being used. In the *Try It Out!* example, the length and width are written in feet, but the height is written in inches and all of the answer options are written in cubic inches. You first must convert all numbers that are to be used for calculating your answer into the same unit of measurement. In this case, looking at the units of measurement in which the answers are written (cubic inches) helps you know to convert any dimensions written in feet into inches.

Remember!

Because area is the measure of square units, or two dimensions (length and width), it is often written with a superscript 2 after the label *(in²)* and is read aloud as "units *squared*" or "square units." Because volume is a measure of cubic units, or three dimensions (length, width, and height), it is often written with a superscript 3 after the label *(ft³)* and is read aloud as "units *cubed*" or "*cubic* units." For example, the answer to the *Try It Out!* might be written 3,640 in³.

On Your Own ■ ■ ■

1. You are a shipping clerk at a post office. A customer wants to know how much space is in a shipping box that measures 11 inches by 8 inches by 5.5 inches. What is the volume of the box?

   A. 16 cubic inches

   B. 24.5 cubic inches

   C. 88 cubic inches

   D. 484 cubic inches

   E. 4,840 cubic inches

2. As an assembler at a garden supply warehouse, you are constructing a cold frame for a customer. The greenhouse is 7 feet, 6 inches long; 3 feet wide, and 24 inches deep. What is the volume of the cold frame?

   F. 15 cubic feet

   G. 22.5 cubic feet

   H. 45 cubic feet

   J. 90 cubic feet

   K. 5,400 cubic feet

3. You are a cost analyst for a paving company. A farmer is installing a gravel driveway that is 7 yards wide and 120 yards long. The road bed needs to be 6 inches thick to handle farm equipment. How many cubic yards of gravel are needed for the job?

   A. 140 cubic yards

   B. 280 cubic yards

   C. 420 cubic yards

   D. 630 cubic yards

   E. 5,040 cubic yards

4. You work for the parks and recreation department as a design engineer. You are planning a new playground that is on a 1.5 acre city lot. The playground will have a sandbox that is 20 feet by 18 feet. The box will be filled 8 inches deep with sand. How much sand do you need to order?

   F. 90 cubic feet

   G. 240 cubic feet

   H. 1,800 cubic feet

   J. 2,240 cubic feet

   K. 4,000 cubic feet

5. You are the owner of a realty management company that rents storage space. You charge $45 per month for a unit that has a volume of 6 feet by 6 feet by 8 feet. You advertise that you have the lowest rate per cubic foot. What is the monthly rate per cubic foot of storage space?

 A. $0.16

 B. $0.18

 C. $0.98

 D. $1.25

 E. $1.54

6. You work at an aquarium as a maintenance supervisor. You are filling an aquarium that measures 2.25 feet by 4 feet by 2 feet. Water weighs about 62 pounds per cubic foot. One gallon of water weighs about 8.6 pounds. What is the weight of the water in the aquaruim?

 F. 155 pounds

 G. 496 pounds

 H. 558 pounds

 J. 840 pounds

 K. 1,116 pounds

7. You work as a foreman for a landscaping company. For an upcoming job, you just purchased 54 cubic feet of mulch at $12 for 2 cubic feet. You are spreading the mulch in an area that is 12 feet long and 6 feet wide. How many inches deep can you spread the mulch?

 A. 6 inches

 B. 8 inches

 C. 9 inches

 D. 12 inches

 E. 13.5 inches

8. As the supervisor in a textbook warehouse, you are helping box books for a large order. The inside dimensions of the boxes that are being used are 18 inches × 11 inches × 9 inches. Each book is 8 inches × 11 inches × 1 inches. How many books can you fit in the box?

 F. 6

 G. 12

 H. 13

 J. 18

 K. 20

9. You are a project engineer designing a storage facility. You sketch this drawing of a floor plan for a facility that has a 10-meter ceiling. How much storage space will be in the facility?

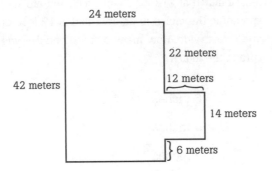

24 meters

22 meters

12 meters

42 meters

14 meters

6 meters

A. 1,680 cubic meters

B. 8,400 cubic meters

C. 10,080 cubic meters

D. 11,760 cubic meters

E. 13,640 cubic meters

10. You are an industrial engineer designing steel pots for use on boats that fish for king crabs. The pots you make have a height of 2 feet and a square opening on top that is 8 feet wide. You receive an order for 300 pots. How much space must the boat have to store the 300 pots?

F. 128 cubic feet

G. 4,800 cubic feet

H. 9,600 cubic feet

J. 19,200 cubic feet

K. 38,400 cubic feet

11. As an assistant curator in a museum, you are packing a fragile glass box inside a larger storage box that has inside dimensions of 10 inches wide, 29 inches long, and 24 inches deep. The glass box is 9 inches wide, 19 inches long, and 12 inches high. All the space between the glass box and storage box will be packed with foam padding. How many cubic inches of the storage box will be filled with foam padding?

A. 120 cubic inches

B. 1,200 cubic inches

C. 2,052 cubic inches

D. 4,908 cubic inches

E. 6,960 cubic inches

12. You are a construction field supervisor building a storage shed to store a crop of soybeans. The shed will need to be large enough to store a crop of 2,000 bushels of soybeans. Each bushel has a volume of 1.25 cubic feet. What is the minimum height for the storage shed if its floor dimensions are 10 feet by 25 feet?

F. 6 feet

G. 8 feet

H. 9 feet

J. 10 feet

K. 12 feet

13. As the facilities manager at an office complex, you are planning floor space for a new tenant. The tenant tells you he will need a storeroom large enough to hold 518 boxes that are 11.75 inches by 7 inches by 4.75 inches. About how much space does the tenant need for storage?

   A. 35 cubic feet

   B. 120 cubic feet

   C. 400 cubic feet

   D. 800 cubic feet

   E. 1,500 cubic feet

14. You work for Beverly Gravel and Stone as an estimator. A customer has asked for a quote to build a wall that is 150 feet long, 3.75 feet wide, and 15 feet high. You charge $55 per cubic yard. How much will the wall cost, rounded to the nearest one hundred dollars?

   F. $3,800

   G. $17,200

   H. $34,400

   J. $154,700

   K. $464,000

15. As the manager at a local bakery, you decide to run a contest in which customers guess the greatest number of brownies that can fit in a box that is 10 inches wide, 10 inches long, and 4 inches high. Each brownie is 3 inches by 4 inches by 1.5 inches high. The brownies cannot be broken to fit. The winner receives the box of brownies. Mary won the brownies. What was her guess?

   A. 2

   B. 18

   C. 22

   D. 23

   E. 7,200

16. You are a product designer for a company that manufactures commercial refrigerators. You receive an order for a refrigerator display case that has a capacity of 210 cubic feet. If the maximum depth front to back of the case is 2 feet, 6 inches and interior height is 7 feet, how long will the case be?

   F. 8 feet

   G. 10 feet, 6 inches

   H. 12 feet

   J. 14 feet, 6 inches

   K. 24 feet

Answers are on page 248.

For a complete list of formulas, including those used in this lesson, refer to the Applied Mathematics Formula Sheet on page 266 of this book

Remember!

When you rearrange a formula, the goal is to isolate the unknown variable on one side of the equation. It is often necessary to perform one or more operations on both sides of the equation in order to isolate the variable. As long as the same thing is done to both sides, the equation remains true.

Lesson 22 ▪▪▪
Rearrange a Formula

Skill: Rearrange a formula before solving a problem

In the workplace, you often encounter problems that require formulas. You may need to rearrange the formula before solving the problem. A landscaper may know the amount of fencing ordered to fence in a rectangular yard (perimeter). By measuring the width, the landscaper can determine the yard's length by rearranging the formula for perimeter into a new equation that is solved for length.

Skill Examples

A shipping company provides a discount rate for boxes that have a maximum perimeter of 140 inches on the largest face. What is the longest box that qualifies for the discount if the width must be 25 inches?

Example 1
Rearrange a formula before calculating.

The formula for perimeter is set up so that you can plug in the length and width.

$$Perimeter = 2(length + width)$$

If you know the perimeter and one dimension, you can rearrange the formula and then solve for the other dimension.

Divide both sides of the equation by 2.

$$\frac{p}{2} = \frac{2(l + w)}{2} = l + w$$

Isolate the length l by subtracting width w from both sides of the equation.

$$\frac{p}{2} - w = l + w - w$$

$$\frac{p}{2} - w = l$$

Plug in the known values and solve.

$$l = \frac{140}{2} - 25 = 70 - 25 = 45$$

$$45 = l$$

The maximum length is 45 inches.

Example 2
Plug numbers into a formula before calculating.

You can also approach this problem by first plugging in those numbers you do know into the perimeter formula.

$$P = 2(l + w)$$

$$140 = 2(l + 25)$$

Because length is the missing variable needed for a complete formula, you must solve for l. The steps you follow are the same as in *Skill Example 1*.

$$\frac{140}{2} = \frac{2(l + 25)}{2}$$

$$70 = l + 25$$

$$70 - 25 = l + 25 - 25$$

$$45 = l$$

Skill Practice

A. Find the third angle of a triangle for which there are two known angles.

Angle A = 63°
Angle B = 55°
Angle C = _____

B. Find the radius of a circle for which the area is known.

Area = 78.5 square inches
Radius = _____

Try It Out! ▪ ▪ ▪

As a sales associate at a flooring and carpeting store, you are completing a carpet order for a customer who wants a beige Berber carpet priced at $1.79 per square foot. On the form given to you by the contractor who measured the rectangular room being carpeted, you are unable to read the measurement for the room's width. The length of the room is 25 feet, and the area of the room is 525 square feet. What is the room's width?

   A. 5 feet   **B.** 15 feet   **C.** 20 feet   **D.** 21 feet   **E.** 50 feet

Step 1 · Understand the Problem ▪ ▪ ▪

Complete the *Plan for Successful Solving*.

Plan for Successful Solving				
What am I asked to do?	**What are the facts?**	**How do I find the answer?**	**Is there any unnecessary information?**	**What prior knowledge will help me?**
Determine the width of the room being carpeted.	The area of the room is 525 square feet. The room's length is 25 feet.	Rearrange the formula for area to solve for width.	The cost and type of the carpeting is not needed.	The formula for calculating area is area = *length × width*.

Step 2 · Find and Check Your Answer ▪ ▪ ▪

- Confirm your understanding of the problem and revise your plan as needed.
- Based on your plan, determine your solution approach: *Since I know the area and the length of the room being carpeted, I will rearrange the area formula to solve for width. I can do this by dividing both sides of the equation by the length.*

   Area = *length × width*   ◄······ Write the formula for area.

   $\frac{Area}{length} = \frac{length \times width}{length}$ ◄······ Divide both sides of the equation by the length to isolate the variable for width.

   $\frac{525}{25} = width$ ◄······ Plug in the measurements for area and length and solve for width.

   21 = *width*

   The room's width is 21 feet.

- Check your answer. Check division by multiplying.

   21 × 25 = 525. The room is 525 square feet.

- **Select the correct answer:**   D. 21 feet

   By dividing both sides of the area formula by the length, the equation is rearranged to one that can be solved for width. Once the measurements for area and length are plugged in, the width can be calculated by simply dividing.

Problem Solving Tip

You can check division by multiplying. If you multiply the answer (quotient) by the number that was used to divide (divisor), the answer should be the number into which you divided (dividend). This is one way to check the answer for the *Try It Out!* example.

Quotient × divisor = dividend

21 × 25 = 525

Remember!

You can also plug in the known measurements into the original formula before rearranging it. To solve the problem in the *Try It Out!* example, you could first plug in the measurements for area and width into the formula for area.

   Area = length × width

   525 =   25   ×   *w*

Then, simply divide both sides of the equation by 25 to isolate and solve for *w*.

   $\frac{525}{25} = \frac{25 \times width}{25}$

On Your Own ▪ ▪ ▪

1. As a designer at a packaging company, you are designing a rectangular box that must have a volume of 5,000 cubic centimeters. If the length and width of the box are specified to be 20 centimeters and 10 centimeters, what will be the height of the box?

   A. 10 cm

   B. 15 cm

   C. 25 cm

   D. 75 cm

   E. 250 cm

2. You are an electrical engineer designing a 60-volt electrical device that uses 5 amps of AC current when it is turned on. You are designing the device to be used in countries with an AC current frequency of 50 hertz. How much power will your device use?

   F. 10 watts

   G. 12 watts

   H. 250 watts

   J. 300 watts

   K. 600 watts

3. As a general contractor, you must secure a rectangular job site with fencing. The entire perimeter measures 196 meters. The length of one side of the site is 55 meters. What length of fencing is needed for one of the short sides of the site?

   A. 4 meters

   B. 7 meters

   C. 22 meters

   D. 28 meters

   E. 43 meters

4. As a landscape architect, you are designing a circular fountain for a client. The base of the fountain will be a circle and it should have an area of 10 square feet in order to match the desired spray pattern. The client wants the fountain to have a spray height of 12 feet. What will be the approximate radius of the fountain, to the nearest tenth of an inch?

   F. 1.8 feet

   G. 2.0 feet

   H. 3.2 feet

   J. 3.8 feet

   K. 5.6 feet

5. You are a design technician at a company that manufactures solar panels for custom installations. You are designing an 85-watt panel that will be used with a battery. What is the approximate voltage of the panel when it is delivering 7 amps of power?

    A.   1

    B.   6

    C.   7

    D.   12

    E.   13

6. As a technician in an industrial quality control lab, you are preparing a solution of a liquid chemical in a solvent. You need to use 8.0 grams of the liquid. According to the label on the bottle, the density of the chemical is 2.0 grams/milliliter. The formula for density is:

$$\text{density} = \frac{\text{mass}}{\text{volume}}$$

What volume of the chemical should you measure for your solution?

    F.   2.0 mL

    G.   4.0 mL

    H.   8.0 mL

    J.   10.0 mL

    K.   16.0 mL

7. You are a construction contractor calculating the dimensions of a new office building for the city planner's office. You know that the floor area of each story of the building is to be 3,000 square meters and that the maximum allowable width is 46 meters. The height of the completed building will be 25 meters. What will be the length of the building if you use the entire permitted width?

    A.   32.8 meters

    B.   65.2 meters

    C.   130.4 meters

    D.   1,300 meters

    E.   1,454 meters

8. As an industrial designer for a power company, your job is to plan a smokestack with a circular base. The circumference of the base is 25 meters. To the nearest tenth of a meter, what is the radius of the smokestack base?

    F.   0.4 meters

    G.   4.0 meters

    H.   8.0 meters

    J.   39.3 meters

    K.   78.5 meters

9. You are a computer-assisted designer for an engineering company. You are designing a drying oven for a manufacturing facility that needs to have an internal volume of 24 cubic meters. The shape of the oven is a rectangular solid. The interior depth from front to back is 1.5 meters and the length is 8 meters. What is the interior height of the drying oven?

   A. 1.5 meters

   B. 2 meters

   C. 4.5 meters

   D. 9 meters

   E. 14.5 meters

10. As a laboratory assistant to a formula chemist, you are trying to figure out the mass of the compound calcium chloride. You know the mass of calcium is 40 grams and that calcium makes up 36% of the mass of calcium chloride. The formula for finding the percent composition of an element in a compound is shown below.

$$percent\ composition = \frac{mass\ of\ element}{mass\ of\ compound} \times 100$$

What is the mass of the calcium chloride?

   F. 76 grams

   G. 111 grams

   H. 114 grams

   J. 144 grams

   K. 360 grams

Energy use is measured in watt-hours and can be calculated using the following formula:

energy use = watts × time

Use this formula for questions 11 and 12.

11. As an electrical design technician, one of your assignments is to design labels for products to help people compare their energy use. You are designing a label for a 600-watt, 120-volt microwave oven. Over a period of how many hours will the oven use 150 watt-hours of energy?

   A. 0.25 hour

   B. 0.8 hour

   C. 1.25 hours

   D. 4 hours

   E. 480 hours

12. As an analyst for a green energy consulting firm, your job is to help companies reduce their energy use. You know that a company's 240-volt color copier draws 0.5 watt of power in the power save mode. You want to recommend that they unplug the copier each night to save power. If the company follows your recommendation, how long will it take for them to save 100 watt-hours?

   F. 50 hours

   G. 120 hours

   H. 200 hours

   J. 480 hours

   K. 500 hours

13. You are an industrial engineer at a refinery. You need to design a transfer pipe to transport fuels from one processing tank to another. The circumference of the pipe is 34 centimeters and it must be 725 centimeters long. What is the diameter of the pipe to the nearest tenth of a centimeter?

    A.   10.8 centimeters

    B.   11.1 centimeters

    C.   21.3 centimeters

    D.   106.8 centimeters

    E.   230.9 centimeters

14. You are a stone cutter at a marble mine. Your job is to cut slabs of marble that have an area of 10 square feet and a thickness of 0.5 foot. The slabs must be 3 feet long. What should the width of the marble slabs be?

    F.   0.33 foot

    G.   3.33 feet

    H.   5 feet

    J.   6 feet

    K.   6.67 feet

15. You are a packaging engineer at a packaging company. Your job is to design plans for a rectangular container that will hold a volume of 1,232 cubic inches. You want the length of the container to be 14 inches and the width to be 11 inches. What must the height of the container be?

    A.   8 inches

    B.   12 inches

    C.   13 inches

    D.   25 inches

    E.   49 inches

16. You are a county surveyor measuring the dimensions of a rectangular property. The perimeter of the property is 1,174 feet. The length of the property is 315 feet. What is the width of the property?

    F.   23 feet

    G.   272 feet

    H.   430 feet

    J.   544 feet

    K.   859 feet

Answers are on page 248.

Remember!

Use multiplication to convert larger units into smaller units. For instance, meters are larger than centimeters. Every meter is a set of 100 centimeters. So, when converting 3 meters to centimeters, think of the 3 meters as 3 sets of 100 centimeters, or

3 meters × 100 = 300 centimeters.

Since division and multiplication are opposite operations, it is logical that you can use division to convert smaller units into larger ones. Again, every meter is a set of 100 centimeters. So, when converting 562 centimeters into meters, think of it as trying to find how many sets of 100 centimeters there are in 562, or

562 centimeters ÷ 100 = 5.62 meters.

Lesson 23 ■ ■ ■
Change from One Unit to Another in the Same Measurement System

Skill: Use two formulas to change from one unit in one system of measurement to a unit in the same system of measurement

When using measurements in the workplace, you sometimes need to convert a measurement from one unit to another. In some instances, this may require using two or more formulas. For example, suppose you need to order fabric by the yard for a particular job. If the measurement you have taken is in feet and inches, you will first need to convert this measurement to inches, then from inches to yards. Understanding when measurements need to be converted and applying the formulas used to calculate these conversions are important workplace skills.

Skill Examples

Example 1
Use formulas to convert a larger unit of measurement to a smaller one.

Convert 5 gallons to cups.

Multiply to convert larger units of measurement into smaller ones. There are 4 quarts in 1 gallon.

5 gallons × 4 = 20 quarts

Since cups are a smaller unit of measurement than quarts, multiply to convert 20 quarts into cups. There are 4 cups in 1 quart.

20 quarts × 4 = 80 cups

By multiplying by 4 to convert from gallons to quarts, then again by 4 to convert from quarts to cups, you find that

5 gallons = 80 cups

Example 2
Use formulas to convert a smaller unit of measurement to a larger one.

Convert 4,000 centimeters to kilometers.

There are 100 centimeters in 1 meter.

4,000 centimeters ÷ 100 = 40 meters

Since kilometers are a larger unit of measurement than meters, a smaller number of kilometers measures the same distance as a larger number of meters. There are 1,000 meters in 1 kilometer.

40 meters ÷ 1,000 = 0.04 kilometers

By dividing by 100 to convert from centimeters to meters, then again by 1,000 to convert from meters to kilometers, you find that

4,000 centimeters = 0.04 kilometers

Skill Practice

A. Change yards to inches. $5\frac{2}{3}$ yards = _____ inches

B. Change fluid ounces to quarts. 23.84 fluid ounces = _____ quarts

C. Change inches to miles. 633,600 inches = _____ miles

Try It Out! ▪ ▪ ▪

In your job as the manager of a commercial property cleaning crew, a total of 74 cups of ammonia are used to clean three buildings over the course of a day. How many gallons of ammonia do you use?

A. 4.625 gallons

D. 18.5 gallons

B. 5.25 gallons

E. 21 gallons

C. 13.25 gallons

Step 1 Understand the Problem ▪ ▪ ▪

Complete the *Plan for Successful Solving.*

Plan for Successful Solving

What am I asked to do?	What are the facts?	How do I find the answer?	Is there any unnecessary information?	What prior knowledge will help me?
Find how much ammonia you need in gallons.	You use 74 cups of ammonia.	Convert cups to quarts, then convert quarts to gallons.	3 buildings are cleaned.	There are 4 cups in a quart and 4 quarts in a gallon.

Step 2 Find and Check Your Answer ▪ ▪ ▪

- Confirm your understanding of the problem and revise your plan as needed.

- Based on your plan, determine your solution approach: *I am going to convert cups to quarts first. Then I am going to convert quarts to gallons.*

  74 cups ÷ 4 = 18.5 quarts ◄······ Divide to convert cups to quarts.
  18.5 quarts ÷ 4 = 4.625 gallons ◄······ Divide to convert quarts to gallons.

- Check your answer. Use opposite operations to check your answer:

  4.625 × 4 = 18.5 × 4 = 74

- **Select the correct answer:** A. 4.625 gallons
  By dividing the number of cups by 4 to convert to quarts, then dividing the result by 4 again to convert to gallons, you convert 74 cups into gallons.

Problem Solving Tip

If you cannot remember whether to multiply or divide when converting measurements, you can also set up a proportion to make the conversion. Using the *Try It Out!* example,

$$\frac{1 \text{ quart}}{4 \text{ cups}} = \frac{x}{74 \text{ cups}}$$

Find cross products:

$$4x = 74$$

Divide both sides of the equation by 4.

$$4x \div 4 = 74 \div 4$$

$$x = 18.5 \text{ quarts}$$

To finish solving the problem, convert 18.5 quarts to gallons by again setting up a proportion of gallons to quarts.

Remember!

As you become more familiar with measurement conversions, you can reduce the number of steps needed to convert measurements. In the *Try It Out!* example, if you know the conversion of 1 gallon = 16 cups, you can solve simply by dividing 74 cups by 16 gallons/cup.

On Your Own ▪ ▪ ▪

1. You are a chromatographer installing a gas chromatograph in a chemistry lab. To supply gases to the instrument, you need $43\frac{1}{3}$ yards of soft copper tubing. The specialty copper tubing that you need comes in 60-foot rolls. You have 2 rolls of tubing in the stockroom. How many more rolls of copper tubing do you need?

    A. 1

    B. 2

    C. 3

    D. 4

    E. 5

2. You are a packing machine operator at a meat packing plant. For one order, you pack 60 kilograms of ground beef in plastic tube packages. Each package holds 0.5 kilogram of ground beef, and the packages are shipped in cases of 20 packages each. How many grams of beef are in each case?

    F. 10 grams

    G. 60 grams

    H. 500 grams

    J. 10,000 grams

    K. 60,000 grams

3. You are a landscape architect planning the layout of a new garden for a commercial client. Among other tasks, your crew will be planting a flower bed that borders a walkway. The garden measures 90 feet in length and 72 inches in width. In order to determine the number of plants to deliver for the bed, you need to know the total area of the bed in square yards. What is the area?

    A. 6 square yards

    B. 36 square yards

    C. 60 square yards

    D. 240 square yards

    E. 540 square yards

4. It is your job as a dental assistant to stock each exam room with the appropriate supplies. There are 4 exam rooms. Each room needs to be stocked with 8 cups of dental rinse daily. The dentist's office is open 5 days a week. How many gallons of dental rinse should you order for June if the office is open for 20 days that month?

    F. 1 gallon

    G. 5 gallons

    H. 10 gallons

    J. 24 gallons

    K. 40 gallons

5. You are a real estate developer laying out two lots in a subdivision. The area of the larger lot is 0.6 acre, and the area of the smaller lot is 0.32 acre. How many square yards bigger is the first lot, rounded to the nearest square yard?

    A.   9 square yards

    B.   1,355 square yards

    C.   1,549 square yards

    D.   2,904 square yards

    E.   4,065 square yards

6. You are the food service manager in a college cafeteria. You want to modify a cupcake recipe that you found in a cookbook to make a larger batch. The recipe calls for $2\frac{1}{2}$ cups milk, but you need to make the equivalent of 13 batches. You also need 8 quarts of milk for other cooking needs today. About how many gallons of milk do you need to have on hand?

    F.   2 gallons

    G.   4 gallons

    H.   6 gallons

    J.   8 gallons

    K.   10 gallons

7. You are a school bus driver transporting students to an event at a football field. Bus drivers have been instructed to park along the sides of the 120-yard football field (including both end zones). They have been instructed to leave the ends of the field open. If each bus is 42 feet long, what is the maximum number of buses that can park on each side of the field?

    A.   3

    B.   7

    C.   8

    D.   12

    E.   16

8. You are a cross-country running coach laying out a practice course for an upcoming race. You measure fifteen 100-meter course segments, followed by twelve 200-meter segments. How many kilometers will your students run on this course?

    F.   2.7 kilometers

    G.   3.9 kilometers

    H.   17 kilometers

    J.   39 kilometers

    K.   3,900 kilometers

9. You are a finish carpenter building a custom storage chest made from cedar planks. To order the supplies, you estimate that you will need six 1 × 4 planks measuring 12 feet in length, four 1 × 6 planks measuring 10 feet in length, and ten 1 × 8 planks measuring 12 feet in length. The home improvement store prices all its cedar planks at $1.39 per board foot. How much money will the supply of cedar cost to complete the chest?

Type of Board	Width	Height
1 × 4	4 inches	1 inch
1 × 6	6 inches	1 inch
1 × 8	8 inches	1 inch

   A. $23.63

   B. $124.00

   C. $172.36

   D. $283.56

   E. $2,068.32

10. In your job as a press operator, you must adjust the printing machine settings to accommodate paper size and align margins correctly. Today you are printing brochures on paper stock that measures 14 centimeters in width and 20 centimeters in length. The margins need to be set at 15 millimeters on all sides. What is the perimeter of the print area?

   F.   0.56 millimeter

   G.   0.68 millimeter

   H.   560 millimeters

   J.   620 millimeters

   K.   680 millimeters

11. As a manager of a salon, you use 10 quarts of liquid monomer per month to make acrylic nails. You can order bottles of liquid monomer from the nail supply catalog in the following sizes: 4 ounces, 8 ounces, $\frac{1}{4}$ gallon, and 1 gallon. If you order three 1–gallon bottles, about how many ounces of liquid monomer will you have left at the end of the month?

   A. $\frac{1}{2}$ ounce

   B. $2\frac{1}{2}$ ounces

   C.   10 ounces

   D.   32 ounces

   E.   64 ounces

12. You are a surveying technician measuring a rural lot. According to your measurements, the area of the lot is 9,400 square yards. A township has an ordinance requiring at least 2 acres for building a horse barn and requires a $165 building permit. The property owner has an adjacent lot and can have the lot lines redrawn to build the barn. How much of the adjacent lot will have to be added to the lot that you surveyed to meet the required size?

   F.   0 square yards

   G.   280 square yards

   H.   560 square yards

   J.   1,080 square yards

   K.   5,120 square yards

13. As a seamstress for a bridal shop, you are making a cathedral veil for a wedding gown. To make the veil, you need a piece of lace 24 inches wide and 90 inches long. You have a bolt of lace that is 12 yards long and $\frac{2}{3}$ yard wide. What is the length of the piece of lace that will remain after you cut the fabric for the veil from the bolt?

A. $2\frac{1}{4}$ yards

B. $3\frac{1}{2}$ yards

C. $8\frac{1}{2}$ yards

D. $9\frac{1}{2}$ yards

E. $9\frac{3}{4}$ yards

14. In your job as a custodian at a hospital, you mix a concentrated cleaning solution with water to make a disinfectant cleaner. The instructions on the bottle say to mix 3 cups concentrated solution with 2 gallons water. There are only $2\frac{1}{4}$ cups of concentrate left in the bottle. How much water should you use to prepare the correct strength of cleaner?

F. 4 quarts

G. 5 quarts

H. $5\frac{1}{2}$ quarts

J. 6 quarts

K. $7\frac{1}{2}$ quarts

15. As a registered nurse, you are administering a common pain medication to a patient. The maximum dose recommended over a 24-hour period is 4 grams. You are giving the medication in tablets containing 325 milligrams each. What is the greatest number of tablets you should give the patient over 24 hours, based on the maximum dose recommendation?

A. 3

B. 4

C. 9

D. 12

E. 15

16. You are a lab technician for a company that produces standard solutions for chemical analysis laboratories. The solution is sold in 2-ounce vials. The vials are then packaged in boxes of 12. How much solution will you need to prepare to fill an order for 16 boxes of the solution?

F. $1\frac{1}{2}$ gallons

G. 3 gallons

H. $4\frac{1}{2}$ gallons

J. 6 gallons

K. 8 gallons

Answers are on page 248.

For a complete list of
measurement conversions,
including those used in
this lesson, refer to the
Applied Mathematics
Formula Sheet on
page 266 of this book.

Remember!

You may not know or
remember when to
multiply and when to
divide when converting
from one unit of
measurement to another.
In these instances, using
the conversion formula to
set up a proportion of two
equal ratios is the most
effective way to convert
correctly. Remember, a
proportion is an equation
that states two ratios are
equal. The cross products
of a proportion are always
equal. In both *Skill
Examples,* the formulas
for converting kilometers
to miles and gallons to
liters are used to set up
proportions of equal
ratios, and then solved for
the missing value.

Lesson 24 ▪ ▪ ▪
Convert from One System of Measurement to Another

*Skill: Use two formulas to change from one unit in one system of
measurement to a unit in another system of measurement*

When using measurements in the workplace, you will typically work within the
same system of measurement. Sometimes, however, you may need to convert
between the customary and metric systems of measurement. For example, if your
company buys some materials from suppliers in the United States and other
materials from suppliers in Europe, you may need to convert weight or volume
measurements.

Skill Examples

Example 1
Convert 10 meters to feet

The two length conversions on your
formula sheet for length are 1 inch =
2.54 centimeters and 1 kilometer ≈
0.62 miles. Since 10 meters is a
relatively short length, it makes sense
to convert to centimeters.

$$1 \text{ meter} = 100 \text{ centimeters}$$

$$10 \text{ meters} = 1{,}000 \text{ centimeters}$$

Use the conversion for centimeters to
inches (1 inch = 2.54 centimeters) to
convert to inches.

$$1{,}000 \div 2.54 = 393.7 \text{ inches}$$

Use the conversion for inches to feet
(1 foot = 12 inches) to convert to feet

$$393.7 \div 12 = 32.8 \text{ feet}$$

Example 2
Convert quarts to liters.

Convert 8 quarts to liters.

Since the conversion formula on your
formula sheet is for gallons to liters, first
convert from quarts to gallons. There are
4 quarts in a gallon, so divide 8 quarts
by 4 to convert.

$$8 \text{ quarts} \div 4 = 2 \text{ gallons}$$

Set up a proportion of two equal ratios of
gallons to liters.

$$\frac{0.264 \text{ gallon}}{1 \text{ liter}} = \frac{2 \text{ gallons}}{n \text{ liters}}$$

Solve the proportion by cross-multiplying.

$$0.264 \times n \approx 2$$

$$n \approx 7.57$$

$$8 \text{ quarts} = 2 \text{ gallons} \approx 7.57 \text{ liters}$$

Skill Practice

A. Convert ounces to grams.
   (nearest gram)

512 ounces ≈ _____ grams

B. Convert liters to quarts.
   (nearest 0.1 quart)

531 liters ≈ _____ quarts

C. Convert ounces to milligrams.
   (nearest 0.1 milligram)

0.25 ounces ≈ _____ milligrams

Try It Out! ▪ ▪ ▪

You are a baker at a sandwich shop. You check your stock of ingredients to be certain you have enough flour for today's breads. You have 25 pounds of whole wheat flour, 15 pounds of buckwheat flour, and 5,000 grams of rice flour. How many pounds of flour do you have in all?

A. 10 pounds   **B.** 23 pounds   **C.** 40 pounds   **D.** 45 pounds   **E.** 51 pounds

 Step 1 **Understand the Problem** ▪ ▪ ▪

Complete the *Plan for Successful Solving.*

Plan for Successful Solving

What am I asked to do?	What are the facts?	How do I find the answer?	Is there any unnecessary information?	What prior knowledge will help me?
Find how many pounds of flour there are in all.	Whole wheat flour = 25 pounds Buckwheat flour = 15 pounds Rice Flour = 5 kilograms	Convert all values to pounds, then add.	No.	1 kilogram = 1,000 grams

 Step 2 **Find and Check Your Answer** ▪ ▪ ▪

- Confirm your understanding of the problem and revise your plan as needed.
- Based on your plan, determine your solution approach: *Convert 5,000 grams to 5 kilograms. I am first going to make sure that all the units are the same before I add. Since two types of flour are already in pounds, I am going to convert 5 kilograms to pounds. I will do this by setting up a proportion using the conversion formula for kilograms to pounds. Then I will add together the weights of all three types of flour to find the total.*

$\frac{5 \text{ kilograms}}{n} = \frac{1 \text{ kilogram}}{2.2 \text{ pounds}}$ ◄······ Set up a proportion of two equal ratios of kilograms to pounds

$n = 5 \times 2.2; n = 11$ pounds ◄······ Cross multiply and solve for *n*.

25 pounds + 15 pounds + 11 pounds = ◄······ Add to find the total.
51 pounds

- Check your answer. The cross products of a proportion will always be equal.

$\frac{5 \text{ kilograms}}{11 \text{ pounds}} = \frac{1 \text{ kilogram}}{2.2 \text{ pounds}}; 1 \times 11 = 5 \times 2.2; 11 = 11$

- **Select the correct answer:** **E.** 51 pounds
  Kilograms can be converted to pounds by setting up and solving a proportion using the formula 1 kilogram ≈ 2.2 pounds. With the weights now in the same unit of measurement, they can be added to find the total pounds of flour.

On Your Own ■ ■ ■

1. The company for which you work as a taxi driver is switching to a metric billing system. You logged 248 kilometers on Monday, 272 kilometers on Tuesday, 280 kilometers on Wednesday, 252 kilometers on Thursday, and 301 kilometers on Friday. You want to know about how many miles per day you drove during the week. What was the average distance in miles?

   A. 168 miles

   B. 226 miles

   C. 276 miles

   D. 1,025 miles

   E. 1,654 miles

2. As a buyer for a large water utility company, you are obtaining bids on pipe for a new main. You will need 3.2 kilometers of large diameter pipe, but some of your suppliers base their bids on customary measurements. What approximate length of pipe should you specify for the alternate bid?

   F. 980 feet

   G. 1,050 feet

   H. 1,500 feet

   J. 3,200 feet

   K. 10,500 feet

3. As the owner and manager of a carpet business, you need to calculate the cost of installing carpet in an office building. The area to be carpeted measures 40 feet by 60 feet. The company that has hired you has chosen an industrial-style carpet manufactured in Canada that comes in metric sizes only. When ordering the carpet for this job, approximately how many square meters should you order?

   A. 100 square meters

   B. 223 square meters

   C. 240 square meters

   D. 732 square meters

   E. 2,400 square meters

4. You are a packaging designer for a cereal company. The standard package size for one of your brands is 1 pound, 2 ounces. The company is expanding to a worldwide market. You have been asked to change the weight listed on the front of the box to grams. Assuming the amount of the cereal will remain the same, what weight should be listed on the new box?

   F. 0.7 gram

   G. 28 grams

   H. 350 grams

   J. 510 grams

   K. 1,200 grams

5. You are a flatbed truck driver. Your truck gets 8 miles to the gallon. It has a 93-gallon tank. You have just crossed the border into Canada, where fuel is sold by the liter. About how many liters of fuel will you need for a 300-mile trip into Canada?

    A.   10 liters

    B.   25 liters

    C.   38 liters

    D.   49 liters

    E.   142 liters

6. The spa where you work as a massage therapist offers hot stone massages. The stones must be heated at 52°C. You use your spa heater to heat both the stones and towels, which you heat at 130°F. The thermometer on the heater reads Fahrenheit. Once you have heated the stones, about how much higher should you set the temperature for heating towels?

    F.   2.9°F

    G.   4.4°F

    H.   54.9°F

    J.   78°F

    K.   126°F

7. You are a truck mechanic working on a truck made in Europe. The manual specifies that you should use 14.5 liters of oil in the engine. Your dispenser measures oil in quarts. How much oil should you use?

    A.   3.8 quarts

    B.   13.7 quarts

    C.   14.5 quarts

    D.   15.3 quarts

    E.   54.9 quarts

8. You are a chemical engineer at a specialty chemical manufacturing company. A research chemist ran a pilot reaction in the lab using a 5,000-milliliter flask. You need to scale up the process so that it can be run in the manufacturing plant in a vessel that has a capacity of 500 gallons. By what factor (rounded to the nearest whole number) should you multiply the quantities of materials used in the pilot batch for your full-scale production run?

    F.   100

    G.   379

    H.   442

    J.   528

    K.   1,000

9. As a pedicurist, you add salts to each foot bath you make. If you add 10.5 grams of salts to each foot bath, how many baths can you make with a 12-pound container of salts?

    A. 28

    B. 38

    C. 518

    D. 5,432

    E. 5,443

10. You are an electrician installing conduit in a building. The architect's drawing specifies an internal diameter of $2\frac{1}{4}$ inches for a large cable. Your supplier uses metric units. Which size conduit could you use if the specified diameter is the minimum acceptable size?

    F. 6 millimeters

    G. 50 millimeters

    H. 55 millimeters

    J. 60 millimeters

    K. 600 millimeters

11. You are a brick mason. Today you are scheduled to build a retaining wall around the perimeter of a garden that measures 8 meters long and 3 meters wide. To check that you have the right amount of brick, you need to know the perimeter of the garden in feet. What is the approximate perimeter of the garden?

    A. 33 feet

    B. 72 feet

    C. 85 feet

    D. 105 feet

    E. 175 feet

12. You are a store manager at a pet store. Each aquarium measures 36 inches long, 24 inches wide, and 16 inches high. You need to fill 4 aquariums with water. About how many liters of water do you need?

    F. 63 liters

    G. 226 liters

    H. 907 liters

    J. 14,600 liters

    K. 55,300 liters

13. As a paramedic, you teach infant CPR training classes. You usually take two mannequins to training classes to simulate emergency situations. Each infant mannequin weighs 7 pounds, 10 ounces. Today's class is unusually large. You need to bring three more mannequins so the training can move quickly. The new mannequins weigh 4 kilograms. About what is the difference in weight between the new and old mannequins?

A. $\frac{1}{8}$ pound

B. 1 pound, 3 ounces

C. 3 pounds

D. 8 pounds, 8 ounces

E. 9 pounds

14. As a medical lab assistant at a hospital, you need to prepare a medication for a patient. The prescribed dosage is 0.2 milligram per kilogram of body weight. Your chart, however, shows the patient's weight is 160 pounds. What dosage should you prepare?

F. 14.5 milligrams

G. 32.0 milligrams

H. 72.7 milligrams

J. 1.45 grams

K. 3.2 grams

15. You are a merchandiser for a specialty detergent company. Every Stuff-Mart that carries your detergent allows you to use 1.25 meters of shelf space. Stuff-Mart and Value Giant are the two leading stores in your region. Value Giant allows you to use 3 feet of shelf space. About how much more shelf space does your product occupy at Stuff-Mart?

A. 6 inches

B. 13 inches

C. 15 inches

D. 18 inches

E. 49 inches

16. In your job as a welder, you notice that there is some damage to the moisture-proof packaging of a new set of electrodes. To use the electrodes, they must be dry. You know that the electrodes should be placed in a drying oven at 820°F. The controls on the drying oven are labeled in Celsius. At about what temperature should you set the oven?

F. 438°C

G. 788°C

H. 852°C

J. 1,476°C

K. 1,508°C

Answers are on page 248.

Not every workplace situation involving rate requires you to simply calculate the rate. In some instances, you may need to use a known rate to calculate something else. For instance, using *Skill Example 1,* suppose you are asked how long it will take to produce 8,000 units. Using the rate of production, you can calculate an answer by setting up the following proportion:

$$\frac{320 \text{ units}}{1 \text{ hours}} = \frac{8,000 \text{ units}}{h}$$

By finding cross products, you can solve for h.

$$320h = 8,000$$

$$\frac{320h}{320} = \frac{8,000}{320}$$

$$h = 25 \text{ hours}$$

Lesson 25 ...
Calculate Multiple Rates

Skill: Calculate multiple rates

When performing common job functions, particularly those involving time or money, you may need to calculate rates. For instance, a supervisor of a manufacturing assembly line needs to be able to calculate the rate at which units are produced. This number can be used to predict how many units will be produced in a day, week, or month. When purchasing products or supplies for a company, calculating the unit price of an item allows you to compare costs and ensure that products are purchased at the lowest unit price possible.

Skill Examples

Example 1
Calculate the rate of production.

If 320 units are manufactured in 5 hours, how many units are manufactured in 40 hours?

To calculate the rate of production, divide the amount or measure of something (units produced) by a unit (time, in hours).

$$r = \frac{\text{number of units}}{\text{hours}}$$

$$r = \frac{320 \text{ units}}{5 \text{ hours}}$$

$$r = 64 \text{ units per hour}$$

Now that you know how many units are produced in 1 hour, you can multiply to determine the number of units that will be produced in 40 hours.

64 units per hour × 40 hours = 2,560 units

Example 2
Calculate the unit price.

What is the price per pound if you buy 2.5 pounds for $4.95?

Unit price is a rate of comparison between the cost of something and the quantity or amount being priced.

$$p = \frac{\text{cost}}{\text{pounds}}$$

$$p = \frac{\$4.95}{2.5 \text{ pounds}}$$

$$p = \$1.98 \text{ per pound}$$

Similar to *Example 1,* once you know the cost per pound (unit price), you can multiply to determine the cost for any number of pounds.

Skill Practice

A. Find the rate when given distance and time.

150 feet in 3 seconds

Rate = _____

B. Find the unit price.

$12\frac{1}{2}$ ounces for $1.50

Per unit price = _____

C. Find the distance when given the rate.

55 miles per hour for 4 hours

Distance = _____

Try It Out! ■ ■ ■

As an office manager at a public relations firm, you are buying stamps. Stamps are sold at the same unit price in rolls of 120, 80, and 40. A roll of 120 stamps costs $57.60. How much does a roll of 80 stamps cost if the cost per stamp is the same?

A. $0.48　　　B. $17.60　　　C. $19.20　　　D. $38.40　　　E. $48.80

Step 1 Understand the Problem ■ ■ ■

Complete the *Plan for Successful Solving.*

Step 2 Find and Check Your Answer ■ ■ ■

- Confirm your understanding of the problem and revise your plan as needed.
- Based on your plan, determine your solution approach: *I am going to divide to find the price per stamp. Then I am going to multiply to find the price of 80 stamps.*

  $57.60 ÷ 120 = $0.48　　◀····· Divide the cost by the number of stamps to find the per unit cost.

  $0.48 × 80 = $38.40　　◀····· Multiply the unit price by the number of stamps in a roll (80) to calculate the total cost.

- Check your answer. Work backward to check your answer.
  $38.40 ÷ 80 = $0.48; $0.48 × 120 = $57.60

- **Select the correct answer:**　D. $38.40
  The unit price of $0.48 per stamp can be determined by dividing the cost of a roll of stamps by the number of stamps. By multiplying the unit price by the number of stamps, you can find the total cost of rolls of stamps of any quantity.

On Your Own ■ ■ ■

1. You are a plumber fixing a leaky pipe. You are charging the customer a flat rate of $255 for what is estimated to be a 3-hour job, so you are making $85 per hour. Upon assessing the leak, you realize that you must return to the office to get a replacement part. Your trip back to the office has added 2 hours to the repair job. By how much has your rate decreased for this job due to the unplanned trip back to your office?

   A. $34.00 per hour

   B. $51.00 per hour

   C. $127.50 per hour

   D. $136.00 per hour

   E. $170.00 per hour

2. As a respiratory therapist, you are checking a patient's vital signs. The patient has 21 heartbeats in 10 seconds. Concerned that this reading may not be accurate because the patient just walked the stairs to your fourth floor office, you let her rest for 10 minutes. When you check again, the patient has 16 heartbeats in 10 seconds. How many beats per minute has this patient's heart rate slowed?

   F. 30 beats per minute

   G. 50 beats per minute

   H. 96 beats per minute

   J. 126 beats per minute

   K. 160 beats per minute

3. As a chef, you buy produce locally for your restaurant. You need 48 pints of strawberries to make strawberry shortcakes for this week's special dessert item and spend $84.00 at one of your produce suppliers doing so. Later, you decide you need 22 additional pints of strawberries to make a strawberry-spinach salad menu item and spend $39.38 at a second produce supplier. About how much more did you pay per pint at the second produce supplier?

   A. $0.04 per pint

   B. $1.75 per pint

   C. $1.79 per pint

   D. $3.54 per pint

   E. $4.62 per pint

4. You are the owner of a floral design shop. You have 32 centerpieces to make for a wedding reception. Each centerpiece will take one and a quarter man-hours to make. You are also making 12 corsages, which will take 20 minutes each. How many man-hours will it take to make the centerpiece and corsages?

   F. 4 man-hours

   G. 40 man-hours

   H. 44 man-hours

   J. 48 man-hours

   K. 240 man-hours

5. As a tile installer, you are installing ceramic floor tiles in a room that measures 9 feet in length and 12 feet in width. You are able to install the tile in 11 hours. Next week, you will be working on a room that measures 15 feet in length and 18 feet in width. If you work at the same rate next week, how long will it take you to install tiles on the entire floor of the second room?

    A. $6\frac{1}{2}$ hours

    B.   18 hours

    C. $20\frac{1}{2}$ hours

    D. $27\frac{1}{2}$ hours

    E.   55 hours

6. You are an editor for a reference book publisher. You log 80 hours editing a 1,200-page manuscript. At this rate, how long will it take to edit an 840-page manuscript?

    F.   11 hours

    G.   23 hours

    H.   56 hours

    J.   76 hours

    K.   84 hours

7. As an electrician, a customer asks you to install 12 deluxe touchpad dimmer switches. After explaining that the total cost for the 12 switches is $179.88, she asks you how much less standard dimmer switches will cost. Standard dimmer switches cost only $6.92 a piece. What is the difference in cost between a standard dimmer switch and a deluxe touchpad dimmer?

    A. $6.92

    B. $8.07

    C. $14.99

    D. $83.04

    E. $96.84

8. You are a lineworker for a large power company. A severe hurricane has downed and disabled power lines in another area to which your company supplies power. You leave at 10:00 A.M. to travel 170 miles to the area to help repair the lines. You drive an average of 60 miles per hour for the first 135 miles of the trip. After stopping for 30 minutes to get food and gas, you estimate that you will only be able to travel 20 miles per hour for the remaining distance because of poor road conditions. At about what time do you reach your destination?

    F.   12:00 P.M.

    G.   12:15 P.M.

    H.   12:25 P.M.

    J.   2:00 P.M.

    K.   2:30 P.M.

9. As an administrative supervisor at an advertising agency, it takes you 29 minutes to type a 1,885-word proposal. At this rate, how long will it take you to type a 2,275-word proposal?

    A.   15 minutes

    B.   29 minutes

    C.   35 minutes

    D.   65 minutes

    E.   99 minutes

10. You are a dispatcher for a telephone company. There is a crew in Area 4 repairing a pole and some lines that were damaged by a fire. At 10 A.M. the crew radios you asking for assistance. When you radio back, you need to tell them when to expect additional help. You have a crew in Area 2 that has finished a repair and is available to help. It is 15 miles to the highway from where this crew just finished working. The speed limit is 30 miles per hour. When the crew reaches the highway, they can travel at 65 miles per hour for the remaining 49 miles of the trip. At what time can you tell the crew in Area 4 to expect help?

    F.   10:30 A.M.

    G.   10:45 A.M.

    H.   11:15 A.M.

    J.   12:00 P.M.

    K.   3:00 P.M.

11. As a purchasing manager for a gift shop, you are trying to find the cheapest supplier of novelty coffee mugs. You are going to charge $9.50 per mug. A supplier in the U.S. will sell you cases of 12 mugs each for $24. A supplier in China will sell you cases of 24 mugs each for $51.60. What is your profit per mug if you buy the mugs from the U.S. supplier?

    A. $2.00

    B. $2.15

    C. $7.45

    D. $7.50

    E. $11.50

12. You are a delivery truck driver. Your old route was 270 miles and took you 6 hours to finish. Today you are starting a new route. You estimate that this route will take you 8 hours to finish. If you plan to drive at the same speed as your old route, how long is the new route?

    F.   56 miles

    G.   180 miles

    H.   303 miles

    J.   360 miles

    K.   540 miles

13. As a photographer, you charge $40 per hour for studio sittings. You charge twice as much for events, such as weddings, because you must cover the cost of travel and other expenses. This week you worked in the studio on Monday, Tuesday, and Thursday for a total of 16 hours. On Saturday you spent 7 hours at a wedding. How much did you make this week?

    A. $80

    B. $560

    C. $640

    D. $920

    E. $1,200

14. As a physician's assistant, you are asked to fill in a prescription order for a common painkiller. The proper dosage for this painkiller is 5 milligrams for every 24 pounds. How much painkiller should you prescribe for a 294-pound man?

    F. 12.25 milligrams

    G. 58.80 milligrams

    H. 61.25 milligrams

    J. 120 milligrams

    K. 1,470 milligrams

15. You are a commercial carpet installer working on a new hotel. It takes you $\frac{1}{2}$ hour to lay 50 square feet of carpet. About how long does it take you to install carpet in a corridor that measures 8 feet in width and 252 feet in length?

    A. 10 hours

    B. 20 hours

    C. 40 hours

    D. 60 hours

    E. 90 hours

16. As a waitress, you make $5.25 per hour in wages plus tips. In a typical week, your tips average to be about 60% of your total take-home pay. You are scheduled to work three shifts this week. If each shift is 6 hours, about how much will you make in tips and wages this week?

    F. $56.70

    G. $94.50

    H. $132.30

    J. $154.50

    K. $236.25

Answers are on page 248.

Apply Formula Rearrangements and Unit Conversions to Calculate Area

Skills: Find areas of basic shapes when it may be necessary to rearrange the formula, convert units of measurement in the calculations, or use the result in further calculations

When dealing with workplace measurements such as area, the numbers that you use to calculate may not always be in the units of measurement needed. In such cases, you need to first convert units before calculating. You may also need to rearrange formulas before calculating to find a missing measurement, such as the length of a piece of sheet metal when the area and width are known. Being able to convert units of measurement and rearrange formulas are key skills when performing workplace calculations.

Remember!

Area is a measure of surface, or two-dimensional, space. It is the number of square units that fit into a space.

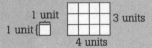

The area of a rectangle 4 units long by 3 units wide is

4 units × 3 units = 12 square units.

When rearranging a formula, the goal is to isolate the variable for which you are solving. In *Skill Example 2*, the formula for the area of a rectangle is rearranged to isolate the unknown variable, which is width in this case.

Skill Examples

Example 1
Calculate area by first converting units of measurement.

Calculate the area of a rectangle that has dimensions 3 feet long and 9 inches wide.

Convert feet to inches so that length and width are in the same unit of measurement.

3 feet = 36 inches

Use the area formula for area to calculate the area of the rectangle.

$A = l \times w$

$A = 36 \text{ inches} \times 9 \text{ inches}$

$A = 324 \text{ square inches}$

Example 2
Rearrange the formula for area to calculate one of a shape's dimensions.

Calculate the width of a rectangle that is 8 yards long and has an area of 40 square yards.

Rearrange the area formula to solve for width.

$A = l \times w$

$\frac{A}{l} = w$

Use the rearranged formula to calculate the width of the rectangle

$w = \frac{40 \text{ square yards}}{8 \text{ yards}}$

$w = 5 \text{ yards}$

Skill Practice

A. Calculate the area of a rectangle by first converting units of measurement.

A rectangle has dimensions 4 yards × 3 feet. Find the area in square feet. _____

B. Rearrange the formula for area to calculate the base of a triangle.

The area of a triangle is 48 square inches. Find the height if the base is 6 inches. _____

Try It Out! ▪ ▪ ▪

You work as a contractor restoring old homes. Your electric floor sander will sand 80 square feet of a hardwood floor in 15 minutes. You need to sand 2 rooms with the dimensions 24 feet, 6 inches × 10 feet and 12 feet, 4 inches × 8 feet. About how many minutes will it take you to sand both rooms?

A. 18   B. 45   C. 65   D. 540   E. 1,792

 Step 1 ## Understand the Problem ▪ ▪ ▪

Complete the *Plan for Successful Solving.*

Plan for Successful Solving

What am I asked to do?	What are the facts?	How do I find the answer?	Is there any unnecessary information?	What prior knowledge will help me?
Calculate the amount of time it takes to sand two rooms.	Room A = 24 feet, 6 inches × 10 feet. Room B = 12 feet, 4 inches × 8 feet. Can sand 80 square feet in 15 minutes.	Find the total area. Then set up a proportion to find the amount of time it takes to sand that area.	No.	Inches can be converted to feet by dividing the number of inches by 12.

 Step 2 ## Find and Check Your Answer ▪ ▪ ▪

▪ Confirm your understanding of the problem and revise your plan as needed.

▪ Based on your plan, determine your solution approach: *I will first calculate the area of the each room and add to find the total area being sanded. I will set up a proportion of two equal ratios of square feet to minutes.*

24 feet, 6 inches = $24\frac{6}{12}$ feet = 24.5 feet ◀······ Convert all
12 feet, 4 inches = $12\frac{4}{12}$ feet ≈ 12.33 feet   measurements to feet.

Area (Room A) = 24.5 × 10 = 245 square feet ◀······ Use the area formula to
Area (Room B) = 12.33 × 8 ≈ 99 square feet   find each room's area.

245 square feet + 99 square feet = 344 square feet ◀······ Add to find the total area.

$\frac{15 \text{ minutes}}{80 \text{ square feet}} = \frac{t}{344 \text{ square feet}}$ ◀······ Set up a proportion.

$80t = 5,160$ ◀······ Cross-multiply and solve.

$t = 64.5 → 65$ minutes

▪ Check your answer. Add the area of both rooms to get the total area. Use the answer of 64.5 in the original proportion. The cross products should be equal.

▪ **Select the correct answer:** C. 65 minutes
The total square footage of the two rooms can be calculated. Use the rate of sanding to set up a proportion to find the total time.

Problem Solving Tip

You can use estimation to determine if your answer is reasonable. In the *Try It Out!* example, once you know that the total square footage of the two rooms is 344 feet, you can estimate by dividing. If you use mental math to divide 344 by 80 (think 320 ÷ 80), you get an answer of about 4. Since it takes about 15 minutes to sand 80 square feet, multiply 15 times 4. This gives you an answer estimate of about 60 minutes.

Remember!

When calculating using measurements that have both feet and inches, you must first convert each measurement to either feet or inches. To convert from feet to inches, simply multiply the number of feet by 12 (12 inches per foot). To convert from inches to feet, simply divide the number of inches by 12.

Inches	Feet
3 in.	0.25 ft.
4 in.	0.33 ft.
6 in.	0.5 ft.
8 in.	0.67 ft.
9 in.	0.75 ft.
12 in.	1 ft.

On Your Own ■ ■ ■

1. As a landscape contractor, you submitted the winning bid to sod a new football field. The field, including the end zone and sideline areas, is 360 feet long and 160 feet wide. The sod you will be using comes in rolls that are 42 inches wide and 128 feet long. How many sod rolls will you need to cover the field?

    A. 10

    B. 11

    C. 65

    D. 125

    E. 129

2. As the contractor of a home renovation, you are installing a new floor. The room measures 16 feet, 6 inches by 21 feet, 4 inches. The laminate flooring costs $8.50 per square foot. About how much does the new floor cost?

    F. $41.41

    G. $321.56

    H. $351.95

    J. $643.11

    K. $2,991.53

3. As an environmental conservationist, you are supervising a crew that is removing an invasive species from a research plot in a state forest. The study involves an area that is 500 feet × 800 feet. The crew can clear about 7,000 square feet each day. About how many days should be scheduled for clearing of the plot?

    A. 7 days

    B. 30 days

    C. 60 days

    D. 120 days

    E. 540 days

4. You are a logging equipment operator using a tractor to clear an area of heavy brush. You are clearing an area that is 73 feet × 42 feet. You charge $7.50 for each square yard and $12.50 for every bush over 5 feet tall. You cleared 7 bushes over 5 feet tall. How much did you charge the customer?

    F. $2,555

    G. $2,643

    H. $4,300

    J. $23,080

    K. $38,370

5. As an environmental scientist, you are studying the late blight that is infecting tomato plants. A farmer calculated that he is losing 90% of his plants to the blight. If each acre has 2,500 tomato plants, about how many plants are lost in a 690 feet × 126 feet field?

    A.   500

    B.   2,250

    C.   4,500

    D.   5,293

    E.   9,000

6. As an architectural drafter, you are designing a walkway around a circular fountain for an office building courtyard. You draw this diagram. What is the area of the walkway? Round your answer to the nearest tenth.

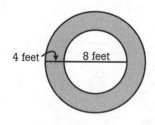

4 feet   8 feet

    F.   62.8 square feet

    G.   150.7 square feet

    H.   163.4 square feet

    J.   251.3 square feet

    K.   452.4 square feet

7. You are part of a team of wildlife biologists tagging and tracking endangered jaguars in a small area of protected Amazon rain forest. Your work covers an area 6 kilometers by 10 kilometers. How many square miles do you cover?

    A.   23.1 square miles

    B.   37.5 square miles

    C.   60 square miles

    D.   96 square miles

    E.   96.8 square miles

8. You work in a marine canvas factory making sails for sailboats. The main sail you are measuring has an area of 22.2 square meters. The bottom of the sail that is along the length of the beam is 3.18 meters. About how tall is the triangular sail?

    F.   3.50 meters

    G.   6.98 meters

    H.   13.96 meters

    J.   35.30 meters

    K.   70.60 meters

9. As a survey crew chief, you are verifying the area of a vacant lot for potential development. You draw this plan of the property. What is the square footage of the property?

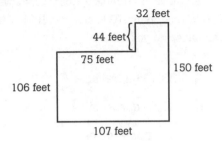

32 feet

44 feet

75 feet

150 feet

106 feet

107 feet

A. 1,176 square feet

B. 11,266 square feet

C. 11,342 square feet

D. 12,750 square feet

E. 16,050 square feet

10. You are a tile setter covering a floor that is 12 feet, 6 inches × 18 feet, 9 inches with ceramic tiles. One box of tiles costs $2.16 per square foot and covers 12.5 square feet. How many boxes do you need?

F. 12

G. 19

H. 38

J. 98

K. 231

11. You are a sales manager for a custom pool and spa company working on a cost estimate. A commercial customer would like you to install a round hot tub with a diameter of 54 inches and a 6-person hot tub that measures 82 inches by 82 inches. What is the combined area of the two hot tubs?

A. 16 square feet

B. 47 square feet

C. 55 square feet

D. 63 square feet

E. 127 square feet

12. As a civil engineering technician, you are drawing a map for a park. The area of the park is 5,000 square yards. You plan a play area that is 25 yards by 50 yards and a fountain that has a diameter of 6 yards. About how much open space is left in the park?

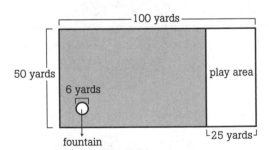

100 yards

50 yards

6 yards

play area

25 yards

fountain

F. 3,722 square yards

G. 3,837 square yards

H. 4,750 square yards

J. 4,887 square yards

K. 4,972 square yards

13. You are a draftsperson designing a custom door with a circular window. The customer tells you that they have a 452.34–square inch circular window that they want to use. The door is 6 feet, 6 inches by 3 feet. What is the diameter of the hole that you need to cut for the window?

    A. 6 inches

    B. 12 inches

    C. 24 inches

    D. 36 inches

    E. 144 inches

14. As a construction estimator, you are developing a bid on a paving project for a parking lot. The site plans are drawn up in meters, but you use the pavement area in square feet for your first estimate of costs. The rectangular parking lot measures 24 meters by 42 meters. In addition, you will be paving a rectangular driveway that measures 6 meters wide by 28 meters long. What is the approximate area, in square feet, of the entire paving project?

    F. 7,500 square feet

    G. 9,150 square feet

    H. 9,800 square feet

    J. 11,750 square feet

    K. 12,650 square feet

15. You are a furniture maker building custom table tops with inlays of different types of wood veneer. A customer wants three tables, each 4 feet by 3 feet, made with triangle patterns of different woods in the dimensions shown below. How many triangles do you need to make each table top?

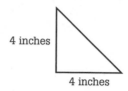

4 inches

4 inches

    A. 18

    B. 96

    C. 108

    D. 216

    E. 648

16. You are the construction manager for a custom building company. The contract allowance for floor coverings is $2.50 per square foot. What is the total amount available for floor coverings if you are to stay within the allowance?

Room	Quantity	Size
Kitchen	1	20 feet × 20 feet
Dining Room	1	15 feet × 20 feet
Living Room	1	25 feet × 25 feet
Bedroom	3	17 feet × 15 feet
Bathroom	2	10 feet × 12 feet

    F. $4,250

    G. $4,330

    H. $4,550

    J. $5,185

    K. $5,825

Answers are on page 248.

Level 6 Performance Assessment

The following problems will test your ability to answer questions at a Level 6 rating of difficulty. These problems are similar to those that appear on a Career Readiness Certificate test. For each question, you can refer to the answer key for answer justifications. The answer justifications provide an explanation of why each answer option is either correct or incorrect and indicate the skill lesson that should be referred to if further review of a particular skill is needed.

1. You are an accountant for a company that wants to switch to using only recycled paper. Paper A costs $31.90 for 10 reams, and Paper B costs $36 for 12 reams. Which is the better deal and what is the savings per ream?

   A. Paper B, $0.19 per ream

   B. Paper B, $1.90 per ream

   C. Paper B, $3.00 per ream

   D. Paper A, $3.19 per ream

   E. Paper A, $4.10 per ream

2. You are a machine shop technician at a bioscience lab. You are working with lab scientists to develop a tank for a specialty incubation chamber. The chamber has a rectangular solid shape with a base that measures 20 centimeters on each side. The volume of the tank must be 5,000 cubic centimeters. What is the height of the tank?

   F. 1.25 centimeters

   G. 12.5 centimeters

   H. 20 centimeters

   J. 125 centimeters

   K. 250 centimeters

3. You manage a storage facility that has 25 occupied units. Each unit is 8 feet by 8 feet by 10 feet. The rate is $1.25 per cubic foot. How much money do you collect per month for all the units?

   A. $800

   B. $2,000

   C. $2,500

   D. $20,000

   E. $80,000

4. You are a corporate analyst reviewing quarterly trends for a client's profits. The current quarter's profits are $13,671. Last quarter's profits were $14,879. The profits for next quarter are projected to be $13,550. What is the difference in profits between last quarter and the current quarter?

   F. −$1,329

   G. −$1,208

   H. $121

   J. $1,208

   K. $1,329

5. As the general contractor of a home renovation, you are installing a new floor. The room measures $14\frac{3}{4}$ feet $\times$ $17\frac{1}{2}$ feet. The hardwood flooring costs $22.50 per square foot. To the nearest dollar, how much does the new flooring cost?

    A. $726

    B. $1,467

    C. $5,355

    D. $5,808

    E. $6,075

6. In your job as a kiln operator, you use coal to power the kiln to 1,042°F. To keep the kiln at this constant temperature, you add coal every 30 minutes. Today on your 12-hour shift, you have put 96 kilograms of coal into the kiln. How much coal would you add to the kiln during a 14-hour shift?

    F. 4 kilograms

    G. 8 kilograms

    H. 112 kilograms

    J. 1,152 kilograms

    K. 1,344 kilograms

7. As a dental assistant, you prepare a sanitizing solution for the dentist's tools. You have prepared 15.3 liters of sanitizing solution. If you fill fourteen 1-quart containers, about how much sanitizing solution will you have left?

    A. 2 quarts

    B. 16 quarts

    C. 30 quarts

    D. 160 quarts

    E. 218 quarts

8. You are a control room operator for a steel mill. The mill is currently producing a particular steel formulation for which the blast furnace temperature is set at 1,100°C. To improve the quality of the steel, you receive instruction from the quality control lab to increase the blast temperature by 24°F. You can set the temperature on the computer using Fahrenheit or Celsius scales. Which temperature setting should you use?

    F. 1,124°F

    G. 1,998°F

    H. 2,004°F

    J. 2,012°F

    K. 2,036°F

9. As a bioscience technician, you need to order microscope slides. A box of 250 costs $50 and a box of 600 costs $100. Which is the better deal, and what is the price per slide?

   A. the box of 250, $0.16

   B. the box of 600, $0.17

   C. the box of 250, $0.20

   D. the box of 250, $0.50

   E. the box of 600, $0.60

10. You are a food service supervisor at a nursing home, and you need to make sure you have enough supplies for the day's menu. You want the cooks to prepare 4 trays of dinner rolls. Each tray requires a double recipe. The recipe for one batch calls for $3\frac{1}{4}$ cups flour. How many cups of flour do you need for 4 trays of dinner rolls?

   F. $6\frac{1}{2}$ cups

   G. $12\frac{3}{4}$ cups

   H. 13 cups

   J. $24\frac{1}{4}$ cups

   K. 26 cups

11. You are a landscape architect designing a water feature for a local park. One of the elements of the feature is a 150–square meter circular pool. What is the radius of the pool?

   A. 0.14 meter

   B. 6.9 meters

   C. 21.7 meters

   D. 38.5 meters

   E. 47.8 meters

12. You are the construction manager for a custom building company. The cost of the house is $120 per square foot. Find the cost of building this house.

Room	Quantity	Size
Kitchen	1	15 feet × 12 feet
Dining Room	1	15 feet × 20 feet
Living Room	1	21 feet × 30 feet
Bedroom	2	15 feet × 15 feet
Bedroom Suite	1	21 feet × 30 feet
Bathroom	2	10 feet × 12 feet

   F. $255,600

   G. $264,600

   H. $277,200

   J. $291,600

   K. $367,200

13. As a food service manager for a college cafeteria, you need to order enough chicken for 595 servings of Wednesday's dinner. Each serving will include 5 ounces of chicken. Chicken is available in 10-pound packages. How many extra 5-ounce servings of chicken will you have?

    A. 13

    B. 18

    C. 19

    D. 45

    E. 65

14. You are a sales manager for a snack company. Your products occupy 18 inches of shelf space in each of 25 grocery stores across your sales region. In those same stores, your competitor's products occupy a total of 50 feet of shelf space. How much shelf space do you need to gain to match your competitor's share of shelf space?

    F. $1\frac{1}{2}$ feet

    G. $12\frac{1}{2}$ feet

    H. $37\frac{1}{2}$ feet

    J. 450 feet

    K. 600 feet

15. You are a fashion designer preparing a dye solution. The ratio of water to dye in the solution needs to be 4:1. You want to make 5 liters of the solution. How much water should you use?

    A. $\frac{1}{5}$ liter

    B. $\frac{4}{5}$ liter

    C. 1 liter

    D. $3\frac{3}{4}$ liters

    E. 4 liters

16. You are a green energy consultant that has been hired by a company to make recommendations for replacing their roof. A green roof will cost $25,000 to install and will result in $3,000 worth of savings in cooling costs each year. A solar roof will cost $40,000 to install and will result in $5,000 worth of savings in electricity costs each year. Based on these factors, which is the better deal for the company over 10 years and why?

    F. The solar roof because it will net a savings of $2,000.

    G. The green roof because it will net a savings of $5,000.

    H. The solar roof because it will net a savings of $10,000.

    J. The green roof because it will net a savings of $30,000.

    K. The solar roof because it will net a savings of $50,000.

17. You are building a cold frame greenhouse for a customer. The customer decides he wants Size P. How much space, in cubic feet, will the customer have to grow plants?

Size	Length	Width	Height
P	8'5"	6'11"	7'4"
T	12'	8'	8'6"
Z	15'6"	9'9"	10'

A. 336 cubic feet

B. 384.3 cubic feet

C. 426.9 cubic feet

D. 577.2 cubic feet

E. 737,704 cubic feet

18. As an electrical engineering technician, you are designing a device that uses 120 volts of electricity and draws 5 amps of current during its use. It runs on an AC current that cycles at 60 hertz (Hz). How much power does the device use?

F. 0.04 watt

G. 10 watts

H. 24 watts

J. 600 watts

K. 36,000 watts

19. You are a city bus driver who works only during the day. You drive your 6-mile route at an average speed of 15 miles per hour. The evening bus driver on the same route drives at an average speed of 20 miles per hour. How many minutes longer than the evening driver does it take you to drive the route?

A. 6 minutes

B. 18 minutes

C. 24 minutes

D. 42 minutes

E. 432 minutes

20. You are a solar energy sales representative and you want to offer customers the best deal. Solar panel A costs $1,305 and has a $250 rebate. Solar panel B costs $1,160 and has a $100 rebate. Which is the better deal and by how much?

F. solar panel B, by $85

G. solar panel B, by $125

H. solar panel A, by $150

J. solar panel B, by $235

K. solar panel A, by $385

21. You are an interior designer working on an entryway to a museum. You want to hang 3 rectangular banners that are each 100 square feet and 21 feet long. What should the width of each banner be?

    A.   0.21 foot

    B.   0.63 foot

    C.   4.76 feet

    D.   14.29 feet

    E.   33.33 feet

22. You work for a mason building brick walls. You are building a brick wall that is to be 4 feet high, 335 feet long, and 4.5 inches deep. You will be using the bricks shown. The rate for a brick wall is $22.75 per cubic foot. About much will the wall cost?

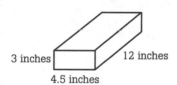

3 inches   12 inches

4.5 inches

    F. $162

    G. $503

    H. $1,143

    J. $11,432

    K. $30,485

23. As an assistant landscape architect, you are helping to design a garden. You decide to put a circular garden in a square plot of land. You sketch the drawing below. What is the area of the land not incorporated into the garden? Round your answer to the nearest hundredth.

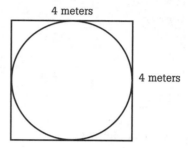

4 meters

4 meters

    A.   3.44 square meters

    B.   12.56 square meters

    C.   16.00 square meters

    D.   28.56 square meters

    E.   34.24 square meters

24. You are the building maintenance manager for a large hotel. To reduce the amount of detergents discharged into the sewer system, you decide to change to a more efficient cleaner. Your crews have been using 12 gallons of cleaning solution concentrate per week. The manufacturer of the new solution advertises that you will need to use just $\frac{1}{3}$ as much. If the new product is packaged in liters instead of gallons, about how many liters of the new product should you order for each week?

    F.   1 liter

    G.   4 liters

    H.   15 liters

    J.   45 liters

    K.   136 liters

25. You are a bookkeeper reviewing your client's balance sheet of monthly income and expenses as shown below.

paycheck	$2,550.45
rent	−$750.00
gas	−$71.23
groceries	−$323.97
insurance	−$225.00
rebate check	$50.00
electricity	−$45.10
phone	−$55.90

What is the client's net profit or loss for this period?

- **A.** $1,079.25
- **B.** $1,129.25
- **C.** $1,471.20
- **D.** $2,600.45
- **E.** $4,071.65

26. As an alarm system installer, you are running a wire along 3 walls. The walls measure 3 meters, 2.625 meters, and 4.125 meters. You have 2 rolls of wire that are each 6 meters long. How much wire will you have left after running the wire?

- **F.** 2.25 centimeters
- **G.** 3.25 centimeters
- **H.** 9.75 centimeters
- **J.** 12 centimeters
- **K.** 225 centimeters

27. You are a surveyor marking the boundaries of a farm lot in a rural area. The plot is rectangular, measuring 2,980 yards by 525 yards. What is the area of the plot?

- **A.** 35.9 acres
- **B.** 107.7 acres
- **C.** 323.2 acres
- **D.** 969.7 acres
- **E.** 3,232 acres

28. You are installing a pool that is 15 feet × 20 feet × 5 feet deep. The pool will be filled $4\frac{1}{2}$ feet deep with water. About how many gallons of water do you need to fill the pool?

- **F.** 300 gallons
- **G.** 1,500 gallons
- **H.** 10,099 gallons
- **J.** 11,220 gallons
- **K.** 2,540,769 gallons

Answers are on page 248.

Level 7 Introduction ...

The lesson and practice pages that follow will give you the opportunity to develop and practice the mathematical skills needed to solve work-related problems at a Level 7 rating of difficulty. The *On Your Own* practice problems provide a review of math skills and instruction for specific problem-solving strategies. The *Performance Assessment* provides problems similar to those you will encounter on a Career Readiness Certificate test. By completing the Level 7 *On Your Own* and *Performance Assessment* problems, you will gain the ability to confidently approach workplace scenarios that require understanding and application of the skills featured in the following lessons:

Lesson 27: Convert Between Systems of Measurement

Lesson 28: Find the Best Deal from Among Several Choices

Lesson 29: Complex Ratios and Proportions

Lesson 30: Calculate Areas and Volumes of Spheres, Cylinders, or Cones

Lesson 31: Solve Problems with Nonlinear Functions and/or
One or More Unknowns

Lesson 32: Apply Basic Statistical and Probability Concepts

These skills are intended to help you successfully understand and solve problems in the workplace requiring more complex mathematics, including linear and nonlinear functions, ratios and proportions, and probability. Solving these types of problems often requires the ability to:

- make a decision based on the results of multiple calculations,
- solve multiple-step problems that require use of both logic and calculation,
- understand information presented in unfamiliar or varied formats.

Through solving problems at this level, you will continue to develop problem-solving approaches and strategies that will help you determine the correct answer in real-world and test-taking situations.

For a complete list of measurement conversions, including those used in this lesson, refer to the Applied Mathematics Formula Sheet on page 266 of this book.

Remember!

If you are uncertain as to how to use the conversion factors for converting from one unit of measurement to another, you can set up a proportion to calculate the conversion. However, if you are familiar with the units with which you are working, you can convert in one simple step.

Lesson 27 ■■■
Convert Between Systems of Measurement

Skill: Convert between systems of measurement that involve fractions, mixed numbers, decimals and/or percentages

When performing workplace calculations, you may need to convert measurements from one system of measurement to another. For example, a production facility that completes work orders in metric measurements may work with a supplier that packages products in containers measured in customary (English) units.

Skill Examples

Example 1
Convert between systems of measurements when the measurement is a mixed number.

$$4\frac{1}{2} \text{ inches} = \underline{\hspace{1cm}} \text{ centimeters}$$

To convert the mixed number to a decimal, first break apart the whole number and fraction.

$$4\frac{1}{2} = 4 + \frac{1}{2}$$

Convert the fraction to its decimal equivalent and add the whole number and the decimal.

$$\frac{1}{2} = 1 \div 2 = 0.5$$

$$4 + 0.5 = 4.5$$

Using the formula for converting inches to centimeters, multiply by 2.54 to find the equivalent measurement in centimeters.

1 inch = 2.54 centimeters

4.5 inches × 2.54 centimeters/inch
= 11.43 centimeters

Example 2
Convert between systems of measurement when a calculation must first be made within the same system of measurement.

$$20 \text{ quarts} = \underline{\hspace{1cm}} \text{ liters}$$

You must first convert 20 quarts to gallons. Begin with the formula for converting quarts to gallons.

1 gallon = 4 quarts

20 quarts ÷ 4 quarts per gallon = 5 gallons

Using the formula for converting gallons to liters, divide by 0.264 to find the equivalent measurement in liters

1 liter ≈ 0.264 gallons

5 gallons ÷ 0.264 gallons per liter ≈ 18.9 liters

Skill Practice

A. Convert from metric to customary units.

$$5 \text{ L} = \underline{\hspace{1cm}} \text{ gallons}$$

B. Convert from customary units to metric units.

$$100 \text{ pounds} = \underline{\hspace{1cm}} \text{ kilograms}$$

Try It Out! ■ ■ ■

As the transportation service manager of a large corporation, you are responsible for the service of a fleet of vehicles. To help determine which brand of engine lubricant to use with your fleet, you decided to compare two types of lubricant. At the completion of the test, you find that, on average, a vehicle burned 5 milliliters of the more expensive synthetic lubricant. The average consumption of regular grade lubricating oil was 64 milliliters. Each vehicle uses 5.8 quarts of engine lubricant. What percentage of the regular oil was lost during the test?

A. 0.5%   B. 1.2%   C. 3.2%   D. 5.6%   E. 9.1%

 Step 1 **Understand the Problem** ■ ■ ■

Complete the *Plan for Successful Solving.*

Plan for Successful Solving

What am I asked to do?	What are the facts?	How do I find the answer?	Is there any unnecessary information?	What prior knowledge will help me?
Find the percent of the regular oil that was consumed.	The engine holds 5.8 quarts. 64 ml of oil was lost.	Convert one measurement to the same system as the other. Calculate the percent that was lost.	5 milliliters of the synthetic lubricant was consumed.	1 gallon = 4 quarts 1 liter ≈ 0.264 gallons 1 liter = 1,000 milliliters

 Step 2 **Find and Check Your Answer** ■ ■ ■

- Confirm your understanding of the problem and revise your plan as needed.

- Based on your plan, determine your solution approach: *I am going to convert the quarts to milliliters and then find the percent of the total that was lost.*

    5.8 quarts ÷ 4 = 1.45 gallons   ◄······ Divide to convert quarts to gallons.

    1.45 gallons ÷ 0.264 ≈ 5.492 liters   ◄······ Divide to convert gallons to liters.

    5.492 liters × 1,000 = 5,492 milliliters   ◄······ Multiply to convert liters to milliliters.

    $\frac{64 \text{ milliliters}}{5{,}492 \text{ milliliters}}$ = 0.012 × 100% = 1.2%   ◄······ Divide the amount of oil that was lost by the initial total to calculate the percent of lubricant consumed.

- Check your answer. You can solve the problem another way by converting the milliliters to quarts and finding the percent.

- **Select the correct answer:** B. 1.2%
    By converting the units of measure to the same system, you can calculate the percent of oil consumed in the test by dividing the amount consumed by the total capacity and multiplying by 100%.

Problem Solving Tip

When solving problems that involve converting from one unit of measurement to another, you typically should first determine to which unit of measurement you should be converting. In the *Try It Out!* example, there are two units of measurement being used—quarts and milliliters. In this problem, however, the answers are listed as percentages. Because of this, you can convert either quarts to milliliters or milliliters to quarts, as long as you use the same unit of measurements for both amounts.

Remember!

The symbol ≈ means "approximately equal to" and is used because the conversion formula between gallons and liters is not exact. When calculating conversions between measurements for which the conversions are not exact, you must take into account the fact that the numbers are often rounded at some point during calculation.

On Your Own ■ ■ ■

1. In your job as art director for a museum, you have been asked to design a 3-column brochure with $\frac{1}{4}$-inch margins on the top and bottom. The text provided for the brochure will not fit however, so you must reduce the top and bottom margins by 20%. If your design software measures margins in picas, and 1 inch = 6 picas, what should you set the top and bottom margins to in your design software?

   A.   0.3 pica

   B.   0.5 pica

   C.   0.7 pica

   D.   1.2 picas

   E.   1.5 picas

Use the following information for questions 2–4.

As a caterer, you have been asked to provide Australian cuisine for a banquet. The client specifically requested lamingtons for dessert. You have found a recipe online that you will use to make the lamingtons. The basic recipe is shown below.

Ingredients	
130 grams butter	190 grams flour
176 grams sugar	2 teaspoons baking
2 eggs	powder
1 teaspoon vanilla	145 milliliters milk
Procedure	
Bake in a conventional oven at 175°C for 25–30 minutes. Serves 20.	

One cup of sugar or flour is equivalent to 110 grams, and $\frac{1}{4}$ cup of butter is equal to 55 grams. You need to prepare for 100 guests at the banquet.

2. How much sugar do you need to make the lamingtons?

   F. $1\frac{1}{2}$ cups

   G.   3 cups

   H. $5\frac{1}{4}$ cups

   J. $6\frac{3}{4}$ cups

   K.   8 cups

3. About how much milk do you need to make the lamingtons?

   A. $1\frac{1}{2}$ cups

   B.   3 cups

   C. $5\frac{1}{4}$ cups

   D. $6\frac{3}{4}$ cups

   E.   8 cups

4. You plan to bake the lamingtons in a convection oven. The general rule is to reduce the temperature by 25°F from the temperature given for a conventional oven. Which temperature is the best choice for a convection oven?

   F.   135°F

   G.   325°F

   H.   335°F

   J.   345°F

   K.   350°F

5. You are a forensic scientist who has been asked to estimate the height of a person, based on the length of a femur. The bone is $19\frac{1}{2}$ inches long. For a female, $h = 61.512 + 2.317F$ and for a male, $h = 69.089 + 2.238F$, where h is the height in centimeters and F is the length of the femur in centimeters. What is the shortest probable height of the person from whom this femur came?

    A.   172.2 centimeters

    B.   176.3 centimeters

    C.   179.9 centimeters

    D.   207 centimeters

    E.   353.9 centimeters

6. In your job as a postsecondary science teacher, you conduct scientific research to be published in professional journals. One journal requires you to provide measurements in both customary and scientific units. The formula to convert Kelvin to Celsius is °C = K − 273.15. If you maintained the solution in your experiment at 305 K, which temperature is equivalent?

    F.   −0.084°F

    G.   31.85°F

    H.   89.33°F

    J.   114.93°F

    K.   1,042.67°F

7. As a pharmacist, you are filling a prescription for nitroglycerin. The doctor prescribed 0.88 milligram of nitroglycerin to treat the patient's symptoms. The nitroglycerin tablets you stock are $\frac{1}{150}$ grain tablets. If 1 gram = 15 grains, how many nitroglycerin tablets should the patient take?

    A. $\frac{1}{2}$ tablet

    B.   1 tablet

    C. $1\frac{1}{2}$ tablets

    D.   2 tablets

    E.   3 tablets

8. As a civil engineer, you are overseeing a project at the municipal airport. The manufacturer's specifications recommend that a particular piece of equipment be stored on a slab of concrete that is at least 23 centimeters thick. You are designing a concrete slab that will measure 30 feet by 15 feet. If you order 10% extra, and round up to the next whole cubic yard, how many cubic yards of concrete should you order?

    F.   14 cubic yards

    G.   32 cubic yards

    H.   167 cubic yards

    J.   499 cubic yards

    K.   4,483 cubic yards

9. In your job as a dietician, you educate people on the foods for the recommended daily allowance of vitamins. The recommended daily allowance for vitamin C is 60 milligrams per day. If there are 70 milligrams of vitamin C in each 100 grams of orange, how many 3-ounce oranges would you recommend that a person eat to meet the weekly requirement?

    A.   1

    B.   2

    C.   4

    D.   5

    E.   8

10. In your job as a nurse practitioner, you need to prescribe an antibiotic for a 50-pound child. The recommended daily dosage for a child is 80 milligrams per kilogram of weight, given in two doses. About how many milligrams of the antibiotic should you prescribe per dose?

    F.   1.6 milligrams

    G.   500 milligrams

    H.   909 milligrams

    J.   1,818 milligrams

    K.   4,400 milligrams

11. You are in charge of shipping for a research institute. You need to ship samples that must be stored at 45°F. Since the shipment is going overseas, it is recommended that you also include the Celsius temperature on the transmittal form. What temperature should you include on the transmittal form?

    A.   7.2°C

    B.   13°C

    C.   23.5°C

    D.   42.8°C

    E.   118.6°C

12. As an editor, you must edit documents for length and layout. You are editing a document that has space saved for a square picture with sides measuring 3.81 centimeters to be inserted. So that the text will fit nicely on the page, you decide that the size of the picture should have sides measuring 1.2 inches instead. By what percent should you scale the picture?

    F.   12.5%

    G.   31.5%

    H.   65%

    J.   80%

    K.   125%

13. In your job as a pressure valve inspector, you are recommending the replacement of an air pressure regulator to control the pressure in a client's liquid cooling system. You need a regulator that has a pressure rating from 15 to 30 psi. The regulators are rated using the bar unit, and 1 bar = 14.5038 psi. Which regulator meets the specifications?

    A.   less than 7.1 bar

    B.   7.1–13.0 bar

    C.   13.0–25.2 bar

    D.   25.2–120 bar

    E.   more than 120 bar

14. As an assistant director of campus planning, you are reviewing the development of 15 acres of property that has been donated to your university for sports and recreational use. The university would like to use some of the property for a 100 meter x 70 meter rugby field, but the donor has requested that no more than 10% of the land be used for any one field. Rounded to the nearest percent, what percent of the recreational area will the rugby field use?

    F.   1%

    G.   4%

    H.   5%

    J.   12%

    K.   16%

15. You are a sales manager for a recreation outfitter that stocks backpacks from several different suppliers. You want to prepare a sales sheet that shows the capacity of each backpack so customers can determine which pack best meets their needs. Some suppliers list the volume by liters, and others list the volume by cubic inches. What is the difference in volume between the largest and the smallest backpack on the table?

Backpack	Volume
Uptop	1,600 cubic inches
Elite	2,441 cubic inches
Vortex	30 liters
Tagalon	24.5 liters

    A.   3.8 liters

    B.   5.5 liters

    C.   15.5 liters

    D.   230.6 cubic inches

    E.   941 cubic inches

16. The sensitive equipment that you use in your job as a lab technician requires that the laboratory be kept between 20°C and 23°C. You know that the temperature in the lab can fluctuate 2 degrees Fahrenheit above or below the temperature set on the thermostat. What is an appropriate temperature for the thermostat in the lab?

    F.   66°F

    G.   68°F

    H.   70°F

    J.   72°F

    K.   74°F

Answers are on page 254.

Lesson 28 ▪ ▪ ▪
Find the Best Deal from Among Several Choices

Skill: Find the best deal when there are several choices

In the workplace, there are a number of situations in which you may need to evaluate the cost of several choices to determine the best deal. When buying items in bulk, the cost per unit of the item for various offers should be evaluated to determine which is the overall better deal. When having items shipped, the cost of the items combined with shipping cost should be evaluated to determine the overall cost for each option. When discounts are offered based on the amount that is purchased or other factors, the discount must be applied to find the final cost before determining the best deal. Knowing what steps to take when finding the best deal is an important skill for reducing costs in the workplace and at home.

Skill Examples

Example 1
Calculate the total after applying a discount.

Find the total cost for a $650 item after applying a 15% discount.

First, convert the percentage to a decimal. A percent tells the amount out of 100 you have.

$$15\% = \frac{15}{100} = 0.15$$

Multiply the original cost by the decimal.

$650 × 0.15 = $97.50

The product is the amount of the *discount*, not the total cost. To apply the discount, subtract.

$650 − $97.50 = $552.50

Example 2
Compare the cost per unit of two items.

Brand A: 5 cases for $65
Brand B: 8 cases for $100

Both of these can be written as a ratio of cases per cost. A ratio can be expressed as a fraction. Cost per unit can be written as $\frac{cost}{unit}$. Place the corresponding numbers and units in the fraction and divide.

$$\frac{\$65}{5} \text{ cases} = \$13 \text{ per case}$$

$$\frac{\$100}{8} \text{ cases} = \$12.50 \text{ per case}$$

The per unit costs can now be compared to determine which is the better deal.

$12.50 < $1,300

Skill Practice

A. Find a discount.	25% of $70	= _____
B. Find the final cost after a discount.	$400 less 10%	= _____
C. Find the cost per gallon.	45 gallons for $116.55	= _____
D. Apply the per unit cost.	20 feet at $14.97 per foot	= _____

Try It Out! ■ ■ ■

In your job as a medical clinic manager, you need to replace the waiting room carpet. The rectangular room measures 15 feet by 24 feet. You have three bids for replacing the carpet. Bid A is $20 per square yard plus a $150 installation fee. Bid B is $2.65 per square foot installed. Bid C is a flat rate of $980, with 5% off for a first time customer. What is the least you can pay to have the carpet replaced?

    A. $800   **B.** $931   **C.** $950   **D.** $954   **E.** $980

 Step 1 **Understand the Problem** ■ ■ ■

Complete the *Plan for Successful Solving.*

Plan for Successful Solving

What am I asked to do?	What are the facts?	How do I find the answer?	Is there any unnecessary information?	What prior knowledge will help me?
Find the least expensive option for replacing the carpet.	Room is 15' x 24' rectangle Bid A: $20 per square yard + $150 Bid B: $2.65 per square foot Bid C: $980, 5% discount	Find the total cost for each bid and compare them to determine the lowest cost.	No.	1 square yard = 9 square feet.

 Step 2 **Find and Check Your Answer** ■ ■ ■

- Confirm your understanding of the problem and revise your plan as needed.

- Based on your plan, determine your solution approach: *I am going to find the total cost for each bid and compare the costs to find the least expensive option.*

    15 × 24 = 360 square feet   ◄······ Calculate the area of the room being carpeted and
    360 ÷ 9 = 40 square yards   convert the area from square feet to square yards.

    40 yd^2 × $20 per yd^2 = $800 ◄······ Multiply the cost per square yard by the number
    $800 + $150 = $950   of square yards, then add the installation fee to
                             find the total cost of Bid A.

    360 ft^2 × 2.65 per ft^2 = $954 ◄······ Multiply the cost per square foot by the number of
                             square feet to find the total cost of Bid B.

    $980 × 0.05 = $49   ◄······ Multiply to calculate the 5% discount, then
    $980 – $49 = $931   subtract to find the total cost of Bid C.

    Bid A = $950 Bid B = $954 ◄······ Compare the costs of the three bids.
    Bid C = $931

- Check your answer. Double-check that the correct units were used.

- **Select the correct answer:** **B.** $931
    By finding the total cost for each bid, you can find which one is the least expensive.

Problem Solving Tip

Before you begin calculating to find the best deal among several options, it is helpful to use a table to organize the information for each option. In the *Try It Out!* example, the following table could be used to help you keep track of the information for each bid.

Bid A	$20 per yd^2 $150 installation
Bid B	$2.65 per ft^2
Bid C	$980 5% discount

Remember!

The cheapest option in one scenario might not be the cheapest option in a different scenario. In the *Try It Out!* example, the per unit cost for carpeting and installation in Bid B is greater than the cost of carpeting for Bid A. However, Bid A also includes an installation cost of $150. Because of this, as the size of the room being carpeted decreases, there is a point where Bid B becomes the cheapest option. The difference between the cost of carpeting and installation using Bid B compared to the cost of the carpeting alone using Bid A is *less than* $150.

On Your Own ■ ■ ■

1. You are a freelance technical writer with three short-term writing projects to consider. Company A offers $20 per hour for a project that will take approximately 16 hours to complete. Company B offers $500 for a project that they estimate will require about 2.5 days to complete. A third company has a 12-page booklet that they will pay you $25 per page to write. If you work an average of 8 hours per day and can complete 4 pages per day, what is the highest pay per hour you can earn on a project?

    A. $15.00 per hour

    B. $18.75 per hour

    C. $20.00 per hour

    D. $25.00 per hour

    E. $27.50 per hour

2. As an electrician wiring a new office building, you need to purchase 75 junction boxes. The local home improvement store sells the junction boxes for $6.50 each, or $155 for a case of 25. The home improvement store offers a 10% discount for contractors. A wholesale catalog lists the same junction box for $5.75 each or $405 for 100. Shipping for any order under $500 is $10. What is the least amount you can spend for the junction boxes?

    F. $399.75

    G. $405.00

    H. $410.25

    J. $415.00

    K. $487.50

Use the following information for questions 3 and 4.

As an occupational health and safety technician, you are asked to advise a company on a program encouraging employees to get a flu shot. You have designed three possible programs.

Plan 1: Reimburse employees for half the cost of a flu shot from their regular doctor. The average cost for a flu shot is $25. You estimate that 75 workers will get a flu shot and file for reimbursement.

Plan 2: Contract with a local pharmacy to provide flu shots on site for employees. They will charge a flat fee of $2,250 for up to 150 shots. To offset the cost, each employee will pay $10 for a flu shot. You estimate that 125 workers will get a flu shot with this plan.

Plan 3: Contract with a local doctor's office to come on site and give flu shots at a discounted rate of $20. The employer will pay half the cost of the shot. You estimate that 125 workers will get a flu shot with this plan.

3. Considering the total cost to the employer, how much will the least expensive plan cost?

    A. $750.00

    B. $875.25

    C. $900.00

    D. $937.50

    E. $1,000.00

4. Considering all the plans, what is the lowest cost per person for the employer?

    F. $5.00

    G. $7.00

    H. $8.00

    J. $10.00

    K. $12.50

5. In your job as an HVAC specialist, you are replacing an air conditioner for a customer. The list price of an air conditioner at Store A is $900, but the store offers a 35% discount for contractors. The same air conditioner is at Store B with a list price of $850 with a 20% discount for contractors. You plan to purchase the air conditioner at the discounted price and charge the customer for the list price of the air conditioner, plus $125 labor. What is the most profit you can make on the job?

    A. $295

    B. $360

    C. $440

    D. $725

    E. $775

6. As an accountant, your job is to evaluate the cost of leasing new office space. You have found three properties that each have 5,000 square feet of office space. You have organized the costs associated with each property in a table.

Bldg.	Rent	Utilities	Insurance
A	$4,000/month	$1,200/month	$1,000/month
B	$36,000/year	$18,000/year	$4,500/quarter
C	$3,500/month	$4,000/quarter	$10,000/year

You have budgeted a total of $13.50 per square foot per year for the new office space, including rent, utilities, and insurance. Identify which building is the best deal and how much it is over or under the amount budgeted.

    F. Building A is $0.56 per square foot per year under budget.

    G. Building A is $1.38 per square foot per year over budget.

    H. Building B is $0.90 per square foot per year over budget.

    J. Building C is $0.20 per square foot per year under budget.

    K. Building C is $0.10 per square foot per year over budget.

Use the following information for questions 7 and 8.

You are a clinical laboratory technician who is setting up a new lab. Your employer requires you to get bids from three different companies for the supplies needed for the lab. The supplies cost $5,750 from Company X. The supplies cost $5,800 from Company Y, who offers a 1% discount if the invoice is paid within 15 days. Company Z charges $6,000 for the supplies, and they offer a 5% discount if the invoice is paid within 10 days, and a 2% discount if the invoice is paid within 20 days.

7. If the accounting department's policy is to pay invoices within 10 days, what is the least you can pay for the supplies?

    A. $5,700

    B. $5,725

    C. $5,742

    D. $5,750

    E. $5,880

8. If the accounting department's policy is to pay invoices within 15 days, what is the least you can pay for the supplies?

    F. $5,700

    G. $5,725

    H. $5,742

    J. $5,750

    K. $5,880

9. As a loan officer for a bank, you often advise customers on loans and refinancing. The Gundersons owe $100,000 on their current home mortgage at 7%. Their current payment is $665.30. You can offer them refinancing on $100,000 at 5.25%, with $3,500 in fees. The new mortgage payment would be $552.20 per month. What is the shortest time they must stay in the home for refinancing to be the best deal?

   A. 5 months

   B. 12 months

   C. 17 months

   D. 20 months

   E. 31 months

10. In your job as a pharmacist, you are researching a new computer program to keep track of patient information. There are several purchase options. Under Option 1, you can purchase the program for $5,000 and receive no technical training. Under Option 2, you can purchase the program for $6,500 and receive 2 free days of training for your staff. Under Option 3, you can purchase the program with free technical support and training at anytime for $10,000. With no training, your staff will require an estimated 25 hours of technical assistance. If they receive 2 days of training, they will require an estimated 5 hours of technical assistance. If technical assistance costs $100 per hour, how much is the least expensive option?

   F. $5,500

   G. $7,000

   H. $7,500

   J. $8,000

   K. $10,000

Use the following information for questions 11 and 12.

As a sales manager for an office supply business, you are responsible for planning the annual sales banquet. You have contacted a local hotel to reserve a banquet room. The banquet room rents for $550 an evening, but that fee is waived if you use the hotel catering. The hotel charges $18.25 per plate for a steak dinner. Another caterer in town will do the same meal for $12.25 per person. A third caterer will provide the meal for $10.50 per person plus $10 per hour for the servers. One server is needed for every 25 people. The caterer estimates that each server will work for 2 hours.

11. If you are expecting 100 people, what is the least you can spend for the room and meal for the banquet?

   A. $1,050

   B. $1,130

   C. $1,225

   D. $1,680

   E. $1,775

12. For which number of people will it be the best deal to use the hotel to cater the meal?

   F. 75

   G. 100

   H. 125

   J. 150

   K. 200

13. You are a graphic designer who is designing a logo for a company shirt to go to their 95 salespeople. You contact several wholesale printers for the price for the shirts. Printer A charges $12.15 per shirt for orders of 1–99 shirts, and $12 per shirt for orders of 100–149 shirts. Shipping is $100 for any order of less than 100 shirts and free for orders 100 shirts or larger. Printer B charges $12.20 per shirt for orders of 1–99 shirts, and $12.05 per shirt for orders of 100 and above. Shipping is 5% of the total cost of the order. What is the least amount you can spend for the shirts so that every salesperson receives a shirt?

 A. $1,154.25

 B. $1,187.50

 C. $1,200.00

 D. $1,254.25

 E. $1,216.95

14. In your job as a surveyor, you are being sent to a remote location to complete a land survey, and you must ship $3,000 worth of equipment. Two carriers will accept your equipment. The first carrier will charge a base rate of $294.11, plus an oversize fee of $45, and surcharges totaling $115.32. The second carrier will charge a base rate of $344.30 and surcharges totaling $30.33. Both carriers will charge $0.65 per $100 of declared value for insurance. What is the least amount you can pay to have your equipment shipped?

 F. $319.45

 G. $374.63

 H. $394.13

 J. $454.48

 K. $473.93

15. In your job as a landscaper, you have just signed contracts to fertilize a 3-acre park 4 times a year and a business park lawn that is 132 feet by 165 feet 6 times a year. You plan to purchase all the fertilizer you will use for the entire year for both properties. One fertilizer is to be applied at the rate of 50 pounds per 15,000 square feet and can be purchased for $28.00 per 50 pounds. Another fertilizer is to be applied at the rate of 65 pounds per acre and sells for $5.15 per 5 pounds. What is the least amount you can spend on fertilizer for the year for the properties?

 A. $234.33

 B. $789.46

 C. $1,004.25

 D. $1,219.68

 E. $1,350.00

16. As a school nurse, you have been asked to research the cost for installing and maintaining hand sanitizer dispensers at 20 locations throughout the school. One company sells automatic dispensing units for $84.99 each or 10 for $687.99. You estimate that you will need 40 liters of hand sanitizer per year that sells for $5.99 per 500 milliliters. Another company sells a push-button dispenser for $22.75 each. These units must be stocked with pre-measured bags of 1,000 milliliters of hand sanitizer. A case of 8 bags sells for $80.49. You estimate that you will use 4 bags per dispenser each year. If there are 600 students and staff at the school, what is the lowest cost per student for purchasing and stocking the units for the first year?

 F. $2.10

 G. $3.09

 H. $3.26

 J. $3.86

 K. $4.01

Answers are on page 254.

Complex Ratios and Proportions

Skill: Set up and manipulate complex ratios or proportions

Complex ratios and proportions are used for calculating in many workplace situations. A ratio is a comparison of two numbers. Ratios may be used when ordering supplies or preparing invoices. An architect or designer uses scale, a ratio that shows the size of an object in a drawing in comparison to the real-life object. A proportion, two equal ratios, can help you determine the cost of a quantity if the price of a smaller quantity of the same item is known.

Remember!

A ratio compares two numbers. There is more than one way to write a ratio.

$$2 \text{ to } 5 \text{ or } 2{:}5 \text{ or } \frac{2}{5}$$

Suppose a supermarket sells three major brands of orange juice. After polling 200 shoppers, 65 said they preferred Brand A, 45 said they preferred Brand B, and 90 said they preferred Brand C.

Comparison of Brand to Total

You can use a ratio to calculate the percentage of shoppers polled that prefer Brand B by dividing.

$$45 \div 200 = 0.225 \times 100$$
$$= 22.5\%$$

Of the shoppers polled, 22.5% preferred Brand B.

Comparison of Brands to Each Other

A comparison of Brand B to Brand C can be written as follows.

$$45 \text{ to } 90, \ 45{:}90, \text{ or } \frac{45}{90}$$

Skill Examples

In a poll of 150 likely voters in an upcoming election, 82 preferred Candidate A. About 12,000 registered voters are likely to cast votes in the election.

Example 1
Set up a ratio.

What is the ratio of voters polled who prefer Candidate A to likely voters polled?

Write a fraction that compares the number of voters polled who prefer Candidate A, 82, with the number of likely voters polled, 150. Write the first number as the numerator. Write the second number as the denominator, and then simplify.

$$\frac{82}{150} = \frac{41}{75}$$

Example 2
Set up a proportion to find an unknown quantity.

What is the projected number of voters who prefer Candidate A?

To find how many likely voters prefer Candidate A, set up a proportion, and solve.

$$\frac{\text{voters who prefer A}}{\text{likely voters}} = \frac{41}{75} = \frac{n}{12,000}$$

$$75n = (41)(12,000) = 492,000$$

$$75n \div 75 = 492,000 \div 75$$

$$n = 6,560$$

Skill Practice

A company makes 3 kinds of cereal. In one month, the company sells 15,000 units of Honey Oats, 8,000 units of Rice Puffs, and 12,000 units of Bran Flakes.

A. Write a ratio comparing a part to a part.

What is the ratio of units of Bran Flakes sold to units of Honey Oats sold? _____

B. Write a ratio comparing a part to a whole.

What is the ratio of units of Rice Puffs sold to total units of cereal sold? _____

Try It Out! ■ ■ ■

As a manufacturing plant manager, you are asked to track the ratio of working parts to defective parts coming off of the assembly line. After two days of monitoring part production, you find that out of 10,500 parts, 500 are defective. There are 23 work days this month. If the ratio of working parts to defective parts is consistent, how many working parts will be made this month?

A. 115,000   **B.** 120,750   **C.** 230,000   **D.** 241,500   **E.** 253,000

Step 1 Understand the Problem ■ ■ ■

Complete the *Plan for Successful Solving*.

Plan for Successful Solving

What am I asked to do?	What are the facts?	How do I find the answer?	Is there any unnecessary information?	What prior knowledge will help me?
Determine how many working parts will be made in one month.	Over two days, 500 of 10,500 parts are defective. There are 23 working days this month.	Determine the ratio of working parts made over two days. Set up a proportion using this ratio.	No.	A rate is a kind of ratio.

Step 2 Find and Check Your Answer ■ ■ ■

- Confirm your understanding of the problem and revise your plan as needed.

- Based on your plan, determine your solution approach: *I need to determine how many working parts will be made in 23 days. I need to subtract to find the number of working parts that were made in two days. Using a ratio of working parts to days, I will set up a proportion and solve to determine how many working parts will be made.*

  $10,500 - 500 = 10,000$ ◄······ Subtract to determine the number of working parts.

  $10,000 : 2$ ◄······ Set up a ratio of working parts to days.

  $\frac{10,000}{2} = \frac{x}{23}$ ◄······ Set up a proportion comparing the number of working parts made in one day to the number or working parts made in 23 days.

  $2x = 230,000$ ◄······ Multiply to find cross products.

  $x = 115,000$ ◄······ Divide both sides by 2 to solve for x.

- Check your answer. Solve the problem a different way. $10,000 \div 2 = 5,000$ working parts per day. $5,000 \times 23 = 115,000$ working parts in 23 days.

- **Select the correct answer:** **A.** 115,000
  By setting up a ratio of number of working parts made to number of days, a proportion can be used to determine the number of parts that will be made for any given number of days.

Problem Solving Tip

Be sure that you read all information carefully. A common mistake in problems is to assume that the number of items produced represents a per day rate. In the *Try It Out!* example, however, the 10,000 working parts are produced in two days, not one day. Because of this, the ratio of working parts to days is 10,000 parts: 2 days.

Remember!

Though the ratio used in the *Try It Out!* example is not a rate, it can be simplified to find the rate of production for working parts per day. To do so, divide both sides by 2. This helps you determine that the number of working parts produced per day is 5,000.

On Your Own ▪ ▪ ▪

1. You are the regional purchasing manager for a children's clothing store. One supplier delivers 48 boys' T-shirts per case. This supplier can deliver no more than 24 cases by the time you will need the T-shirts. Another supplier delivers 32 boys' T-shirts per case. You plan to order 2,208 T-shirts. If you order 24 cases from the first supplier, how many cases do you need to order from the second supplier?

   A. 22

   B. 33

   C. 46

   D. 69

   E. 92

2. As a market analyst, you conduct a survey for a restaurateur who plans to open a vegetarian restaurant. Of the 250 people who responded, 18 said that they do not eat meat or fish, and 21 said that they eat fish but not meat. An additional 26 people said that they eat meat but enjoy eating vegetarian food. These three groups are considered likely customers. If the people who responded to the survey are representative of the town of 34,500 people, how many townspeople are likely to be customers?

   F. 19

   G. 26

   H. 65

   J. 8,970

   K. 22,425

3. You are a pharmacy technician. You have 5 liters of a 10% solution of a chemical. You need to reduce the concentration of the chemical in this solution to 5%. How much water do you need to add?

   A. 0.5 liter

   B. 1 liter

   C. 2.5 liters

   D. 5 liters

   E. 95 liters

4. In your role as a customer service manager, you and your team are responsible for replying to customer requests in writing. Alice can typically handle about 48 requests during a 4-hour morning shift, and James can typically handle about 80 requests during his 8-hour workday. You ask Alice and James to take care of the 143 requests that have been logged so far this week. If they work together, about how long will it take them to reply to all the requests?

   F. $6\frac{1}{2}$ hours

   G. 23 hours

   H. $71\frac{1}{2}$ hours

   J. 120 hours

   K. 121 hours

5. As a sales representative for a moving company, you are preparing a quote. You estimate that the move will require 6 hours for 4 movers. The charge for a move is $108 per hour for 3 movers, plus $30 per hour for any additional movers. In the quote, you also need to include a charge for 15 boxes, which are sold for $6 for a package of 5. What should be the total charge on the quote?

    A. $144

    B. $354

    C. $678

    D. $846

    E. $918

6. You are the staff accountant for a housewares shop. The shop has 3 investors—Amy, Bob, and Carla. The 3 investors agree to share the profits from the shop in proportion to their investments. Amy invested $5,000, Bob invested $8,000, and Carla invested $12,000. The shop has a profit of $60,000. What is Carla's share of the profit?

    F. $7,200

    G. $20,000

    H. $28,800

    J. $47,000

    K. $48,000

7. You are the production supervisor at a small candy factory. Of the total production of chocolate at the factory, 70% should be milk chocolate and 30% should be dark chocolate. At the end of one day, you find that the actual production that day was 85% milk chocolate and 15% dark chocolate. You plan to adjust the production tomorrow so the proportion over today and tomorrow is corrected. Assuming that the same amount of chocolate is produced both days, what percent of the chocolate produced on the second day should be dark chocolate?

    A.   15%

    B.   30%

    C.   45%

    D.   55%

    E.   70%

8. As a research assistant, you are comparing actual changes in air temperature to a theoretical model. According to the model, the temperature should rise 4°C every 3 hours from sunrise until about noon and then should rise 1°C every hour from noon until about 3:00 P.M. When the sun rises at 6:00 A.M., you find that the temperature is 21°C. According to the model, what should the temperature be at 3:00 P.M.?

    F.   10°C

    G.   11°C

    H.   26°C

    J.   32°C

    K.   33°C

Use this graph for questions 9 and 10.

Book Shop Revenue, April

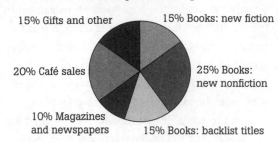

15% Gifts and other

15% Books: new fiction

20% Café sales

25% Books: new nonfiction

10% Magazines and newspapers

15% Books: backlist titles

Total revenue = $384,000

9. As the manager of a bookstore, you are reviewing the sales figures from April. What was the revenue earned from non-book sales?

    A. $45,000

    B. $172,800

    C. $192,000

    D. $211,200

    E. $339,000

10. You want to increase book sales so that the ratio of revenue from book sales to revenue from non-book sales is 3:2. If you meet this goal and the revenue from non-book sales for one month remains the same, what would be the revenue from book sales for one month?

    F. $115,200

    G. $259,200

    H. $432,000

    J. $576,000

    K. $633,600

11. As a registered nurse you want to check the dosage of medicine prescribed for a patient. The recommended dosage is 0.5 milligram per 5 kilograms of the patient's weight. The patient weighs 70 kilograms. What is the recommended dosage for this patient?

    A. 0.7 milligram

    B. 7 milligrams

    C. 15.4 milligrams

    D. 35 milligrams

    E. 154 milligrams

12. As a machine operator, you manage a canning machine that fills and seams 300 cans of juice per minute. The machine is in operation for 12 hours every day. If a planned change in production methods takes place, the canning machine will be slowed down so that it fills and seams only 250 cans per minute. For how much time each day does the machine need to operate at the slower rate to fill the same number of cans as before the change?

    F. 14 hours

    G. 14 hours, 4 minutes

    H. 14 hours, 24 minutes

    J. 22 hours

    K. 24 hours

13. As a farm manager, you are reviewing a purchase of fencing for a pasture. You have calculated that you need 12,000 feet of fencing for a pasture that measures 250 feet by 750 feet. If a 150-foot roll of fence costs $29.80, how much will you have to pay to buy the fencing for the pasture?

    A. $596

    B. $1,788

    C. $2,384

    D. $3,576

    E. $37,250

14. You are a building manager. A five-room apartment needs to be repainted before it can be leased. It takes Alex 6 hours to paint a room, and it takes Pat 9 hours to paint a room. How many hours will it take Alex and Pat to paint the apartment if they work together?

    F.   3 hours

    G.   15 hours

    H.   18 hours

    J.   45 hours

    K.   75 hours

15. As a procurement clerk, you find that 40 cases of copy paper were used at your firm over the past 2 weeks. You want to place an order for enough paper for 3 months, or 13 weeks. The charge is $32 per case, and there is a 5% discount for orders of 100 cases or more. What will be the charge for your order?

    A. $1,216

    B. $1,280

    C. $3,040

    D. $3,648

    E. $7,904

16. As a commercial interior designer, you are purchasing fabric for drapes. You need to have 12 drapes made, and you need $3\frac{1}{2}$ yards of fabric for each drape. The price for the fabric is $15 per yard or $40 per 3 yards. What will be the lowest cost of the fabric?

    F. $180

    G. $480

    H. $560

    J. $630

    K. $1,680

Answers are on page 254.

For a complete list of measurement conversions, including those used in this lesson, refer to the Applied Mathematics Formula Sheet on page 266 of this book.

Remember!

Surface Area of a Cylinder

Open cylinder

diameter

height

area ≈ (3.14 × diameter) × *height*

Closed cylinder, including ends

diameter

height

area ≈ 2 × 3.14 × *radius* × (*radius + height*)

Surface Area of a Cone

Open cone

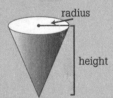

radius

height

area ≈ 3.14 × *radius* × $\sqrt{radius^2 + height^2}$

Closed cone, including ends

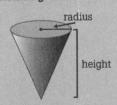

radius

height

area ≈ 3.14 × *radius* × (*radius* + $\sqrt{radius^2 + height^2}$)

Lesson 30 ▪ ▪ ▪
Calculate Areas and Volumes of Spheres, Cylinders, or Cones

Skill: Calculate multiple areas and volumes of spheres, cylinders, or cones

In performing workplace calculations, you may need to find the surface area or volume of an object that has the shape of a sphere, cylinder, or cone. For example, you may need to know the capacity of a cylindrical container or calculate the amount of paint needed to cover a cone-shaped piece of equipment.

When calculating the volume of cylinders and cones, you will first need to determine whether you need the area of the circular ends of the figure or only the sides. Then use the formulas on this page to make the calculations.

Skill Examples

Example 1
Calculate the volume of a sphere.

Find the volume of a sphere that has a diameter of 4 feet.

Divide the diameter by 2 to calculate the radius.

4 feet ÷ 2 = 2 feet

Write the formula for volume of a sphere from the formula sheet.

volume ≈ $\frac{4}{3}$ × 3.14 × (*radius*)³

Plug in the radius and solve. Calculate exponents first.

volume ≈ $\frac{4}{3}$ × 3.14 × (2 feet)³

volume ≈ $\frac{4}{3}$ × 3.14 × 8 feet³ ≈ 33.5 feet³

Example 2
Calculate the surface area of a cylinder.

Find the surface area of a closed cylindrical can that is 4 inches tall and 3 inches in diameter,

Divide the diameter by 2 to calculate the radius.

3 inches ÷ 2 = 1.5 inches

Write the cylinder surface area formula.

surface area ≈ 2 × 3.14 × 1.5 inches × (1.5 inches + 4 inches) ≈ 51.8 inches²

Skill Practice

A. Find the volume of a cone.

Volume of a cone with a radius of 4 inches and a height of 8 inches = _____ inches³

B. Find the surface area of a closed cone.

Surface area of a closed cone with a 2-inch radius and 6-inch height = _____ inches²

Try It Out! ▪ ▪ ▪

You are a mechanical engineer designing a production facility that will make solid spheres of plastic for a specialty bearing. Your company has an initial order for 500,000 spheres with a 6-centimeter diameter. In order to size the production equipment, you first will need to determine the volume of plastic in each spherical bearing. What is the volume, in cubic centimeters, of each of the spherical bearings?

A. 27　　　　B. 36　　　　C. 85　　　　D. 113.04　　　　E. 70,817

Problem Solving Tip

When calculating areas and volumes of shapes that have a circular cross-section, remember to use the radius when calculating, not the diameter.

Step 1　Understand the Problem ▪ ▪ ▪

Complete the *Plan for Successful Solving.*

Plan for Successful Solving				
What am I asked to do?	**What are the facts?**	**How do I find the answer?**	**Is there any unnecessary information?**	**What prior knowledge will help me?**
Calculate the volume of a plastic sphere.	The diameter of the sphere is 6 centimeters.	Use the formula for the volume of a sphere.	Yes. The initial order is 500,000 spheres.	The radius of a sphere is one-half its diameter.

Step 2　Find and Check Your Answer ▪ ▪ ▪

- Confirm your understanding of the problem and revise your plan as needed.

- Based on your plan, determine your solution: *Since I know the diameter of the sphere, I will divide it by 2 to determine the radius. Then I will use the formula for finding the volume of a sphere to determine the volume of each plastic sphere.*

  radius = 6 ÷ 2 = 3 centimeters　　◀······ Divide the diameter by 2 to calculate the radius of the sphere.

  volume ≈ $\frac{4}{3}$ × 3.14 × (*radius*)³　　◀······ Write the equation for the volume of a sphere.

  volume ≈ $\frac{4}{3}$ × 3.14 × (3)³　　◀······ Set up the equation using the radius.

  volume ≈ $\frac{4}{3}$ × 3.14 × 27　　◀······ Calculate the exponents first.

  volume ≈ $\frac{4}{3}$ × 3.14 × 27 ≈ 113.04 cubic centimeters　　◀······ Multiply to solve.

- Check your answer. From the original equation, you can see that the radius is approximately equal to the cube root of one-fourth of the volume. One-fourth of the volume is 28.25, which is close to 3 cubed (27).

- **Select the correct answer:**　D. 113.04
  By applying the formula for the volume, you can find the volume of each sphere.

Remember!

Watch the units involved. If the volume is wanted in cubic centimeters, make sure all your measurements are in centimeters before you plug them into a formula.

On Your Own ▪ ▪ ▪

1. In your job as a chemical engineer, you are writing specifications for a cone-shaped funnel to feed materials into a dryer that has a capacity of 28 cubic meters. The largest funnel that will fit into the space available will measure 2 meters across the open end and 4.5 meters high. What is the approximate volume of material will this funnel hold?

    A.   1.50 meters^3

    B.   4.71 meters^3

    C.   9.42 meters^3

    D.   14.13 meters^3

    E.   18.84 meters^3

2. As an atmospheric scientist, you need to use a helium balloon to carry instruments to an altitude of 28,000 feet. To control the balloons' altitude, you need to know the volume of the balloon in a specified temperature and pressure range so that you can use the correct amount of helium. At 28,000 feet, the balloon will have a spherical shape and a diameter of 12 meters. To the nearest cubic meter, what is the volume of the balloon under the conditions that it will encounter at 28,000 feet?

    F.   25 meters^3

    G.   151 meters^3

    H.   302 meters^3

    J.   904 meters^3

    K.   7,235 meters^3

3. You are a mechanical engineer working for a company that manufactures specialty fiberglass tanks. A customer has specified a cylindrical tank that has inside measurements of 10 meters tall and 5 meters in diameter. You will coat the inside of the wall and floor of the tank with an epoxy sealant. To calculate the amount of sealant to order, you need to find the surface area of the inner surfaces of the tank. What is the total area of the inner wall and the floor of the tank rounded to the nearest meter?

    A.   177 meters^2

    B.   353 meters^2

    C.   361 meters^2

    D.   377 meters^2

    E.   5,511 meters^2

4. As a product manager for a cosmetics company, you are proposing a new fragrance that will be packaged in a unique bottle. Your packaging supplier can provide a cone-shaped bottle, which has interior dimensions of 4 centimeters high and a 3-centimeter diameter at the base of the cone. What volume of perfume will the bottle hold? (Note: 1 milliliter = 1 cubic centimeter)

    F.   6.3 milliliters

    G.   9.4 milliliters

    H.   14.1 milliliters

    J.   28.3 milliliters

    K.   87.3 milliliters

Use the following information for questions 5 and 6.

You are a fireworks manufacturer making a new type of shell. The material that carries the shell upward is packed into a cylindrical tube, and the shell itself is a sphere attached to the top of the tube. The rocket body is 16 inches long with a radius of 2.5 inches and the shell on top has a diameter of 8 inches. The rocket is designed to reach an altitude of about 1,150 feet before the shell explodes.

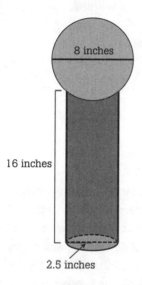

8 inches

16 inches

2.5 inches

5. What is the approximate volume of propellant in the rocket tube if the tube is completely filled?

    A.   314 inches³

    B.   502 inches³

    C.   942 inches³

    D.   1,256 inches³

    E.   2,010 inches³

6. What is the approximate volume of the spherical shell on top of the rocket?

    F.   50 inches³

    G.   268 inches³

    H.   512 inches³

    J.   804 inches³

    K.   2,143 inches³

7. You are a drilling technician working on a research ship that is taking cylinder–shaped core samples from the sea floor. To determine how much space will be needed to store the samples you will be collecting on an expedition, you need to know the volume of each core sample. Each sample is 20 centimeters in diameter and 50 meters long. What is the approximate volume of each sample?

    A.   0.5 meter³

    B.   1.6 meters³

    C.   6.3 meters³

    D.   26 meters³

    E.   52.3 meters³

8. As a marketing design specialist, you are sketching a new label for a client's line of canned vegetables. The standard can that the client uses is $3\frac{1}{2}$ inches in diameter and $5\frac{3}{4}$ inches tall. What is the approximate area of the label that will wrap around the can?

    F.   22.0 square inches

    G.   63.2 square inches

    H.   126.4 square inches

    J.   110.6 square inches

    K.   442.3 square inches

9. In your job as a packaging technician for a cannery, you are setting up a filling machine to fill a cylindrical can with tomato paste. The inside dimensions of the can are 4 inches in diameter and 7 inches in height. The filling machine can process 2,025 cans of this size in one hour when it is properly adjusted. What is the approximate volume of tomato paste in each can?

    A.   29 cubic inches

    B.   88 cubic inches

    C.   112 cubic inches

    D.   352 cubic inches

    E.   615 cubic inches

10. You are a park facilities manager in charge of a number of local municipal parks. One of the water parks has a play area that includes three cone-shaped containers that fill with water and then tip over and pour the water out. In order to determine a safe structure to disperse the water when it spills, you need to know the volume of water that must be handled. The cones are 8 feet tall and the diameter of the large end is 5 feet. What is the volume of each cone?

    F.   16.7 cubic feet

    G.   52.3 cubic feet

    H.   138.2 cubic feet

    J.   167.5 cubic feet

    K.   209.3 cubic feet

11. You are a road construction foreman whose crew is preparing a worksite for the start of construction next week. To mark off the site, you have decided to use a new type of cone that is filled with water to make it more stable. In order to fill the cones, you must calculate the amount of water to have delivered to the site. If the cones are 26 inches tall with a 12-inch diameter base, about how much water will you need per cone? (One gallon is equal to 231 cubic inches.)

    A.   4 gallons

    B.   4.25 gallons

    C.   6 gallons

    D.   13 gallons

    E.   25 gallons

12. You are a landscape architect designing a large public garden. One feature that the garden administrator wants to include in the garden is a row of decorative granite spheres that are 1.2 meters in diameter. To design support structures for the spheres, you need to know the mass of each sphere. The density of granite is about 2,700 $\frac{kg}{m^3}$. What is the approximate mass of each sphere? (density = $\frac{mass}{volume}$)

    F.   230 kilograms

    G.   380 kilograms

    H.   520 kilograms

    J.   2,442 kilograms

    K.   5,500 kilograms

13. As part of your job as a medical technician, you are calculating how long an oxygen cylinder should last. To do so, you need to know the volume of the cylinder. You determine that the inside measurements are 22 inches long by 18 inches in circumference. What volume should you use for your calculations?

    A.   396 cubic inches

    B.   567 cubic inches

    C.   622 cubic inches

    D.   1,244 cubic inches

    E.   5,595 cubic inches

14. You are a packaging specialist for a company that makes novelty gifts. One of the products for which you need to design a package is a crystal sphere with an image etched inside it by a laser. The diameter of the sphere is 20 centimeters. You want to pack it in a cube-shaped box that measures 30 centimeters on each side and use foam filler in the remaining space. About how much foam will you need for each box?

    F.   4,190 cubic centimeters

    G.   6,500 cubic centimeters

    H.   13,450 cubic centimeters

    J.   19,170 cubic centimeters

    K.   22,800 cubic centimeters

15. You are a mechanical engineer on a team designing a new aircraft. You have specified the dimensions of a hydraulic cylinder as part of the automatic control for a large cargo door. The inner diameter of the tube is 25 centimeters and its length is 80 centimeters. About how much hydraulic fluid will be needed to fill the cylinder? (1,000 cubic centimeters = 1 liter)

    A.   3.14 liters

    B.   13.08 liters

    C.   39.25 liters

    D.   78.5 liters

    E.   157 liters

16. As the manager of a municipal water company, you need to have a new storage tank added to the supply grid. The capacity of the tank is to be about 100,000 cubic yards. It has a cylindrical shape with a base that is 210 feet in diameter. About how tall will the tank be?

    F.   35 feet

    G.   47 feet

    H.   56 feet

    J.   63 feet

    K.   78 feet

Answers are on page 254.

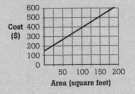
Lesson 31 ▪ ▪ ▪
Solve Problems with Nonlinear Functions and/or One or More Unknowns

Skill: Solve problems that include nonlinear functions and/or that involve more than one unknown.

In performing workplace calculations, you may need to solve problems that have a nonlinear function or a function with more than one variable. A nonlinear function is one whose graph is not a straight line. Some examples of nonlinear functions are quadratic, exponential, and radical.

Quadratic Function	Exponential Function	Radical Function
$y = ax^2 + bx + c$	$y = b^x$	$y = \sqrt{x}$
x is the unknown	x is the unknown	x is the unknown
a, b, and c are constants (numbers)	b is a constant called the base	

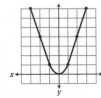 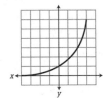 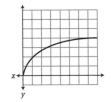

Skill Example

Example

Solve problems that include nonlinear functions and/or more than one variable.

Evaluate the function $y = ax^2 + bx + c$ for $x = 2$, $a = 5$, $b = -1$, $c = 3$

Replace the unknowns in the function with their numerical values

$$y = ax^2 + bx + c$$

$$= (5 \times 2^2) + (-1 \times 2) + 3$$

$$= 20 + (-2) + 3$$

$$= 21$$

Skill Practice

A. $y = \sqrt{x + 30}$ Find the value of the _____ function when $x = 6$

B. $y = b^x$ Find the value of the _____ function when $b = 0.2$ and $x = 3$

Try It Out! ▪ ▪ ▪

You design packaging for a marketing company. You are asked to design a box that is 10 inches long and has a volume of 490 cubic inches. The width and the height are the same measurement. What is the width and height of the box?

A. 4.9 inches B. 7 inches C. 14 inches D. 24.5 inches E. 49 inches

 Step 1 **Understand the Problem** ▪ ▪ ▪

Complete the *Plan for Successful Solving.*

Plan for Successful Solving				
What am I asked to do?	**What are the facts?**	**How do I find the answer?**	**Is there any unnecessary information?**	**What prior knowledge will help me?**
Find the height and width of the box.	Length = 10 inches Volume = 490 cubic inches	Rearrange the volume formula to solve for the height and width. Substitute the known values for unknowns.	No.	Equation for calculating the volume of a rectangular prism is volume = *length* × *width* × *height*

 Step 2 **Find and Check Your Answer** ▪ ▪ ▪

- Confirm your understanding of the problem and revise your plan as needed.

- Based on your plan, determine your solution approach: *I will begin with the volume formula and will rearrange it to solve for the unknown x, which represents the width and the height of the box. I will then replace the known values to find the missing value.*

  $volume = length \times width \times height$ ◀⋯⋯ Volume formula for a rectangular prism.

  $volume = length \times x^2$ ◀⋯⋯ Replace *width* and *height* with *x*.

  $\pm\sqrt{\dfrac{volume}{length}} = x$ ◀⋯⋯ Rewrite the formula to solve for *x*.

  $x = \pm\sqrt{\dfrac{490}{10}}$ ◀⋯⋯ Plug in the values for *length* and *volume*.

  $x = \pm 7$ ◀⋯⋯ Divide and find the square root to solve. Since the dimensions for the box cannot be negative, choose the positive answer

- Check your answer. Plug your answer into the original equation.
  volume = 10 × 7 × 7 = 490. The volume of the box is 490 cubic inches.

- **Select the correct answer:** B. 7 inches
  The width and height are the same measurement, so there should only be one answer.

Problem Solving Tip

In the *Try It Out!* example, you can also plug the known numbers into the equation before rearranging it to solve for *x*.

Remember!

Equations must always stay "balanced." When working to isolate the variable in algebraic equations, you can often use opposite operations (multiplication/division and addition/subtraction) to do so. However, when working with quadratic equations as in the *Try It Out!* example, you must use roots to eliminate the exponent. Since *x* is squared in this example, you must find the square root of both sides in order to isolate *x*. The ± is here because the square root of a number can theoretically be negative since a negative number multiplied by a negative number equals a positive number.

On Your Own ■ ■ ■

1. You are designing a circular pond for a new park. You give the specifications that the maximum depth is 4 feet and the volume is 20,000 cubic feet. What is the largest possible diameter of the pond? Round your answer to the nearest foot.

   A. 39 feet

   B. 40 feet

   C. 80 feet

   D. 398 feet

   E. 796 feet

2. As the bread maker in a bakery, you use the formula, $T = r^2 + h$ where r is the radius and h is the length of the baked loaf in inches to estimate the baking time T in minutes. You get an order for the largest 5-inch long loaf possible to be ready within the next hour. What is the radius of the loaf of bread?

   F. 2 inches

   G. 3 inches

   H. 4 inches

   J. 7 inches

   K. 8 inches

3. You are a professional fireworks technician setting up a display of stars. Aerial fireworks carry "stars" upward, ignite them, and project them into the air. The star's height is given by the function $h = -16t^2 + 72t + 520$, where h is the star's height in feet and t is the time in seconds. How high will the star be after 2.25 seconds?

   A. 520 feet

   B. 601 feet

   C. 646 feet

   D. 738 feet

   E. 763 feet

4. You are a financial analyst. You invest $1,500 of a client's money in a savings account where the interest is compounded annually. The interest rate on the account averages 6.5% a year. To the nearest dollar, how much money will the client have in 10 years? Use the formula $B = p(1 + r)^x$, where B is the balance, r is the interest rate, x is the number of years invested, and p is the initial amount invested.

   F. $1,598

   G. $2,323

   H. $2,816

   J. $3,425

   K. $15,975

5. As a mechanical engineer designing radio towers, you must calculate how much cable is needed to support a tower that is 260 feet high. The cable is attached to the tower half the distance from the base to the top. The anchor base for the cable is placed 54 feet from the tower. How long is the cable? Use the function $C^2 = t^2 + a^2$, where C is the cable length, t is the height where the cable is attached to the tower, and a is the length of the anchor base. Round your answer to the nearest foot.

   A. 117 feet

   B. 128 feet

   C. 141 feet

   D. 145 feet

   E. 266 feet

6. You are a firefighter. When putting out a fire, the rate you can spray water on the fire depends on the nozzle pressure. You find the flow rate using the function $f = 120 \sqrt{p}$, where f is the flow rate in gallons per minute and p is the pressure in pounds per square inch. What is the flow rate when the pressure is 64 pounds per square inch?

   F. 701 gallons per minute

   G. 960 gallons per minute

   H. 1,800 gallons per minute

   J. 3,840 gallons per minute

   K. 7,680 gallons per minute

7. As a photographer, you determine optimal lighting placement with the formula $I = \frac{445}{x^2}$, where I is the intensity of light in lumens at a distance x feet from a light bulb with 445 watts. How far away from the 445-watt bulb should an object be to have an intensity of 17.8 lumens?

   A. 5 feet

   B. 7 feet

   C. 10 feet

   D. 44.5 feet

   E. 89 feet

8. You are a carpenter building a barn door that measures 5 feet wide and 12 feet high. To cut diagonal braces for the door, you use the formula $d^2 = w^2 + h^2$ to compute the length of the diagonals. How long must the diagonals for your door be?

   F. 4 feet

   G. 13 feet

   H. 17 feet

   J. 24 feet

   K. 25 feet

9. You are the marketing manager for an auto company. The sales forecasting model for a new car is $S = p(54 - 0.75p)$, where S is the total sales in thousands of dollars and p is the price in thousands of dollars. You set the price of the car at $36,000. How close will the company come to making $1,000,000 with the car?

   A. $972

   B. $27,000

   C. $28,000

   D. $971,250

   E. $972,000

10. You are a display designer at a science museum. You are building a display about the history of timekeeping. One of the items in the display is a clock operated by a pendulum that is 54 inches long. As you write your display description, you want to include information about the physics of the pendulum, including how long it takes for the pendulum to swing back and forth. The formula for finding the period T in seconds is $T = 2\pi \sqrt{\frac{L}{32}}$, where L is the length of the pendulum in feet. What is the period for this pendulum?

   F. 1.44 seconds

   G. 2.355 seconds

   H. 4.08 seconds

   J. 8.16 seconds

   K. 11.5 seconds

11. You are an architect designing a building with a viewing area on the top floor. The building will be 509 meters high. How many miles can a person see to the horizon from the top of the building? Use the formula $d = \sqrt{1.5h}$ to estimate the distance d in miles to a horizon where h is the height of the viewer's eyes above the ground in feet.

   A. 15 miles

   B. 28 miles

   C. 45 miles

   D. 50 miles

   E. 2,511 miles

12. You are the designer for a new roller coaster to be built at a theme park. The equation $v - 8\sqrt{h \quad 2r}$ gives the velocity v in feet per second of a car at the top of a loop of a roller coaster, where r is the radius of the loop and h is the height of the hill the car has just come down. If the loop is 40 feet in diameter, about how high should the hill be in order for the car to reach its maximum velocity of 30 feet per second?

   F. 10 feet

   G. 12 feet

   H. 14 feet

   J. 54 feet

   K. 94 feet

13. As a research assistant in a sports lab, you are studying how long it takes for a ball to hit the ground. The equation $h = -16t^2 + 60t$ models the altitude, in feet, a ball will reach t seconds after it is kicked. How high will the ball be after 3 seconds?

    A.   36 feet

    B.   56 feet

    C.   90 feet

    D.   120 feet

    E.   132 feet

14. You are a builder who has been hired by an ice cream company to build a large fiberglass ice cream cone as a promotion for a new flavor. On top of the cone will be half of a sphere that has a volume of about 91 cubic feet. What is the radius of the top of the cone if the height is 10 feet and the volume is 128 cubic feet?

    F.   3.5 feet

    G.   5 feet

    H.   6 feet

    J.   10 feet

    K.   12 feet

15. You work as the assistant to the Chief Financial Officer of a company. A new bank is offering customers an interest rate of 6% compounded yearly on a 15-month CD with a deposit of $50,000. How much interest will the money earn? Use the formula $B = p(1 + r)^x$, where B is the balance, r is the interest rate, x is the number of years invested, and p is the initial amount invested.

    A. $894.00

    B. $3,777.71

    C. $39,974.61

    D. $53,777.71

    E. $69,827.90

16. As a police detective reconstructing vehicle accident scenes, you use the formula $r = 2\sqrt{5L}$, where r is the approximate speed, in miles per hour, of a car that leaves a skid mark of length L in feet. A car left a skid mark that is 40 feet long. About fast was the car going?

    F.   10 miles per hour

    G.   14 miles per hour

    H.   15 miles per hour

    J.   20 miles per hour

    K.   28 miles per hour

Answers are on page 254.

Lesson 32 ▪ ▪ ▪
Apply Basic Statistical and Probability Concepts

Skill: Apply basic statistical concepts

In performing workplace calculations, you may need to apply basic concepts of statistics to understand and analyze a set of data. There are several different ways you can interpret data in the workplace. You can organize and summarize the data using *measures of central tendency,* which include the mean, median, and mode. These measures are used to describe an entire set of data using only a few numbers. This can be useful when you describe the characteristics of a production run or the responses of a group of patients to a treatment.

Probability is another concept that is often used in the workplace. Probability is a way to describe the likelihood that something will occur, either as a fraction, ratio, or percent.

Skill Examples

Example 1
Calculate the mean of a set of data.

Determine the mean of the data set:

26, 35, 28, 22, 36, 30

First, find the sum of the values in the set:

$26 + 35 + 28 + 22 + 36 + 30 = 177$

Divide the sum by the number of data points.

$177 \div 6 = 29.5$

The mean is 29.5.

Example 2
Determine the probability of an event occurring.

Overtime shifts are determined by drawing beads. 24 people will get overtime and 72 will not. If you go first, what is the chance of drawing an overtime bead?

Find the fraction of times that the event occurs compared to total observations.

$$\frac{\text{occurrences}}{\text{total events}} = \frac{24}{24 + 72} = \frac{24}{96} = \frac{1}{4}$$

Divide, then multiply the decimal by 100% to find the percentage.

$\frac{1}{4} = 0.25$

$0.25 \times 100\% = 25\%$

The probability of drawing an overtime bead is 1 in 4 or 25%.

Skill Practice

A. Find the mean of a set of data.   75, 38, 43, 120, 65, 48, 52 = _____

B. Find the median of a set of data.   12, 15, 19, 24, 21, 28, 11 = _____

Try It Out! ■ ■ ■

You are a quality control inspector for a circuit board manufacturer. In order to assess the quality of a new production process, you pull 500 circuit boards from the line at random for testing. In that sample, 451 boards pass the inspection. What is the probability that a randomly selected board will pass the test criteria?

A. 9.02% **B.** 9.8% **C.** 90.2% **D.** 110% **E.** 902%

Step 1 Understand the Problem ■ ■ ■

Complete the *Plan for Successful Solving.*

Plan for Successful Solving				
What am I asked to do?	**What are the facts?**	**How do I find the answer?**	**Is there any unnecessary information?**	**What prior knowledge will help me?**
Find the probability that a circuit board, chosen at random, will pass quality inspection.	Of 500 tested circuit boards, 451 passed the test.	Divide the number of samples that passed inspection by the total number of tested samples.	No.	To convert a decimal to a percent, multiply by 100%.

Step 2 Find and Check Your Answer ■ ■ ■

- Confirm your understanding of the problem and revise your plan as needed.

- Based on your plan, determine your solution approach: *I am going to divide the number of circuit boards that have no defects, and therefore passed inspection, by the total number of circuit boards inspected.*

  $$P(\text{pass test}) = \frac{\text{number of samples that passed inspection}}{\text{total number of samples}} = \frac{451}{500}$$ ◄······ Set up an equation for calculating the probability of selecting a sample board that passed inspection and plug the data into the equation.

  $$= 0.902 \times 100\% = 90.2\%$$ ◄······ Divide, then multiply by 100% to find the percentage.

- Check your answer. Since there were some defects in the circuit boards inspected, the percent should be less than 100%. Since more circuit boards passed inspection than did not pass inspection, the probability should be between 50% and 100%.

- **Select the correct answer:** C. 90.2%
  By dividing the number of circuit boards that passed inspection by the total number of circuit boards that were tested, you find the probability of selecting a circuit board that will pass inspection.

Problem Solving Tip

When solving problems involving probability, remember that the probability of an event occurring can only fall between 0 and 1 (or 0% and 100%). Using this knowledge, in the *Try It Out!* example, you can eliminate answer options D and E because both are greater than 100%.

Remember!

The probability of an event occurring is

$$P(\text{event}) = \frac{\text{favorable outcome(s)}}{\text{possible outcomes}}$$

The probability of an event not occurring is
$P(\text{not event}) = 1 - P(\text{event})$.

When you add the probability of an event occurring to the probability of that same event *not* occurring, the total should be 1.

On Your Own ■ ■ ■

1. You are a geologist studying activity beneath Yellowstone National Park. You collect data on the amount of time between eruptions of Old Faithful geyser. You record the following times between eruptions: 35 minutes, 59 minutes, 90 minutes, 45 minutes, 65 minutes, 75 minutes, 83 minutes, 45 minutes, 95 minutes, and 68 minutes. What is the average time between eruptions according to your data?

   A. 45 minutes

   B. 60 minutes

   C. 66 minutes

   D. 66.5 minutes

   E. 68 minutes

2. You work as a property assessment specialist in a real estate office. A broker has asked you to research recent homes for sale in a Boston neighborhood. You find homes that sold for $344,000, $532,700, $225,900, $314,500, $532,700, $401,900, $1,034,900, and $299,900. Based on your data, what is the median home sale price for this area?

   F. $344,000

   G. $372,950

   H. $401,900

   J. $532,700

   K. $809,000

Use the following information to answer questions 3 and 4.

As a respiratory therapist, you are doing research on the effect of a new drug to treat asthma. There are 25 patients enrolled in the study. You ask each participant to record their peak flow measurements when they get up in the morning before taking any medication. Here are 30 days of the results for Participant 5 in liters per minute.

Sun.	Mon.	Tue.	Wed.	Thur.	Fri.	Sat.
550	525	475	550	550	450	500
325	350	350	400	450	550	550
550	500	450	450	500	550	500
475	450	375	400	425	500	550
575	600					

3. What is the mean of the peak flow readings for this patient?

   A. 275 liters/minute

   B. 481 liters/minute

   C. 488 liters/minute

   D. 550 liters/minute

   E. 600 liters/minute

4. What is the median value of peak flow for this patient?

   F. 475 liters/minute

   G. 480 liters/minute

   H. 487.5 liters/minute

   J. 500 liters/minute

   K. 600 liters/minute

5. You are a systems analyst working in the human resources department of a large corporation. The company is structured in 4 different divisions, each of which has a number of work units that are evaluated annually. The managers' salaries for a particular work unit are: $85,000, $82,000, $75,000, $100,000, $74,800, $70,500, $92,000, and $89,000. What is the median salary of the managers?

A. $29,500

B. $83,500

C. $83,538

D. $86,000

E. $87,400

6. You are a department supervisor in charge of inventory at a book warehouse. There are 9,524 book titles in the warehouse. Based on several years of publishers' statistics, the probability that a randomly chosen book is a work of fiction is 75%. How many book titles in the warehouse are likely to be works of fiction?

F. 71 books

G. 714 books

H. 7,143 books

J. 71,430 books

K. 717,300 books

7. You are a paralegal working in a large law firm that specializes in foreclosures. You need to compile data on activity this year to date. What is the average monthly number of foreclosures the firm handled in the first six months of this year?

Month	Number of Foreclosures
January	15
February	19
March	28
April	36
May	10
June	31

A. 23

B. 26

C. 29

D. 46

E. 149

8. You are a human resources supervisor in a health services corporation. In addition to the medical staff, there are 567 employees in the company. For a report, you are collecting data on the number of employees who have completed a 4-year college program. Of the nonmedical staff, 351 have a degree. What is the probability of randomly selecting a non-medical staff employee who does not have a 4-year degree for an interview?

F. 37%

G. 38%

H. 62%

J. 162%

K. 263%

9. You are a marketing director for a grocery chain. In order to compare your prices with your competitors, you research sales prices of 125 products at other stores each week. In one week, you see the prices below for a particular brand of frozen corn. What price is the mode of this data set?

Store	Price
A	$1.89
B	$1.98
C	$1.75
D	$1.89
E	$1.89
F	$1.49
G	$1.89
H	$1.64
I	$1.79
J	$1.89

   A. $1.64

   B. $1.79

   C. $1.81

   D. $1.89

   E. $1.98

10. As a credit analyst for a large bank, you are analyzing mortgages granted in the last month. You have approved mortgages of $245,000, $659,500, $325,900, $614,200, $268,700, $175,000, $312,500, and $397,200. What is the median amount of the loans that were approved?

   F. $312,500

   G. $319,200

   H. $325,900

   J. $360,000

   K. $374,750

11. You are a quality auditor at a plant that fabricates fiberglass parts for boats. To determine whether one drilling machine is aligning pieces correctly, you measure the distance between the holes on each end of the part. The measurements (in millimeters) are the following: 325, 326, 330, 325, 325, 329, 325, 326, 326, and 325. What is the mode of the data set of these measurements?

   A.   325 millimeters

   B.   326 millimeters

   C.   326.2 millimeters

   D.   327 millimeters

   E.   330 millimeters

12. You are a horticulturist studying seed germination for a major seed supplier currently working with 15 different strains of soybeans. For one strain you planted 28 flats with 64 seeds per flat. Of these, 1,636 seeds germinated. Based on this sample, what is the probability that a seed of this strain will germinate, rounded to the nearest percent?

   F.   13%

   G.   84%

   H.   87%

   J.   91%

   K.   96%

13. You are a social science technician studying diabetes rates. You have registered the following people to be in the case pool for your study. What is the probability that you will randomly select a person from the pool who does not have diabetes?

Diabetes Study Case Pool	
People Who Have Type 1 Diabetes	53
People Who Have Type 2 Diabetes	104
People Who Have Pre-Diabetes	72
People Who Do Not Have Diabetes	29

    A.   11%

    B.   21%

    C.   28%

    D.   40%

    E.   89%

14. You work as a safety inspector for the federal government helping investigate accidents on construction jobs. The numbers of investigations for each of the past 12 months were the following: 14, 7, 4, 8, 5, 9, 6, 5, 12, 4, 6, and 4. Find the average monthly number of accidents you investigated over that time.

    F.   4

    G.   6

    H.   7

    J.   8

    K.   10

15. As a financial officer at a small university, you want to compare your charges for tuition and fees to those of similar schools. Your tuition and fees for one semester are $9,685. You survey 5 other schools and find the following costs: $8,500, $9,266, $8,884, $9,450, and $10, 615. How do the costs for your students compare to the mean of the costs at the other schools?

    A. $342 lower

    B. $342 higher

    C. $419 lower

    D. $419 higher

    E. $1,185 higher

16. As a private accountant, you oversee the balance sheets of eight small businesses. These businesses have total assets of $1.4M, $2.29M, $2.14M, $1.76M, $1.84M, $1.97M, $1.43M, and $1.84M. The president of another business with $17.4M in assets wants to use your services. If you add this new client, what is true about the worth of your small-business client base?

    F.   The median worth of your client base increases.

    G.   The mode worth of your client base increases.

    H.   The median worth of your client base remains unchanged.

    J.   The mean worth of your client base remains unchanged.

    K.   The median worth will be higher than the mean worth.

Answers are on page 254.

Level 7 Performance Assessment

The following problems will test your ability to answer questions at a Level 7 rating of difficulty. These problems are similar to those that appear on a Career Readiness Certificate test. For each question, you can refer to the answer key for answer justifications. The answer justifications provide an explanation of why each answer option is either correct or incorrect and indicate the skill lesson that should be referred to if further review of a particular skill is needed.

1. You are a veterinary assistant preparing a dog for surgery. The dog weighs 45 pounds. The prescribed dose of the anesthetic is 12 milligrams of anesthetic per kilogram of body weight. The concentration of the anesthetic solution is 200 milligrams/milliliter. How many milliliters of solution are needed to prepare the dog for surgery?

   A. 0.85 milliliter

   B. 1.2 milliliters

   C. 5.9 milliliters

   D. 340 milliliters

   E. 1,650 milliliters

2. As an aeronautical engineer, you are designing a weather balloon to carry an instrument package to an altitude of 15,000 meters above a South Pole research station. You know that if the temperature does not change, the helium in the balloon expands as the pressure decreases, based on the equation $P_s V_s = P_a V_a$ where P is pressure, V is volume, and the subscripts indicate these measurements at the surface and at altitude. If the pressure at the surface is $1.00 \frac{kg}{cm^2}$ and the gas volume at the surface is 75 liters, what is the approximate volume of the balloon at 15,000 meters, where the pressure is $0.12 \frac{kg}{cm^2}$, assuming the same temperature?

   F. 0.0016 liter

   G. 0.11 liter

   H. 9 liters

   J. 75 liters

   K. 625 liters

Use the following information for questions 3 and 4.

You work as a training specialist in the computer industry. You need to advertise a new training class that you are going to teach in a metropolitan area. There are two major newspapers in the community. The *City News* charges $783 per column inch for advertising and has 40,000 subscribers, while the *City Tribune* charges $585 per column inch and has 22,500 subscribers. The *City Tribune* has a special price of $7,200 for an ad that covers two 10-inch columns. Your planned ad covers three 5-inch columns, but it can be adjusted to two 10-inch columns if the price is better.

3. What is the least you can spend on advertising in one paper?

   A. $1,755

   B. $2,925

   C. $4,680

   D. $7,200

   E. $8,775

4. What is the least you can spend on advertising per subscriber?

   F. $0.29

   G. $0.32

   H. $0.39

   J. $2.90

   K. $3.20

5. As a floral designer, you are arranging trailing plants for a unique cone-shaped hanging basket. The top of the basket has a diameter of 24 inches and the cone is 18 inches deep. If you are planting 100 baskets, how many cubic yards of potting mix will you need to prepare? If necessary, round your answer up to the nearest whole number.

    A. 6

    B. 18

    C. 24

    D. 157

    E. 279

6. As a general contractor, you have been asked to prepare an estimate for the cost to replace the chain-link fence around a playground. The length of the playground is 40 yards, and the ratio of the length to the width of the playground is 2:3. The chain-link fence costs $130 for each 48-inch length. What will be the cost of the fencing?

    F. $6,500

    G. $9,750

    H. $19,500

    J. $23,400

    K. $31,200

7. You are a contractor building a circular base for a fountain. According to the plans, the diameter of the base is 6 feet. The basin will hold about 24,416 cubic inches of water. The plan does not include the depth of the water. What do you calculate the water depth to be?

    A. 1.5 inches

    B. 6 inches

    C. 69 inches

    D. 215 inches

    E. 864 feet

8. You are the manager of a hand-made furniture store. Gina can construct a medium-sized bookcase in 4 hours, and Tom can construct one in 6 hours. Your shop needs to produce 15 medium-sized bookcases this week. How many hours will it take Gina and Tom to make them if they work together?

    F. $1\frac{1}{2}$ hours

    G. 3 hours

    H. 36 hours

    J. 75 hours

    K. 150 hours

9. In your job as a boiler inspector, you check the pressure valves for boilers. You record the following pressures: 12 psi, 13 psi, 13 psi, 14.5 psi, 14 psi, 13 psi, 16 psi, 14.5 psi, 15 psi, and 13 psi. What is the mean reading of the pressure valve?

    A. 4 psi

    B. 13 psi

    C. 13.5 psi

    D. 13.8 psi

    E. 14.1 psi

10. As a data analyst for a news organization, you decide to compare the speed of the winner of the 1,500-meter race to the speed of the world record holder in the 1-mile race. In a recent men's 1,500-meter world championship race, the winning time was 3 minutes, 35.93 seconds. If the fastest 1-mile time is 3 minutes, 32.94 seconds, what is the difference in speed between the world record 1-mile time and the winning time of the recent men's 1,500-meter world championship race?

    F. 1.4 feet per second

    G. 2.0 feet per second

    H. 17.5 feet per second

    J. 20.5 feet per second

    K. 22.3 feet per second

11. You are an interior designer who is purchasing fabric for custom drapes. You have located two stores that carry the fabric the client has chosen. A local store sells the fabric for $25 per yard. A catalog store sells the same fabric for $30 per yard for orders up to 25 yards, with a $10 shipping fee. It also sells fabric for $20 per yard for orders over 25 yards, with a $15 shipping fee. If you need 30 yards of fabric, what is the least amount you can pay for the fabric?

    A. $515

    B. $600

    C. $610

    D. $615

    E. $750

12. You are a chemical engineer designing a milling process for crushing a product into a powder. The mill that you are using mixes the solid material with hard ceramic balls and then tumbles them to get the desired powder size. You need to know the volume of each ceramic ball to determine how many balls to add for the desired volume. The balls you will use in a particular milling process are 5 centimeters in diameter. What is the volume of each ball?

    F. 19.6 cm^3

    G. 26.2 cm^3

    H. 49.1 cm^3

    J. 65.4 cm^3

    K. 523.3 cm^3

13. You are a marketing copywriter for a television manufacturer. The size of a television screen is defined by its diagonal measurement. Your company is marketing a new large-screen television monitor that measures 64 inches wide and 36 inches high. Using the formula $D = \sqrt{l^2 + h^2}$, where D is the diagonal measure, l is the length, and h is the height, calculate the size of the screen. Round up to the nearest whole number, if necessary.

    A.   10 inches

    B.   28 inches

    C.   48 inches

    D.   74 inches

    E.   100 inches

14. As the purchasing director of a clothing store, you notice that a new style of jeans is selling well. The store had 480 pairs of the jeans 2 weeks ago and now has only 24 pairs left. You expect that the jeans will sell at the same rate for 3 more weeks. If the jeans are shipped in cases of 32 pairs per case, how many cases should you order?

    F.   20

    G.   21

    H.   22

    J.   23

    K.   42

15. You have just taken a job as the curator of a museum. The museum uses wood display cases, which emit chemical compounds that can damage the museum artifacts. The industry standard is to place a sheet of polyester film under the artifacts to create a barrier from the acids in the wood. One company sells 3-mil polyester film in rolls that are 48 inches by 100 feet for $108.30. Another company sells 3-mil film in rolls that are 150 centimeters by 75 meters for $300. What is the cost per square foot of the less expensive roll?

    A. $0.03/sq. ft.

    B. $0.25/sq. ft.

    C. $0.27/sq. ft.

    D. $0.41/sq. ft.

    E. $3.69/sq. ft.

16. You work in a real estate office. A broker has asked you to research recent homes sale figures in a neighborhood of Denver. You find that in the past year, homes in this neighborhood sold for $142,000; $214,700; $168,900; $190,500; $210,000; $175,000; $149,100; and $380,200. Based on sales from the past year, what is the median home sale price in this neighborhood?

    F. $175,000

    G. $182,750

    H. $190,500

    J. $203,800

    K. $238,200

17. You work as a packaging technician for a company that provides consulting services to shippers. One of your clients wants to design a label for a tube-shaped package. The label will completely cover the side of the tube but not the end caps. If the cardboard tube is 16 centimeters in diameter and 50 centimeters long, what is the total area of the label?

   A.   402 centimeters^2

   B.   1,256 centimeters^2

   C.   2,512 centimeters^2

   D.   5,024 centimeters^2

   E.   10,048 centimeters^2

18. In your position as an education administrator, you must approve textbook purchases for the district. For one class, there are two possible textbooks. One company offers the student edition for $64, the teacher edition for $107.25, and a student workbook for $15.25. With the purchase of at least 100 student books, you get 2 teacher editions free and a free workbook for each student book. Another company offers the student edition for $75, the teacher edition for $125, and the workbook for $8.25. Regardless of which company you choose, after the first year, new workbooks must be purchased. You expect to have an enrollment of 125 students per year and need 4 teacher editions. If you plan to use the same textbook for 6 years and provide new workbooks each year, what is the least you can pay per student per year over 6 years?

   F. $14.54

   G. $21.42

   H. $23.66

   J. $23.95

   K. $26.20

19. You are performing quality assurance for a computer manufacturer. You inspect 3 batches of computer chips. The chart below shows your findings.

Batch	Total chips	Defective
1	100	5
2	96	8
3	87	3

If all three batches are combined, what is the probability that you will select a chip that is defective? Write your answer as a percent.

   A.   3.4%

   B.   5.7%

   C.   8.3%

   D.   16%

   E.   94.3%

20. You have been hired as a database administrator to transfer a bank's records over to electronic form. Because you have to maintain some paper records, you need a secure storage area. The unit must be between 1,500 and 2,500 cubic feet, and the cost for rental must be no more than $6,000 per year. Three different units are available. Unit 1 is 10 feet by 15 feet by 8 feet and rents for $250 per month. Unit 2 is 15 feet by 12 feet by 10 feet and rents for $415 per month. Unit 3 is 16 feet by 18 feet by 8 feet and rents for $500 per month. What is the lowest rate per cubic foot for a storage unit that meets the requirements?

   F. $0.21 per month

   G. $0.22 per month

   H. $0.23 per month

   J. $0.58 per month

   K. $4.61 per month

21. As a petroleum engineer, you are designing a more efficient distillation tower for a refinery. The tower has the shape of a cylinder with an inside diameter of 6 meters and a height of 40 meters. Inside the cylinder are ten cooling pipes, which are cylinders with an outside diameter of 0.5 meter extending the entire height of the tower. Vapors condense in the chamber formed by the volume of space around the cooling pipes. To the nearest cubic meter, what is the volume of the condensation chamber?

    A.   1,052 cubic meters

    B.   1,123 cubic meters

    C.   1,130 cubic meters

    D.   1,209 cubic meters

    E.   11,089 cubic meters

22. As a pharmacy technician, you prepare prescription labels for medication that is dispensed. One children's liquid medication is prescribed for 3 teaspoons per dose, 4 times a day. The liquid-measuring syringe that you provide with the medicine measures in milliliters. If 5 milliliters = 1 teaspoon, how much medicine should the child receive per day?

    F.   2.4 milliliters

    G.   12 milliliters

    H.   15 milliliters

    J.   20 milliliters

    K.   60 milliliters

23. As a financial analyst, you invest $25,000 of a customer's money in a CD for which the interest is compounded annually. The interest rate on the account averages 4.5% a year. To the nearest dollar, how much money will the customer have in 3 years? Use the function $B = p(1 + r)^x$ where B is the balance, r is the interest rate as a decimal number, x is the number of years invested, and p is the initial amount invested.

    A. $25,002

    B. $26,125

    C. $28,529

    D. $76,216

    E. $78,375

24. You are a biologist studying the deer population in a protected area. When you began studying the population, there were about 15 deer living in the area. Based on characteristics of the environment, you expect exponential population growth, with a 150% annual increase. Such growth is modeled by the equation $y = a \times b^t$ where y is the population at a given time, a is the initial population, b is the periodic growth rate as a decimal, and t is the time that has elapsed, in years. What do you estimate the deer population will be 3 years into the study?

    F.   7

    G.   23

    H.   51

    J.   68

    K.   6,750

25. In your job as a construction engineer, you make recommendations for vapor barriers to block moisture. The building code in your area requires a vapor barrier that is 0.15–0.25 millimeters thick under a concrete slab. Vapor barriers are sold by thickness that is measured in mils. If 1 mil = $\frac{1}{1,000}$ inch, which vapor barrier thickness will meet the building code?

   A. 7 mil

   B. 63.5 mils

   C. 98 mils

   D. 635 mils

   E. 984 mils

26. You are a lab technician. You have 2 liters of a 4% saline solution. You need to dilute the solution to make a 2.5% saline solution. How much water do you need to add?

   F. −0.36 liter

   G. 1 liter

   H. 1.2 liters

   J. 1.28 liters

   K. 3.12 liters

Use the following information for questions 27 and 28.

You are a psychologist doing a study of the relationship between political attitudes and social interactions during aging. The ages of people in the oldest of your survey groups are: 78, 92, 78, 84, 86, 73, 85, 95, 101, 74, 75, 80, 81, 82, 78, 74.

27. What is the median value of the age data of the participants in this group?

   A. 28

   B. 78

   C. 80

   D. 80.5

   E. 82.25

28. What is the mean age of the participants in this group?

   F. 28

   G. 78

   H. 80.5

   J. 82

   K. 82.25

Answers are on page 254.

Answer Key ■ ■ ■

Level 3

Lesson 1 (pp. 2–7)
Skills Practice:

   A. 43   B. 108   C. 120   D. 8

On Your Own:

1. D	5. C	9. E	13. D
2. J	6. G	10. G	14. J
3. B	7. D	11. B	15. C
4. J	8. H	12. J	16. G

Lesson 2 (pp. 8–13)
Skills Practice:

   A. $1.65   B. $1.50   C. 135   D. 1, 40

On Your Own:

1. E	5. C	9. D	13. C
2. H	6. J	10. G	14. J
3. D	7. B	11. C	15. C
4. J	8. G	12. J	16. H

Lesson 3 (pp. 14–19)
Skills Practice:

   A. 0.20   B. $\frac{1}{2}$ C. $3\frac{1}{3}$ D. $\frac{6}{10} \longrightarrow \frac{3}{5}$

On Your Own:

1. C	5. C	9. E	13. C
2. J	6. K	10. H	14. G
3. C	7. C	11. D	15. A
4. H	8. G	12. J	16. J

Lesson 4 (pp. 20–25)
Skills Practice:

   A. –38   B. 47   C. –19   D. 0

On Your Own:

1. A	5. B	9. D	13. A
2. H	6. K	10. J	14. J
3. C	7. D	11. A	15. A
4. H	8. G	12. H	16. F

Level 3 Performance Assessment (pp. 26–32)

1. Subtract the required clearance from the width of the opening. *(Lesson 1)*

   A. Incorrect: 37 – 12 = 25 (subtracted twice the width of the clearance)

   B. **Correct:** 37 inches – 6 inches = 31 inches

   C. Incorrect: 37 – 2 = 35 (subtracted 2 inches from 37 inches)

   D. Incorrect: 37 (did not subtract the clearance from the opening)

   E. Incorrect: 37 + 6 = 43 (added the clearance to the opening)

2. Add the values of each group of coins to find a total of 87 cents. *(Lesson 2)*

   F. Incorrect: 2 quarters, 2 dimes, and 2 pennies (coins add up to 72 cents)

   G. Incorrect: 2 quarters, 3 dimes, and 2 pennies (coins add up to 82 cents)

   H. Incorrect: 3 quarters, 1 nickel, and 2 pennies (coins add up to 82 cents)

   J. **Correct:** 75 cents + 10 cents + 2 cents = 87 cents

   K. Incorrect: 4 quarters, 1 dime, and 2 pennies (coins add up to $1.12)

3. Change 60% to a decimal. *(Lesson 3)*

   A. Incorrect: 0.06 = 6% (0.06 = 6%, not 60%)

   B. **Correct:** 0.60 = 60%

   C. Incorrect: 6.0 = 600% (6.0 = 600%, not 60%)

   D. Incorrect: 60.0 = 6,000% (60.0 = 6,000%, not 60%)

   E. Incorrect: 600.0 = 60,000% (600.0 = 60,000%, not 60%)

4. Change $\frac{8}{3}$ into a whole number and a fraction that is less than one and then add 8 to the whole number. *(Lesson 3)*

   F. **Correct:** $\frac{8}{3} = \frac{6}{3} + \frac{2}{3} = 2\frac{2}{3}$; 8 cups + $2\frac{2}{3}$ cups = $10\frac{2}{3}$ cups

   G. Incorrect: 11 cups (incorrectly converted the fraction $\frac{8}{3}$)

   H. Incorrect: $11\frac{2}{3}$ cups (incorrectly converted the fraction $\frac{8}{3}$)

   J. Incorrect: $12\frac{2}{3}$ cups (incorrectly converted the fraction $\frac{8}{3}$)

   K. Incorrect: $13\frac{1}{3}$ (incorrectly converted the fraction $\frac{8}{3}$)

5. Multiply the number of areas by the number of trees in one area. *(Lesson 1)*

   A. Incorrect: $40 - 25 = 15$ (subtracted the number of areas from the number of trees)

   B. Incorrect: $40 + 25 = 65$ (added the number of areas to the number of trees)

   C. Incorrect: $25 \times 4 = 100$ (multiplied by 4 instead of 40)

   D. **Correct:** $25 \times 40 = 1,000$

   E. Incorrect: $25 \times 400 = 10,000$ (multiplied by 400 instead of 40)

6. Add the drop in temperature as a negative number to the day's high temperature; or, subtract the amount of the drop in temperature as a positive number from the day's high temperature. *(Lesson 4)*

   F. Incorrect: $-34 + (-16) = -50$ (incorrect sign on the first number)

   G. Incorrect: $-34 + (-16) = -28$ (incorrect sign on the first number; added incorrectly)

   H. Incorrect: $-34 + 16 = -18$ (reversed signs on numbers)

   J. **Correct:** $34°F + (-16°F) = 18°F$; or, $34°F - 16°F = 18°F$

   K. Incorrect: $34 + 16 = 50$ (incorrect sign on the second number)

7. Add the elapsed time in hours and minutes to the starting time. Convert the minutes into hours and minutes and add to the number of hours. *(Lesson 2)*

   A. Incorrect: $1:45 + 0:30 = 1:75 = 1:00 + 1:15 = 2:15$ A.M. (added $\frac{1}{2}$ hour)

   B. Incorrect: $1:45 + 1:00 = 2:45$ A.M. (added 1 hour)

   C. Incorrect: $1:45 + 1:15 = 2:60 = 2:00 + 1:00 = 3:00$ A.M. (added 1 hour, 15 minutes)

   D. **Correct:** $1:45 + 1:30 = 2:75 = 2:00 + 1:15 = 3:15$ A.M.

   E. Incorrect: $1:45 + 2:00 = 3:45$ A.M. (added 2 hours)

8. Add the lengths of the three sections to find the total length needed. *(Lesson 1)*

   F. Incorrect: 35 inches (measured only one of the three lengths)

   G. Incorrect: $35 + 12 = 47$ inches (added only two of the three lengths)

   H. Incorrect: $35 + 28 = 63$ inches (added only two of the three lengths)

   J. **Correct:** 35 inches + 28 inches + 12 inches = 75 inches

   K. Incorrect: $3 \times 35 = 105$ inches (multiplied the longest measure by 3)

9. Change 5% to a decimal to find the tax for a purchase of 100 cents. (Lesson 3)

   A. **Correct:** 5% of 100 cents = $0.05 \times 100 = \$0.05$

   B. Incorrect: $0.07 (equal to 7% tax or 0.07×100)

   C. Incorrect: $0.10 (equal to 10% tax or 0.10×100)

   D. Incorrect: $0.15 (equal to 15% tax or 0.15×100)

   E. Incorrect: $0.50 (equal to 50% tax or 0.5×100)

10. Divide the total weight of ground beef by the weight in one package. *(Lesson 1)*

    F. **Correct:** 72 pounds ÷ 3 pounds/package = 24 packages

    G. Incorrect: $72 - 3 = 69$ (subtracted the weight per package from the total weight)

    H. Incorrect: 72 (used the number of pounds instead of the number of packages)

    J. Incorrect: $72 + 3 = 75$ (added the weight per package to the total weight)

    K. Incorrect: $3 \times 72 = 216$ (multiplied the number of packages by the weight per package)

11. Divide the pounds needed by the number of pounds in one bag to find the number of bags. *(Lesson 1)*

    A. Incorrect: $420 ÷ 70 = 6$ (divided by the wrong weight per bag)

    B. **Correct:** 420 pounds ÷ 60 pounds/bag = 7 bags

    C. Incorrect: $420 ÷ 60 = 8$ (divided incorrectly)

    D. Incorrect: $420 ÷ 6 = 70$ (divided by the wrong value)

    E. Incorrect: $420 + 60 = 480$ (added the total weight to the weight of each bag)

12. Add the amount of the two withdrawals. Both numbers should be negative. *(Lesson 4)*

    F. **Correct:** $-\$120 + (-\$275) = -\$395$

    G. Incorrect: $120 + (-275) = -\$155$ (missing the negative sign before the first number)

    H. Incorrect: $-120 + 275 = \$155$ (missing the negative sign before the second number)

    J. Incorrect: $120 + 275 = \$395$ (missing the negative signs)

    K. Incorrect: $120 + 275 = \$405$ (missing the negative signs and added incorrectly)

13. Subtract the temperature change from the original temperature; or, add the temperature change (as a negative number) to the original temperature. *(Lesson 4)*

   A. Incorrect: 35°C (used the temperature change instead of the final temperature)

   B. **Correct:** 150° − 35° = 115°C; or, 150° + (− 35°) = 115°C

   C. Incorrect: 150 − 25 = 125°C (did not borrow correctly during subtraction)

   D. Incorrect: 150°C (used the original temperature instead of the final temperature)

   E. Incorrect: 150 + 35 = 185°C (added the temperature change to the original temperature)

14. Change 20% to a fraction by dividing by 100 and reducing the fraction. *(Lesson 3)*

   F. Incorrect: $\frac{1}{6}$ ($\frac{1}{6} = 16\frac{1}{2}\%$)

   G. **Correct:** 20% = $\frac{20}{100} = \frac{1}{5}$

   H. Incorrect: $\frac{1}{4}$ ($\frac{1}{4} = 25\%$)

   J. Incorrect: $\frac{1}{3}$ ($\frac{1}{3} = 33\frac{1}{3}\%$)

   K. Incorrect: $\frac{1}{2}$ ($\frac{1}{2} = 50\%$)

15. Multiply the number of bulbs in one square foot by the number of square feet in the bed. *(Lesson 1)*

   A. Incorrect: 27 ÷ 9 = 3 (divided by 9 instead of multiplying)

   B. Incorrect: 27 − 9 = 18 (subtracted 9 instead of multiplying)

   C. Incorrect: 27 + 9 = 36 (added 9 instead of multiplying)

   D. Incorrect: 27 × 3 = 81 (multiplied by 3 instead of 9)

   E. **Correct:** 27 square feet × 9 bulbs/square foot = 243 bulbs

16. Convert 1 minute into 60 seconds and add 20 to the number of seconds. *(Lesson 2)*

   F. Incorrect: 20 seconds (1 minute was not converted into seconds and added)

   G. Incorrect: 60 seconds (forgot to add 20 seconds to 1 minute)

   H. **Correct:** 60 seconds + 20 seconds = 80 seconds

   J. Incorrect: 120 seconds (converted 1 minute incorrectly to 100 seconds)

   K. Incorrect: 140 seconds (used conversion to seconds for 2 minutes instead of 1)

17. Add the combined values of each set of bills and coins to find the total amount of money. *(Lesson 2)*

   A. Incorrect: 20 + 30 + 12 + 3.25 = $65.25 (did not count one of the $20 bills)

   B. Incorrect: 40 + 30 + 12 = $82 (did not count the quarters)

   C. Incorrect: 40 + 30 + 12 + 2.25 = $84.25 (counted quarters incorrectly)

   D. **Correct:** $40 + $30 + $12 + $3.25 = $85.25

   E. Incorrect: 40 + 30 + 12 + 3.75 = $85.75 (counted quarters incorrectly)

18. Add the amount paid out as a negative number from the starting balance. *(Lesson 4)*

   F. Incorrect: −7,924 + (−8,126) = −$16,050 (used incorrect sign for first number)

   G. Incorrect: −7,924 + 8,126 = −$1,808 (used incorrect sign for both numbers and added incorrectly)

   H. **Correct:** $7,924 + (−$8,126) = −$202

   J. Incorrect: −7,924 + 8,126 = $202 (used incorrect sign for both numbers)

   K. Incorrect: 7,924 + 8,126 = $16,050 (used incorrect sign for second number)

19. Find the money combination that is equal to $1.50. *(Lesson 2)*

   A. Incorrect: 0.80 + 0.15 = $0.95 (value does not match cost of postcards)

   B. Incorrect: 0.75 + 0.25 = $1.00 (value does not match cost of postcards)

   C. Incorrect: 0.75 + 0.30 = $1.05 (value does not match cost of postcards)

   D. Incorrect: 1.00 + 0.40 = $1.40 (value does not match cost of postcards)

   E. **Correct:** 6 quarters × $0.25 = $1.50

20. Subtract the height of the fence from the height of the fence post. Depth of hole is a positive number. *(Lesson 4)*

   F. Incorrect: −4 + (−6) = −10 feet (incorrect sign on the first number)

   G. Incorrect: 4 + (−6) = −2 feet (depth of hole should be positive)

   H. **Correct:** 4 feet + (−6) feet = −2 feet; absolute value of −2 feet = 2 feet

   J. Incorrect: 4 (height of the fence)

   K. Incorrect: 4 + 6 = 10 feet (incorrect sign on second number)

21. Add the cost of each item and find the result that has the same value. *(Lesson 1)*

    A. Incorrect: 0.85 − 0.50 = $0.35 (subtracted the costs)

    B. Incorrect: 0.50 + 0.50 = $1.00 (added the costs of two nuts)

    C. **Correct:** $0.85 + $0.50 = $1.35

    D. Incorrect: 0.85 + 0.85 = $1.70 (added the cost of two bolts)

    E. Incorrect: 0.85 + 0.85 + 0.50 = $2.20 (added the cost of two bolts and one nut)

22. Convert the decimal part of the measurement to a fraction and then simplify the fraction. *(Lesson 3)*

    F. Incorrect: $1\frac{1}{16}$ inches ($\frac{1}{16}$ = 0.0625)

    G. Incorrect: $1\frac{1}{8}$ inches ($\frac{1}{8}$ = 0.125)

    H. **Correct:** 1.25 inches = $1\frac{25}{100}$ inches = $1\frac{1}{4}$ inches

    J. Incorrect: $1\frac{3}{8}$ inches ($\frac{3}{8}$ = 0.375)

    K. Incorrect: $1\frac{1}{2}$ inches ($\frac{1}{2}$ = 0.5)

23. Convert two weeks into the number of days (14 days) and add that number to the current date. *(Lesson 2)*

    A. Incorrect: April 5 + 7 days = April 12 (added 1 week to current date)

    B. Incorrect: April 5 + 9 days = April 14 (added 9 days to current date)

    C. **Correct:** April 5 + 14 days = April 19

    D. Incorrect: April 5 + 16 days = April 21 (added 16 days to current date)

    E. Incorrect: April 5 + 21 days = April 26 (added 3 weeks to current date)

24. Add the weights together. *(Lesson 4)*

    F. Incorrect: 85 + (−100) = −15 pounds (reversed signs on both numbers)

    G. Incorrect: 86 + (−100) = −14 pounds (added incorrectly)

    H. Incorrect: 90 + (−100) = −10 pounds (added incorrectly)

    J. Incorrect: 100 + (−90) = 10 pounds (added incorrectly)

    K. **Correct:** 100 + (−85) = 15 pounds

25. Convert $\frac{1}{4}$ to a decimal number and add 4. *(Lesson 3)*

    A. Incorrect: 4.20 pounds (0.20 is equal to $\frac{1}{5}$, not $\frac{1}{4}$)

    B. **Correct:** $\frac{1}{4}$ pound = 1.00 ÷ 4 = 0.25 pound; 4 + 0.25 = 4.25 pounds

    C. Incorrect: 4.40 pounds (0.40 is equal to $\frac{2}{5}$, not $\frac{1}{4}$)

    D. Incorrect: 4.50 pounds (0.50 is equal to $\frac{1}{2}$, not $\frac{1}{4}$)

    E. Incorrect: 4.75 pounds (0.75 is equal to $\frac{3}{4}$, not $\frac{1}{4}$)

26. Add the number of televisions shipped (as a negative number) to the original number of televisions; or, subtract the number of televisions shipped from the original number of televisions. *(Lesson 4)*

    F. Incorrect: 0 + (−20) = −20 (added incorrect numbers and used incorrect sign with 20)

    G. Incorrect: −10 + 0 = −10 (did not add the number of televisions from the beginning of the week)

    H. **Correct:** 20 + (−10) = 10

    J. Incorrect: 10 + 10 = 20 (added the incorrect numbers)

    K. Incorrect: 10 + 20 = 30 (did not write the number of televisions shipped as a negative number)

27. Simplify the fraction to find the whole number value of the mixed number. *(Lesson 3)*

    A. Incorrect: 3 cups (subtracted 1 from 4 cups instead of adding)

    B. Incorrect: 4 cups (did not include the value of the fraction $\frac{2}{2}$)

    C. Incorrect: $4\frac{1}{4}$ cups (incorrectly converted the fraction $\frac{2}{2}$ to $\frac{1}{4}$)

    D. **Correct:** 4 cups + $\frac{2}{2}$ cup = 4 cups + 1 cup = 5 cups

    E. Incorrect: $5\frac{1}{2}$ cups (incorrectly converted the fraction $\frac{2}{2}$ to $1\frac{1}{2}$)

28. Convert the percent value to a fraction. *(Lesson 3)*

    F. Incorrect: = $\frac{1}{1,000}$ ($\frac{1}{1,000}$ is equal to 0.1%)

    G. Incorrect: $\frac{1}{100}$ ($\frac{1}{100}$ is equal to 1%)

    H. **Correct:** $\frac{10}{100}$ = $\frac{1}{10}$

    J. Incorrect: $\frac{20}{100}$ = ($\frac{1}{5}$ is equal to 20%)

    K. Incorrect: $\frac{100}{100}$ = ($\frac{100}{100}$ is equal to 100%)

Level 4

Lesson 5 (pp. 34–39)

Skill Practice:

A. $1\frac{1}{4}$ B. 0.75   C. 40%

On Your Own:

1. D	5. D	9. D	13. D
2. G	6. J	10. G	14. J
3. E	7. B	11. E	15. E
4. K	8. H	12. F	16. K

Lesson 6 (pp. 40–45)

Skill Practice:

A. $\frac{4}{5}$ B. $\frac{5}{8}$ C. $\frac{11}{9}$ ⤳ $1\frac{2}{9}$

On Your Own:

1. E	5. D	9. D	13. D
2. K	6. J	10. H	14. J
3. E	7. E	11. D	15. C
4. J	8. J	12. J	16. K

Lesson 7 (pp. 46–51)

Skill Practice:

A. $1\frac{1}{10}$ B. $7\frac{1}{2}$ C. $3.75

On Your Own:

1. E	5. D	9. E	13. D
2. J	6. K	10. J	14. H
3. E	7. C	11. D	15. D
4. K	8. G	12. G	16. H

Lesson 8 (pp. 52–57)

Skill Practice:

A. 34   B. 15   C. $76

On Your Own:

1. D	5. C	9. B	13. B
2. K	6. G	10. K	14. H
3. D	7. D	11. B	15. B
4. G	8. H	12. J	16. H

Lesson 9 (pp. 58–63)

Skill Practice:

A. 7,479 B. 78

On Your Own:

1. C	5. D	9. D	13. B
2. H	6. H	10. K	14. J
3. E	7. C	11. D	15. C
4. G	8. K	12. H	16. J

Lesson 10 (pp. 64–69)

Skill Practice:

A. 37   B. 96

On Your Own:

1. C	5. D	9. B	13. C
2. J	6. H	10. K	14. J

3. E	7. E	11. C	15. A
4. K	8. G	12. H	16. J

Lesson 11 (pp. 70–75)

Skill Practice:

A. −72   −72   −28   −20

B. 75   75   60   60

On Your Own:

1. A	5. C	9. A	13. B
2. G	6. G	10. G	14. J
3. A	7. E	11. B	15. A
4. F	8. H	12. G	16. F

Level 4 Performance Assessment (pp. 76–82)

1. Add the measures of the sides that do not border the house. *(Lesson 5)*

   A. Incorrect: 3.75 + 4 = 7.75 meters (did not add all the sides not bordering the house)

   B. Incorrect: 10.25 + 3.75 + 4 = 18 meters (did not add all the sides not bordering the house)

   C. **Correct:** 10.25 meters + 3.75 meters + 4 meters + 8.5 meters = 26.5 meters

   D. Incorrect: 10.25 + 3.75 + 15.5 = 29.5 meters (added incorrectly)

   E. Incorrect: 10.25 + 3.75 + 15.5 + 4 + 8.5 = 42 meters (added all the sides, including the one bordering the house)

2. Add the numerators of the four fractions. Then simplify the answer. *(Lesson 6)*

   F. Incorrect: $\frac{3}{8} \times \frac{1}{8} = \frac{3}{64}$ inch (multiplied fractions)

   G. Incorrect: $\frac{1}{8}$ inch (did not add fractions)

   H. Incorrect: $\frac{3}{8} - \frac{1}{8} = \frac{2}{8}$ inch (subtracted fractions)

   J. Incorrect: $\frac{4}{8}$ inch (did not add all the fractions)

   K. **Correct:** $\frac{3}{8}$ inch + $\frac{3}{8}$ inch + $\frac{1}{8}$ inch + $\frac{1}{8}$ inch = 1 inch

3. Convert the mixed number to a fraction and multiply the numerator by the number of crowns; or, convert the mixed number to a whole number and a fraction, multiply both by 3, and add the sums $(6 + 1\frac{1}{2})$. *(Lesson 7)*

   A. Incorrect: $2\frac{1}{2}$ minutes (curing time for one crown)

   B. Incorrect: $2\frac{1}{2} + 3 = 5\frac{1}{2}$ minutes (added 3 to curing time instead of multiplying)

   C. Incorrect: $3 \times 2 + \frac{1}{2} = 6\frac{1}{2}$ minutes (multiplied whole number, but not fraction)

   D. **Correct:** $2\frac{1}{2} = \frac{5}{2}$; $\frac{5}{2}$ minutes × 3 = $\frac{15}{2}$ minutes = $7\frac{1}{2}$ minutes

   E. Incorrect: $\frac{5}{2} \times 3 = \frac{15}{2} = 8\frac{1}{2}$ minutes (incorrectly simplified fraction)

4. Set up a proportion to solve for the missing width. *(Lesson 8)*

   F. Incorrect: $\frac{4.5}{2} = \frac{18}{x}$; $= \frac{18}{2 \times 4.5}$; $x = 2$ inches (calculated cross product incorrectly)

   G. **Correct:** $\frac{4.5 \text{ inches}}{2 \text{ inches}} = \frac{18 \text{ inches}}{x \text{ inches}}$; $x = \frac{2 \times 18}{4.5}$; $x = 8$ inches

   H. Incorrect: $18 + 4.5 = 22.5$ inches (added instead of using proportion)

   J. Incorrect: $\frac{4.5}{2} = \frac{18}{x}$; $x = \frac{18 \times 4.5}{2}$; $x = 40.5$ inches (calculated cross product incorrectly)

   K. Incorrect: $x = 18 \times 4.5 \times 2 = 162$ inches (multiplied instead of using proportion)

5. Multiply $\frac{1}{3}$ by the number of cases sold in August (2,352). *(Lesson 9)*

   A. Incorrect: $\frac{1}{3} \times 1,932 = 644$ (calculated the number of cases sold in July, not August)

   B. Incorrect: $\frac{1}{3} \times 2,130 = 710$ (calculated the number of cases sold in June, not August)

   C. **Correct:** $\frac{1}{3} \times 2,352 = 784$

   D. Incorrect: $\frac{2}{3} \times 2,130 = 1,420$ (calculated the number of cases sold in June to specialty markets, not grocery stores)

   E. Incorrect: $\frac{2}{3} \times 2,352 = 1,568$ (calculated the number of cases sold in August to specialty markets, not grocery stores)

6. Multiply the length by 2. Multiply the seam allowance by 2. Subtract the total seam allowance from the total length. *(Lesson 10)*

   F. Incorrect: $(2 \times 18) - (2 \times \frac{1}{4}) = 34\frac{1}{2}$ (subtracted incorrectly)

   G. Incorrect: $(2 \times 18) - (2 \times \frac{1}{4}) = 35$ (multiplied fraction incorrectly)

   H. **Correct:** $(2 \times 18) - (2 \times \frac{1}{4}) = 35\frac{1}{2}$ inches

   J. Incorrect: $(2 \times 18) = 36$ inches (did not subtract the seam allowance)

   K. Incorrect: $(2 \times 18) + (2 \times \frac{1}{4}) = 36\frac{1}{2}$ inches (added seam allowance instead of subtracting it)

7. Multiply the number of items that came in different from estimated by the difference in cost from the estimation to the actual cost. *(Lesson 11)*

   A. **Correct:** $2 \times -\$100 = -\$200$ or $200 less than estimated

   B. Incorrect: $1 \times -100 = -\$100$ or $100 less than estimated (multiplied by wrong number of items that had different costs)

   C. Incorrect: $0 \times -100 = \$0$ or $0 less than estimated (multiplied by wrong number of items that had different costs)

   D. Incorrect: $1 \times 100 = \$100$ or $100 more than estimated (used the wrong number to multiply by number of items that had different costs)

   E. Incorrect: $2 \times 100 = \$200$ or $200 more than estimated (used the wrong number to multiply by number of items that had different costs)

8. Add the percentages of the two crops that failed. *(Lesson 5)*

   F. Incorrect: $25 + 10 = 35$; $65 - 35 = 30\%$ (added percentages of crops that failed and subtracted it from percentage of crops that passed)

   G. **Correct:** $25\% + 10\% = 35\%$

   H. Incorrect: $10 + 65 = 75\%$ (added one of the percentages that failed to the percentage of crops that passed)

   J. Incorrect: $25 + 65 = 90\%$ (added one of the percentages that failed to the percentage of crops that passed)

   K. Incorrect: $25 + 10 + 65 = 100\%$ (added all three of the percentages together)

9. Multiply the number of repairs by $-\$50$ and add to the starting account balance. *(Lesson 11)*

   A. Incorrect: $24 \times 50 = -1,200 + 500 = -\$700$ (multiplied number of inspections instead of repairs)

   B. Incorrect: $3 \times -50 = -\$150$ (forgot to add starting account balance)

   C. **Correct:** $3 \times -\$50 = -\$150 + \$500 = \$350$

   D. Incorrect: $3 \times -50 = -150 + 600 = \$450$ (used incorrect starting account balance)

   E. Incorrect: $\$500$ (did not subtract amount of repairs from starting account balance)

10. Multiply the number of revised products by the number of training modules. Add the product to the number of new training modules written. *(Lesson 10)*

   F. Incorrect: $5 + 4 = 9$ (forgot to multiply the number of training modules by the number of revised software products)

   G. Incorrect: $5 \times 4 = 20$ (multiplied the number of revised software products by the number of new training modules)

   H. Incorrect: $4 \times 13 = 52$ (calculated the number of training modules for the revised software products, but forgot to add the number of modules for the new product)

   J. **Correct:** $5 + 4 \times 13 = 57$

   K. Incorrect: $5 + 4 \times 13 = 117$ (performed calculations from left to right without regard to correct order of operations)

11. Divide to find how many crews are sent each hour. Then multiply to find how many people are sent out within 2 hours. *(Lesson 9)*

   A. Incorrect: $60 \div 15 = 4$ (number of crews sent per hour, not the number of people sent in two hours)

   B. Incorrect: $60 \div 15 = 4$; $4 \times 3 = 12$ (number of people sent within 1 hour, not 2 hours)

   C. Incorrect: $15 + 3 + 2 = 20$ (added all the numbers in the problem)

   D. **Correct:** $[(60 \div 15) \times 2] \times 3 = 24$ [(number of dispatches per hour) × number of hours] × number of people per dispatch

   E. Incorrect: $15 \times 3 \times 2 = 90$ (multiplied all the numbers in the problem)

12. Find the sum of the test scores. Then divide by the number of tests. *(Lesson 8)*

   F. Incorrect: $85 + 93 + 91 + 81 + 89 = 439$; $439 \div 6 = 73.2$ (divided by wrong number of tests)

   G. **Correct:** $85 + 93 + 91 + 81 + 89 = 439$; $439 \div 5 = 87.8$

   H. Incorrect: 89 (chose middle value instead of arithmetic mean)

   J. Incorrect: $85 + 93 + 91 + 81 + 89 = 439$; $439 \div 4 = 109.8$ (divided by wrong number of tests)

   K. Incorrect: $85 + 93 + 91 + 81 + 89 = 439$ (did not divide by number of tests)

13. Convert the mixed number to a fraction and multiply the numerator by 2 for the borders on both sides. *(Lesson 7)*

   A. Incorrect: $2\frac{3}{8}$ inches (this is the border on one side only)

   B. Incorrect: $2\frac{3}{8} = \frac{16}{8}$; $\frac{16}{8} \times 2 = \frac{32}{8} = 4$ inches (did not convert whole number to a fraction correctly)

   C. Incorrect: $2 \times 2 = 4$; $4 + \frac{3}{8} = 4\frac{3}{8}$ inches (multiplied the whole number by 2, but not the fraction)

   D. Incorrect: $2\frac{3}{8} = \frac{19}{8}$; $\frac{19}{8} \times 2 = \frac{38}{8} = 4\frac{4}{8} = 4\frac{1}{2}$ inches (did not convert fraction to a mixed number correctly)

   E. **Correct:** $2\frac{3}{8}$ inches $= \frac{19}{8}$ inches; $\frac{19}{8}$ inches × $2 = \frac{38}{8}$ inches $= 4\frac{6}{8}$ inches $= 4\frac{3}{4}$ inches

14. Add the numerators of the three fractions. *(Lesson 6)*

   F. Incorrect: $\frac{1}{4} + \frac{1}{4} = \frac{1}{2}$ hour (added only two fractions)

   G. **Correct:** $\frac{1}{4}$ hour $+ \frac{1}{4}$ hour $+ \frac{1}{4}$ hour $= \frac{3}{4}$ hour

   H. Incorrect: 1 hour (added incorrectly)

   J. Incorrect: $1\frac{1}{4}$ hours (added incorrectly)

   K. Incorrect: $\frac{1}{4} + \frac{1}{4} + \frac{1}{4} + \frac{1}{4} + \frac{1}{4} + \frac{1}{4} = 1\frac{1}{2}$ hours (added the fractions twice)

15. Add the amount of extra space needed on each side to each dimension. *(Lesson 5)*

   A. Incorrect: $(48) \times (28\frac{3}{8} + \frac{2}{8}) = 48$ inches × $28\frac{5}{8}$ inches (did not add the extra space to one of the dimensions)

   B. Incorrect: $(48 + \frac{1}{8}) \times (28\frac{3}{8} + \frac{1}{8}) = 48\frac{1}{8}$ inches × $28\frac{1}{2}$ inches (incorrectly added the amount of extra space to both of the dimensions)

   C. Incorrect: $(48 + \frac{1}{4}) \times (28\frac{3}{8}) = 48\frac{1}{4}$ inches × $28\frac{3}{8}$ inches (did not add the extra space to one of the dimensions)

   D. Incorrect: $(48 + \frac{1}{4}) \times (28\frac{3}{8} + \frac{1}{8}) = 48\frac{1}{4}$ inches × $28\frac{1}{2}$ inches (incorrectly added the amount of extra space to one of the dimensions)

   E. **Correct:** $(48$ inches $+ \frac{2}{8}$ inch$) \times (28\frac{3}{8}$ inches $+ \frac{2}{8}$ inch$) = 48\frac{1}{4}$ inches × $28\frac{5}{8}$ inches

16. Add the numerators of the three fractions. Then change to a mixed number. *(Lesson 6)*

   F. Incorrect: $\frac{2}{5} + \frac{4}{5} + \frac{1}{5} = \frac{1}{15}$ gallon (added denominators, not numerators)

   G. Incorrect: $\frac{2}{5} + \frac{4}{5} + \frac{1}{5} = \frac{7}{15}$ gallon (added numerators and denominators)

   H. Incorrect: $\frac{1}{5} + \frac{4}{5} = 1$ gallon (only added two fractions)

   J. Incorrect: $\frac{2}{5} + \frac{4}{5} = 1\frac{1}{5}$ gallons (only added two fractions)

   K. **Correct:** $\frac{2}{5}$ gallon $+ \frac{4}{5}$ gallon $+ \frac{1}{5}$ gallon $= \frac{2 + 4 + 1}{5}$ gallons $= \frac{7}{5}$ gallons $= 1\frac{2}{5}$ gallons

17. Convert the mixed number to a fraction and multiply by $\frac{1}{3}$. *(Lesson 7)*

   A. Incorrect: $4\frac{1}{2} = \frac{5}{2}$; $\frac{5}{2} \times \frac{1}{3} = \frac{5}{6}$ cup (incorrectly converted mixed number to a fraction)

   B. **Correct:** $4\frac{1}{2} = \frac{9}{2}$; $\frac{9}{2} \times \frac{1}{3} = \frac{9}{6} = 1\frac{3}{6} = 1\frac{1}{2}$ cups

   C. Incorrect: $4\frac{1}{2} = \frac{9}{2}$; $\frac{9}{2}$ cups × $\frac{1}{3} = \frac{9}{4}$ cups $= 2\frac{1}{4}$ cups (incorrectly multiplied)

   D. Incorrect: $4\frac{1}{2} = \frac{9}{2}$; $\frac{9}{2} \times \frac{1}{3} = \frac{9}{6} = 2\frac{3}{6} = 2\frac{1}{2}$ cups (incorrectly converted fraction to a mixed number)

   E. Incorrect: $4\frac{1}{2} = \frac{9}{2}$; $\frac{9}{2} \times \frac{3}{1} = \frac{27}{2} = 13\frac{1}{2}$ cups (multiplied by 3 instead of $\frac{1}{3}$)

18. Multiply the rate of square meters per hour by the number of hours; or, set up problem as a proportion where 3.5 meters/1 hour = x/8 hours, then find cross products to solve for x. *(Lesson 8)*

   F. Incorrect: $8 \div 3.5 = 2.3$ square meters (divided instead of multiplying)

   G. Incorrect: $8 - 3.5 = 4.5$ square meters (subtracted instead of multiplying)

   H. Incorrect: $8 + 3.5 = 11.5$ square meters (added instead of multiplying)

   J. Incorrect: $8 \times 3 = 24$ square meters (multiplied by 3 instead of 3.5)

   K. **Correct:** 8 hours $\times$ 3.5 square meters per hour = 28 square meters

19. Add the cost of all the materials and labor to find the total estimate. *(Lesson 9)*

   A. Incorrect: $680 + 450 + 1{,}200 + 2{,}400 \neq$ $1,630 (added incorrectly)

   B. Incorrect: $680 + 450 + 1{,}200 = \$2{,}330$ (did not include cost of labor)

   C. Incorrect: $680 + 450 + 2{,}400 = \$3{,}530$ (did not include cost of other materials)

   D. Incorrect: $450 + 1{,}200 + 2{,}400 = \$4{,}050$ (did not include cost of pump)

   E. **Correct:** $\$680 + \$450 + \$1{,}200 + \$2{,}400 = \$4{,}730$

20. Add the amount it costs to ship packages each day. *(Lesson 5)*

   F. Incorrect: $3{,}504.50 + 2{,}497.75 = \$6{,}002.25$ (added only the amount for the first 2 days)

   G. Incorrect: $3{,}504.50 + 2{,}497.75 + 5{,}000.25 = \$11{,}002.50$ (added only the amount for the first 3 days)

   H. Incorrect: $3{,}504.50 + 2{,}497.75 + 5{,}000.25 + 2{,}389.75 + 4{,}731.00 \neq \$12{,}229.00$ (added incorrectly)

   J. Incorrect: $3{,}504.50 + 2{,}497.75 + 5{,}000.25 + 2{,}389.75 = \$13{,}392.25$ (added only the amount for the first 4 days)

   K. **Correct:** $\$3{,}504.50 + \$2{,}497.75 + \$5{,}000.25 + \$2{,}389.75 + \$4{,}731.00 = \$18{,}123.25$

21. Find the sum of the total number of tons that need to be moved. Divide by 6 and multiply by 2 to find the number of pulleys needed to move the containers. *(Lesson 10)*

   A. **Correct:** $(40 + 52 + 46 + 39 + 63) \div 6 \times 2$

   B. Incorrect: $(40 + 52 + 46 + 39 + 63) \div 6 + 2$ (added the number of pulleys needed per 6 tons instead of multiplying)

   C. Incorrect: $(40 + 52 + 46 + 39 + 63) \div 6$ (did not multiply to find the number of pulleys needed)

   D. Incorrect: $(40 + 52 + 46 + 39 + 63) \div 2$ (this was the total number of tons divided in half, not the number of pulleys needed)

   E. Incorrect: $(40 \times 52 \times 46 \times 39 \times 63) \div 6 \times 2$ (the number of tons per container have been multiplied together instead of added)

22. Multiply the number of spending categories by the amount you spent less in each category and add to the new budget difference. *(Lesson 11)*

   F. Incorrect: $6 \times -1{,}000 = -\$6{,}000$ or $6{,}000 under budget (did not add the difference in the new budget)

   G. Incorrect: $-\$5{,}000$ or $5,000 under budget (only used the difference in the new budget)

   H. **Correct:** $6 \times -\$1{,}000 = -\$6{,}000 + \$5{,}000 = -\$1{,}000$ or $1,000 under budget

   J. Incorrect: $6 \times 1{,}000 = 6{,}000 + -5{,}000 = \$1{,}000$ or $1,000 over budget (multiplied by a positive number instead of a negative number; subtracted the difference in the new budget instead of adding)

   K. Incorrect: $6 \times 1{,}000 = 6{,}000 + 5{,}000 = \$11{,}000$ or $11,000 over budget (multiplied by a positive number instead of a negative number)

23. Add the numerators of the three fractions. *(Lesson 6)*

   A. Incorrect: $\frac{3}{8} + \frac{1}{8} = \frac{1}{2}$ inch (added only two fractions)

   B. Incorrect: $\frac{3}{8} + \frac{3}{8} + \frac{1}{8} \neq \frac{5}{8}$ inch (added incorrectly)

   C. Incorrect: $\frac{3}{8} + \frac{3}{8} = \frac{3}{4}$ inch (added only two fractions)

   D. **Correct:** $\frac{3}{8} + \frac{3}{8} + \frac{1}{8} = \frac{7}{8}$ inch

   E. Incorrect: $\frac{3}{8} + \frac{3}{8} + \frac{1}{8} \neq 1$ inch (added incorrectly)

24. Convert the mixed number to a fraction and multiply by 30. *(Lesson 7)*

   F. Incorrect: $1\frac{1}{4} = \frac{5}{4}; \frac{5}{4} \times 30 = \frac{150}{120} = 1\frac{30}{120} = 1\frac{1}{4}$ hours (incorrectly multiplied)

   G. Incorrect: 30 hours (only included appointment time)

   H. Incorrect: $1\frac{1}{4} = \frac{5}{4}; \frac{5}{4} \times 30 = \frac{150}{4} = 35$ hours (incorrectly converted mixed number to a whole number)

   J. **Correct:** $1\frac{1}{4} = \frac{5}{4}; \frac{5}{4} \times 30 = \frac{150}{4} = 37\frac{2}{4} = 37\frac{1}{2}$ hours

K. Incorrect: $1\frac{1}{4} = \frac{5}{2}$; $\frac{5}{2}$ hours × 30 sessions = $\frac{150}{2}$ hours = 75 hours (incorrectly converted mixed number to a fraction)

25. Divide the estimated cost for labor by the number of hours to be billed. *(Lesson 8)*

    A. Incorrect: 185 ÷ 5 = $37 per installer (did not measure rate in units of time)

    B. **Correct:** $185 ÷ 5 hours = $37 per hour

    C. Incorrect: 185 ÷ 1 = $185 per day (did not use the unit of time specified in the question)

    D. Incorrect: 185 ÷ 1 = $185 per hour (divided by the wrong number of hours)

    E. Incorrect: 185 × 5 = $925 per installation (multiplied by the number of hours instead of dividing)

26. Subtract the number of testing strips used from the number ordered. *(Lesson 9)*

    F. **Correct:** 200 − 83 = 117

    G. Incorrect: 200 − 54 = 146 (subtracted number of test tubes ordered, not number of testing strips used)

    H. Incorrect: 200 − 12 = 188 (subtracted amount of hydrochloric acid used, not number of testing strips used)

    J. Incorrect: 200 − 3 = 197 (subtracted number of microscopes ordered)

    K. Incorrect: 200 − 83 ≠ 217 (subtracted incorrectly)

27. Add the cost of the cut to the product of twice the amount of the cut. Then add the tip to the sum. *(Lesson 10)*

    A. Incorrect: 60 + 36 = $96 (forgot to add the cost of the dye job)

    B. Incorrect: 60 + (60 × 1) + 36 = $156 (multiplied the cost of the cut by the wrong number to find the cost of the dye job)

    C. Incorrect: 60 + (60 × 2) = $180 (forgot to add the tip)

    D. Incorrect: 60 + 60 + (36 × 2) = $192 (multiplied the cost of the tip instead of the dye job)

    E. **Correct:** $60 + ($60 × 2) + $36 = $216

28. Multiply the number of inches of mercury per hour the pressure drops by the number of hours it drops. Add the answer to the starting pressure. *(Lesson 11)*

    F. Incorrect: (0.06 × 24) = 1.44 − 30.95 = −29.51 inches of mercury (subtracted the starting pressure from the amount the pressure dropped)

    G. Incorrect: 1.44 inches of mercury (only the amount of pressure drop)

    H. **Correct:** 30.95 + (−0.06 × 24) = 29.51 inches of mercury

    J. Incorrect: 30.95 − (−1.44) = 32.39 inches of mercury (subtracted the pressure drop instead of adding it)

    K. Incorrect: 30.95 × 1.44 = 44.57 inches of mercury (multiplied the starting pressure by the amount the pressure dropped in 24 hours)

Level 5

Lesson 12 (pp. 84–89)
Skill Practice:

  A. 1,186 centimeters or 11.86 meters
  B. 10
  C. 182 ounces or 11 pounds, 6 ounces
  D. 18

On Your Own:

1. D	5. D	9. C	13. D
2. H	6. H	10. H	14. G
3. C	7. B	11. B	15. A
4. G	8. J	12. J	16. F

Lesson 13 (pp. 90–95)
Skill Practice:

  A. 20 square inches B. 113 square meters

On Your Own:

1. E	5. D	9. D	13. B
2. J	6. K	10. H	14. J
3. C	7. E	11. A	15. B
4. H	8. H	12. H	16. G

Lesson 14 (pp. 96–101)
Skill Practice:

  A. Cereal is sold in 18-ounce boxes.
  B. Divide by 12.

On Your Own:

1. D	5. B	9. B	13. E
2. H	6. K	10. H	14. H
3. E	7. C	11. A	15. B
4. K	8. G	12. F	16. G

Lesson 15 (pp. 102–107)
Skill Practice:

  A. 20 quarts   C. 38.1 centimeters
  B. 0.792 gallon

On Your Own:

1. B	5. C	9. C	13. C
2. G	6. F	10. H	14. J
3. C	7. B	11. A	15. A
4. F	8. K	12. G	16. F

Lesson 16 (pp. 108–113)
Skill Practice:

  A. $1,250

  B. $1,350

  C. The designer who charges $250 per day
    for 5 days will cost less, at $1,250.

On Your Own:

1. B	5. B	9. C	13. D
2. J	6. G	10. H	14. H
3. C	7. D	11. D	15. B
4. H	8. G	12. F	16. G

Lesson 17 (pp. 114–119)
Skill Practice:

  A. $52; $36   B. $412; $22.68

On Your Own:

1. C	5. D	9. D	13. C
2. J	6. K	10. H	14. J
3. E	7. B	11. B	15. B
4. H	8. F	12. J	16. H

Lesson 18 (pp. 120–125)
Skill Practice:

  A. −11   B. −6   C. 4

On Your Own:

1. C	5. D	9. B	13. B
2. G	6. H	10. K	14. G
3. D	7. D	11. C	15. B
4. G	8. H	12. F	16. H

Level 5 Performance Assessment (pp. 126–132)

1. Use the formula 1 kilogram ≈ 2.2 pounds to convert kilograms to pounds, and then convert the decimal part of the product to ounces. *(Lesson 15)*

  A. Incorrect: 3.4 − 2.2 ≈ 1.2 = 1 pound, 2 ounces (applied the formula incorrectly and subtracted; and then incorrectly interpreted 1.2 pounds as equal to 1 pound, 2 ounces)

  B. Incorrect: 3.4 ÷ 2.2 ≈ 1.5 = 1 pound, 5 ounces (applied the formula incorrectly and divided; and then incorrectly interpreted 1.5 pounds as equal to 1 pound, 5 ounces)

  C. Incorrect: 3.4 + 2.2 ≈ 5.6 = 5 pounds, 6 ounces (applied the formula incorrectly and added; and then incorrectly interpreted 5.6 pounds as equal to 5 pounds, 6 ounces)

  D. Incorrect: 3.4 × 2.2 ≈ 7.48 ≈ 7 pounds, 5 ounces (interpreted 7.5 pounds as equal to 7 pounds, 5 ounces)

  E. **Correct:** 3.4 kilograms × 2.2 pounds per kilogram ≈ 7.48 pounds; 7 pounds + (0.48 pounds × 16 ounces per pound) ≈ 7 pounds, 8 ounces

2. Multiply the depth of the work surface by its width to find its area. *(Lesson 14)*

  F. Incorrect: 2 square feet; 4 ÷ 2 = 2 (divided instead of multiplying)

  G. Incorrect: 5 square feet; $2\frac{1}{2} \times 2 = 5$ (multiplied the depth of the work surface by its height)

  H. **Correct:** 2 feet deep × 4 feet wide = 8 square feet

J. Incorrect: 10 square feet; $2\frac{1}{2} \times 4 = 10$ (multiplied the width of the work surface by its height)

K. Incorrect: 20 square feet; $2\frac{1}{2} \times 4 \times 2 = 20$ (multiplied the width of the work surface by its depth then multiplied the product by its height)

3. Find the difference between the current price and the price 6 months ago and divide by 6. Because the price decreased, the change is negative. *(Lesson 18)*

A. Incorrect: $54.90 – $64.20 = –$9.30 (only found the difference between the current price and the price 6 months ago)

B. **Correct:** ($54.90 – $64.20) ÷ 6 months = –$9.30 ÷ 6 = –$1.55 per month

C. Incorrect: $54.90 ÷ 6 = $9.15 (divided the current price by 6)

D. Incorrect: $64.20 ÷ 6 = $10.70 (divided the price 6 months ago by 6)

E. Incorrect: ($64.20 + $54.90) ÷ 6 = $19.85 (added the price 6 months ago and the current price, and then divided by 6)

4. Multiply the monthly price offered by each vendor by 12, add the installation fee to the result for the second vendor, and compare. *(Lesson 16)*

F. Incorrect: $250 × 12 = $3,000 (multiplied the one-time installation fee by 12)

G. Incorrect: $399 × 12 = $4,788 (multiplied the monthly price offered by the second vendor by 12 but did not add the one-time installation fee)

H. **Correct:** $425 per month × 12 months = $5,100; ($399 per month × 12 months) + $250 = $4,788 + $250 = $5,038; $5,100 > $5,038

J. Incorrect: $425 × 12 = $5,100 (found the price per year offered by the building, which is not the lower price)

K. Incorrect: ($399 + $250) × 12 = $649 × 12 = $7,788 (added the one-time installation fee to the monthly price offered by the second vendor, and multiplied the sum by 12)

5. Subtract 1.197 meters from 1.2 meters and convert difference to millimeters. *(Lesson 12)*

A. Incorrect: 0.003 millimeter; 1.200 meters – 1.197 = 0.003 (did not convert to millimeters)

B. **Correct:** 1.200 meters – 1,197 millimeters = 0.003 meter × 1,000 mm/m = 3 millimeters

C. Incorrect: 195 millimeters; 1.197 meters – 1.002 = 0.195 × 1,000 = 195 (added zeroes incorrectly to 1.2)

D. Incorrect: 397 millimeters; 1.197 meters – 1.200 = 0.397 × 1,000 = 397 (added instead of subtracting values after decimal point)

E. Incorrect: 2,397 millimeters; 1.197 meters + 1.200 = 2.397 × 1,000 = 2,397 (added instead of subtracting)

6. Subtract the current number of orders filled (720) from the goal (792) and divide the result by the number of workers (8). *(Lesson 14)*

F. Incorrect: 792 – 720 = 72; 72 ÷ 9 = 8 (found the difference between the current number of orders filled and the goal, and then divided by the number of hours per shift)

G. **Correct:** 792 orders – 720 orders = 72 orders; 72 orders ÷ 8 workers = 9 orders per worker

H. Incorrect: 720 ÷ 8 = 90; 90 ÷ 9 = 10 (divided the current number of orders filled by the number of workers and then by the number of hours per shift)

J. Incorrect: 792 – 720 = 72; 72 ÷ 4 = 18 (found the difference between the current number of orders filled and the goal, and then divided by the number of weeks to meet the goal)

K. Incorrect: 792 – 720 = 72 (found the difference between the current number of orders filled and the goal)

7. Find the current cost and the increase in cost for shipping a 5-pound package. Divide the increase by the current cost and multiply by 100% to find the percentage increase. *(Lesson 17)*

A. Incorrect: 0.18%; $0.35 + (4 × $0.10) = $0.75; $0.75 ÷ $4.10 = 0.18 (did not multiply by 100%)

B. Incorrect: 1.8%; $0.35 + (4 × $0.10) = $0.75; $0.75 ÷ $4.10 = 0.18 × 100% = 1.8% (multiplied incorrectly)

C. Incorrect: 14%; $0.35 ÷ $2.50 = 0.14 × 100% = 14% (calculated increase for one-pound package)

D. Incorrect: 15%; $0.45 ÷ $2.90 = 0.15 × 100% = 15% (calculated increase for two-pound package)

E. **Correct:** 18%; $0.35 + (4 × $0.10) = $0.75; $0.75 ÷ $4.10 = 0.18 × 100% = 18%

8. Subtract to find the gallons that need to be ordered, and then use the formula 1 liter ≈ 0.264 gallon to convert gallons to liters. Finally, divide by 4 and interpret the remainder correctly to find the number of containers needed. *(Lesson 15)*

F. Incorrect: (40 – 9) × 0.264 = 31 × 0.264 = 8.184; 8.184 ÷ 4 = 2.046; 2 containers plus one more needed = 3 (applied the formula incorrectly by multiplying instead of dividing)

G. Incorrect: 40 ÷ 4 = 10 (divided the total number of gallons needed by the number of liters in each container)

H. Incorrect: (40 − 9) ÷ 0.264 = 31 ÷ 0.264 ≈ 117.424; 117.424 ÷ 4 = 29.356; 29 containers needed (interpreted the remainder/decimal incorrectly and dropped it)

J. **Correct:** (40 gallons − 9 gallons) ÷ 0.264 gallon per liter = 31 gallons ÷ 0.264 gallon per liter ≈ 117.424 liters; 117.424 liters ÷ 4 liters per container = 29.356 containers; 29 containers plus one more needed = 30

K. Incorrect: (40 − 9) ÷ 0.264 = 31 ÷ 0.264 ≈ 117.424; 117 containers plus one more needed = 118 (found the number of liters needed and interpreted it as the number of containers needed)

9. Find the perimeter in feet, convert to inches, and divide by 3. *(Lesson 13)*

A. Incorrect: (6 × 3) ÷ 3 = 6 (found area instead of perimeter and did not convert to inches)

B. Incorrect: 6 + 3 = 9 (found the length of two sides in feet and did no other steps)

C. Incorrect: 2(6 + 3) = 18 (found the perimeter in feet and did no other steps)

D. Incorrect: 2(6 + 3) = 18; 18 × 3 = 54 (found the perimeter in feet and multiplied by 3)

E. **Correct:** 2(6 feet + 3 feet) = 18 feet; 18 feet × 12 inches per foot = 216 inches; 216 inches ÷ 3 inches per light bulb = 72 light bulbs

10. Use the formula 1 kilometer ≈ 0.62 mile to convert kilometers to miles, and then divide the distance in miles by the rate to find the travel time. *(Lesson 15)*

F. Incorrect: (178 − 55) × 0.62 = 76.26 ≈ 1 hour, 16 minutes (subtracted the rate from the distance in kilometers and then applied the formula, misinterpreting the result as representing time)

G. Incorrect: 178 × 0.62 = 110.36 ≈ 1 hour, 50 minutes (applied the formula and misinterpreted the result as representing time)

H. **Correct:** (178 kilometers × 0.62 mile per kilometer) ÷ 55 miles per hour = 110.36 miles ÷ 55 miles per hour ≈ 2 hours

J. Incorrect: 178 ÷ 55 ≈ 3.24 ≈ 3 hours, 14 minutes (did not convert kilometers to miles)

K. Incorrect: 178 ÷ 0.62 ≈ 287.10; 287.10 ÷ 55 ≈ 5.2 ≈ 5 hours, 12 minutes (applied the formula incorrectly, dividing instead of multiplying)

11. Find the discount, subtract the discount from the original price, and multiply by 55. *(Lesson 17)*

A. **Correct:** $12 − ($12 × 0.60) = $12 − $7.20 = $4.80; $4.80 × 55 = $264

B. Incorrect: $12 × 0.60 = $7.20; $7.20 × 55 = $396 (found the amount of the discount and treated it as the price after the discount)

C. Incorrect: $12 − 0.60 = $11.40; $11.40 × 55 = $627 (subtracted the percent of the discount from the original price and then multiplied by the number of manuals)

D. Incorrect: $12 × 55 = $660 (found the cost of the manuals without the discount)

E. Incorrect: 60 × 55 = $3,300 (multiplied the percent of the discount by the number of manuals)

12. Subtract 4 from 40 to find the target weight, and then subtract the target weight from the current weight. *(Lesson 14)*

F. Incorrect: 40 − 38.8 = 1.2 pounds (subtracted the current weight from the original weight)

G. **Correct:** 40 pounds − 4 pounds = 36 pounds; 38.8 pounds − 36 pounds = 2.8 pounds

H. Incorrect: 38.8 − (40 − 6) = 38.8 − 34 = 4.8 pounds (subtracted 6 months from the original weight, and subtracted the result from the current weight)

J. Incorrect: (40 − 38.8) + 4 = 1.2 + 4 = 5.2 pounds (subtracted the current weight from the original weight and added the weight to be lost)

K. Incorrect: 40 − 4 = 36 pounds (subtracted to find the goal weight)

13. Add the distances and convert inches to feet *(Lesson 12)*

A. Incorrect: 34 feet; 7 + 15 + 12 = 34 (did not add inches)

B. Incorrect: 35 feet, 6 inches; 7 + 15 + 12 = 34 feet; 10 + 8 + 8 = 26 inches = 1 foot, 6 inches (incorrectly converted inches to feet)

C. **Correct:** 36 feet, 2 inches; 7 + 15 + 12 = 34 feet; 10 + 8 + 8 = 26 inches = 2 feet, 2 inches; 34 feet + 2 feet, 2 inches = 36 feet, 2 inches

D. Incorrect: 36 feet, 6 inches; 7 + 15 + 12 = 34 feet; 10 + 8 + 8 = 26 inches = 2 feet, 6 inches (divided inches by 10 instead of 12)

E. Incorrect: 37 feet; 8 + 16 + 13 = 37 (rounded to nearest foot instead of adding inches)

14. Find the first company's estimate by multiplying $450 by 3 and $200 by 2 and adding the two products. Find the second company's estimate by multiplying $85 by 20. Compare the two estimates. *(Lesson 16)*

F. Incorrect: $450 + $200 = $650 (added the first company's estimates for just one larger room and one smaller room)

G. Incorrect: ($450 × 3) + $200 = $1,350 + $200 = $1,550 (found the first company's estimate to paint the 3 larger rooms, but added the estimate to paint only 1 smaller room)

H. **Correct:** ($450 per larger room × 3 larger rooms) + ($200 per smaller room × 2 smaller rooms) = $1,350 + $400 = $1,750; $85 per hour × 20 hours = $1,700; $1,750 > $1,700

J. Incorrect: ($450 × 3) + ($200 × 2) = $1,350 + $400 = $1,750 (found the first company's estimate, which is not the lower estimate)

K. Incorrect: ($450 + $200) (3 + 2) = $650 × 5 = $3,250 (added the first company's estimate to paint one larger room to the estimate to paint one smaller room and multiplied the sum by the total number of rooms)

15. Multiply the hours worked by the rate per hour. *(Lesson 14)*

A. Incorrect: 38 + 18 = $56 (added the number of hours worked to the rate per hour)

B. Incorrect: 5 × 18 = $90 (multiplied the number of items produced by the number of hours worked)

C. Incorrect: 5 × $38 = $190 (multiplied the number of items produced by the rate per hour)

D. **Correct:** 18 hours × $38 per hour = $684

E. Incorrect: 18 × 5 × $38 = $3,420 (multiplied the number of hours worked by the items produced and the rate per hour)

16. Find the difference between the number of members 12 months ago and the number of members now and divide by 12. Because the number of members decreased, the change is negative. *(Lesson 18)*

F. Incorrect: 20,040 − 24,360 = −4,320 (found only the total change in membership)

G. **Correct:** 20,040 members − 24,360 members = −4,320 members; −4,320 members ÷ 12 months = −360 members per month

H. Incorrect: 20,040 ÷ 12 = 1,670 (divided the current membership by 12)

J. Incorrect: 24,360 ÷ 12 = 2,030 (divided the original membership by 12)

K. Incorrect: (24,360 + 20,040) ÷ 12 = 3,700 (added the original and current membership and divided by 12)

17. Find the total length by adding 2 meters to the length of the garden and the total width by adding 2 meters to the width of the garden and then multiply length by width. *(Lesson 13)*

A. Incorrect: 5 + 3.5 + 1 = 9.5 square meters (added the numbers given in the problem)

B. Incorrect: 5 × 3.5 = 17.5 square meters (found the area of the garden without the path)

C. Incorrect: (5 + 2)(3.5 + 2) − (5 × 3.5) = 38.5 square meters − 17.5 square meters = 21 square meters (found the area of the path without the garden)

D. Incorrect: (5 + 1)(3.5 + 1) = 27 square meters (added 1 to the length and width of the garden and then multiplied)

E. **Correct:** (5 + 2)(3.5 + 2) = 38.5 square meters (found the area of the rectangle created by the outer edges of the stone path)

18. Use the formula 1 ounce ≈ 28.350 grams to convert ounces to grams, and then subtract the result from the total grams needed. *(Lesson 15)*

F. Incorrect: (450 − 12) ÷ 28.350 = 438 ÷ 28.350 ≈ 15.4 grams (subtracted the number of ounces from the total grams needed and divided to apply the formula)

G. Incorrect: 450 ÷ 12 = 37.5 grams (divided the number of grams needed by the number of ounces)

H. **Correct:** 450 grams − (12 ounces × 28.350 grams per ounce) = 450 grams − 340.2 grams = 109.8 grams

J. Incorrect: 450 − 12 = 438 grams (subtracted the number of ounces from the total grams needed)

K. Incorrect: (450 − 12) × 28.350 = 438 × 28.350 = 12,417.3 grams (subtracted the number of ounces from the total grams needed and multiplied to apply the formula)

19. Find the difference between the weight 12 months ago and the weight now and divide by 12. Because the weight decreased, the change is negative. *(Lesson 18)*

    A. Incorrect: 138 −186 = −48 pounds (found the total change in weight)

    B. Incorrect: 12 months = −12 pounds (selected the number of months as a negative quantity)

    C. **Correct:** 138 pounds − 186 pounds = −48 pounds; −48 pounds ÷ 12 months = −4 pounds per month

    D. Incorrect: 138 ÷ 12 = 11.5 pounds (divided the current weight by the number of months)

    E. Incorrect: 186 ÷ 12 = 15.5 pounds (divided the original weight by the number of months)

20. Divide the cost of each pallet by the number of boxes on the pallet and compare. *(Lesson 16)*

    F. Incorrect: $840 ÷ 40 = $21 (divided the price for the pallet with 24 boxes by the number of pounds per box)

    G. Incorrect: $840 ÷ 36 ≈ $23.33 (divided the price for the pallet with 24 boxes by 36)

    H. Incorrect: $1,224 ÷ 40 = $30.60 (divided the price of the pallet with 36 boxes by the weight of the boxes)

    J. **Correct:** $1,224 ÷ 36 boxes = $34 per box; $840 ÷ 24 boxes = $35 per box; $34 < $35

    K. Incorrect: $840 ÷ 24 = $35 (found the price per box on the pallet with 24 boxes, which is not the lowest price)

21. Divide the cost of each case by the number of boxes in the case and compare the costs per box. *(Lesson 16)*

    A. Incorrect: $73.90 ÷ 100 ≈ $0.74 (divided the price of a case by the number of gloves in a box)

    B. Incorrect: $87 ÷ 100 = $0.87 (divided the price of a case by the number of gloves in a box)

    C. **Correct:** $73.90 ÷ 10 boxes = $7.39 per box; $87 ÷ 12 boxes = $7.25 per box; $7.39 > $7.25

    D. Incorrect: $73.90 ÷ 10 = $7.39 (found the price per box in the case with 10 boxes, which is not the lower price)

E. Incorrect: $73.90 < $87 (incorrectly identified the cost of the case as the lower per box cost)

22. Find the radius of the wading pool, and then use the formula for the area of a circle: 3.14 × (radius)². *(Lesson 13)*

    F. Incorrect: 10 ÷ 2 = 5, 3 × 5 = 15 square feet (found radius correctly, but applied the formula incorrectly by not squaring the radius; also used incorrect value for pi)

    G. Incorrect: 10 ÷ 2 = 5; 3.14 × 5 = 15.7 square feet (found the radius correctly, but applied the formula incorrectly by not squaring the radius)

    H. Incorrect: 10 ÷ 2 = 5; 3.14 × (5 × 2) = 3.14 × 10 = 31.4 square feet (found the radius correctly, but applied the formula incorrectly by multiplying the radius by 2 instead of squaring it, finding the circumference instead)

    J. **Correct:** 10 feet ÷ 2 = 5 feet; 3.14 × (5 feet)² = 3.14 × 25 square feet = 78.5 square feet

    K. Incorrect: 3.14 × 10² = 3.14 × 100 = 314 square feet (squared the diameter instead of the radius)

23. Find the change in hourly rate and multiply by 25. *(Lesson 17)*

    A. Incorrect: $0.08 × 25 = $2 (interpreted 8% as equal to $0.08 and multiplied by the number of hours)

    B. Incorrect: $14 + ($14 × 0.08) = $14 + $1.12 = $15.12 (found the new hourly rate)

    C. **Correct:** $14 × 0.08 = $1.12; $1.12 per hour × 25 hours = $28

    D. Incorrect: $8 × 25 = $200 (interpreted 8% as equal to $8)

    E. Incorrect: $14 + ($14 × 0.08) = $14 + $1.12 = $15.12; $15.12 × 25 = $378 (found the total amount earned in 25 hours at the new hourly rate)

24. Convert 4 hours, 30 minutes to minutes, then divide by 18 to find the number of interviews that can be done in this time. Subtract that number from 20 to find the number of interviews that still need to be conducted. *(Lesson 12)*

    F. **Correct:** (4 hours × 60 minutes per hour) + 30 minutes = 240 minutes + 30 minutes = 270 minutes; 270 minutes ÷ 18 minutes per interview = 15 interviews; 20 customers to be interviewed − 15 interviews = 5 interviews

G. Incorrect: $(4 \times 60) + 30 = 240 + 30 = 270$; $270 \div 18 = 15$ (found the number of interviews that can be done in 4 hours, 30 minutes, not the number that will need to be conducted afterward)

H. Incorrect: $(4 \times 60) + 30 = 240 + 30 = 270$; $270 \div 18 = 15$; $20 - 15 = 5$; $5 + 20 = 25$ (added the correct result to 20)

J. Incorrect: $(4 \times 60) + 30 = 240 + 30 = 270$; $270 \div 18 = 15$; $20 + 15 = 35$ (added number of interviews that can be done in 4 hours, 30 minutes to 20 instead of subtracting)

K. Incorrect: $(4 \times 60) + 30 = 240 + 30 = 270$; $270 - 20 = 250$ (converted 4 hours, 30 minutes to minutes, and then subtracted 20)

25. Add the cost of the fabric, and, because the total is greater than $150, find the 10% discount and subtract. Finally, add the cost of shipping. *(Lesson 17)*

A. Incorrect: $75 + $120 + $109 = $304; $304 - $150 = $154 (found the total cost and subtracted $150)

B. Incorrect: $75 + $120 + $109 = $304; $304 - ($304 \times 0.1) = $304 - $30.40 = $273.60 (did not add the cost of shipping)

C. **Correct:** $75 + $120 + $109 = $304; $304 - ($304 \times 0.1) = $304 - $30.40 = $273.60; $273.60 + $12 = $285.60

D. Incorrect: $75 + $120 + $109 = $304 (found the total cost without the discount or shipping)

E. Incorrect: $75 + $120 + $109 = $304; $304 + $12 = $316 (found the total cost and added shipping; did not find or subtract the discount)

26. Add the temperatures and divide the sum by 4 to find the average. *(Lesson 18)*

F. Incorrect: $(-20°C) + (-18°C) + (-17°C) + (-17°C) = -72°C$; $-72°C \times 4 = -288°C$ (multiplied instead of dividing the sum by 4)

G. Incorrect: $(-20°C) + (-18°C) + (-17°C) + (-17°C) = -72°C$ (found the sum of the 4 temperatures)

H. **Correct:** $(-20°C) + (-18°C) + (-17°C) + (-17°C) = -72°C$; $-72°C \div 4 = -18°C$

J. Incorrect: $(-20°C) + (-18°C) + (-17°C) + (-17°C) = -72°C$; $-72°C \div 4 = 18°C$ (interpreted the quotient of a negative divided by a positive number as positive)

K. Incorrect: $(-20°C) + (-18°C) + (-17°C) + (-17°C) = 72°C$ (found the sum of the 4 temperatures and dropped the negative sign)

27. Use the formula to find the circumference of a circle (3.14 × diameter). *(Lesson 13)*

A. Incorrect: $3.14 \times \sqrt{9} = 3.14 \times 3 = 9.42$ inches (used the square root of the diameter in the formula)

B. Incorrect: $3.14 + 9 = 12.14$ inches (added instead of multiplying)

C. Incorrect: $3.14 \times \frac{9}{2} = 14.3$ inches (multiplied pi by the radius instead of the diameter)

D. **Correct:** 3.14×9 inches $= 28.26$ inches

E. Incorrect: $3.14 \times 9 \times 2 = 56.52$ inches (multiplied the circumference by the width)

28. Convert 40 quarts to gallons and subtract from 36 gallons to find how many more are needed. *(Lesson 12)*

F. Incorrect: $40 \div 4 = 10$; $36 \div 4 = 9$; $10 - 9 = 1$ gallon (incorrectly divided the number of gallons needed by 4 and subtracted that amount from the number of gallons delivered)

G. **Correct:** 40 quarts $\div$ 4 quarts per gallon $= 10$ gallons; 36 gallons $-$ 10 gallons $= 26$ gallons

H. Incorrect: $40 \div 4 = 10$; $40 - 10 = 30$ gallons (subtracted from the number of gallons ordered instead of from the number of gallons needed)

J. Incorrect: $40 \times 4 = 160$; $160 - 40 = 120$ gallons (multiplied instead of dividing to convert from quarts to gallons, then subtracted the number of gallons ordered)

K. Incorrect: $40 \times 4 = 160$; $160 - 36 = 124$ gallons (multiplied instead of dividing to convert from quarts to gallons, then subtracted the number of gallons needed)

Level 6

Lesson 19 (pp. 134–139)
Skill Practice:

A. $44.90
B. $39
C. $49.80
D. $3.62

On Your Own:

1. C	5. C	9. D	13. A
2. G	6. F	10. G	14. G
3. A	7. D	11. C	15. C
4. H	8. G	12. J	16. G

Lesson 20 (pp. 140–145)
Skill Practice:

A. $500.00
B. $31,250.00
C. −46

On Your Own:

1. D	5. D	9. E	13. B
2. J	6. G	10. J	14. J
3. E	7. E	11. B	15. D
4. G	8. H	12. G	16. F

Lesson 21 (pp. 146–151)
Skill Practice:

A. 84 cubic centimeters
B. 0.125 cubic feet

On Your Own:

1. D	5. A	9. D	13. B
2. H	6. K	10. K	14. G
3. A	7. C	11. D	15. B
4. G	8. K	12. J	16. H

Lesson 22 (pp. 152–157)
Skill Practice:

A. 62°   B. 5 inches

On Your Own:

1. C	5. D	9. B	13. A
2. J	6. G	10. G	14. G
3. E	7. B	11. A	15. A
4. F	8. G	12. H	16. G

Lesson 23 (pp. 158–163)
Skill Practice:

A. 204 inches   C. 10 miles
B. 0.745 quart

On Your Own:

1. A	5. B	9. A	13. D
2. J	6. G	10. H	14. J
3. C	7. C	11. E	15. D
4. K	8. G	12. G	16. G

Lesson 24 (pp. 164–169)
Skill Practice:

A. 14,515 grams   C. 7,087.5 milligrams
B. 561 quarts

On Your Own:

1. A	5. E	9. C	13. B
2. K	6. G	10. J	14. F
3. B	7. D	11. B	15. B
4. J	8. G	12. H	16. F

Lesson 25 (pp. 170–175)
Skill Practice:

A. 50 feet per second
B. $0.12 per ounce
C. 220 miles

On Your Own:

1. A	5. D	9. C	13. E
2. F	6. H	10. H	14. H
3. A	7. B	11. D	15. B
4. H	8. K	12. J	16. K

Lesson 26 (pp. 176–181)
Skill Practice:

A. 36 square feet   B. 16 inches

On Your Own:

1. E	5. C	9. D	13. C
2. K	6. G	10. G	14. K
3. C	7. A	11. D	15. D
4. G	8. H	12. F	16. K

Level 6 Performance Assessment (pp. 182–188)

1. First, divide to find out the cost per ream of Paper A and Paper B and choose the one with the lowest cost. Then subtract to compare the cost per ream to find out the savings per ream. *(Lesson 19)*

   A. **Correct:** $31.90 ÷ 10 = $3.19; $36 ÷ 12 = $3; $3.19 − $3 = $0.19; Paper B, $0.19 per ream.

   B. Incorrect: Paper B, $1.90 per ream (placed decimal points incorrectly during subtraction)

   C. Incorrect: $36 ÷ 12 = Paper B, $3 per ream (calculated the cost per ream of Paper B, rather than the difference in the cost per reams)

   D. Incorrect: $31.90 ÷ 10 = Paper A, $3.19 per ream (found the cost per ream of Paper A, rather than the difference in the cost per reams)

   E. Incorrect: $36 − $31.90 = Paper A, $4.10 per ream (subtracted the case price, rather than the price per ream)

2. Solve for height in the formula for volume of a rectangular solid. Height = volume ÷ (*width* × *length*). *(Lesson 21)*

   F. Incorrect: 500 cubic centimeters ÷ (20 centimeters × 20 centimeters) = 1.25 centimeters (used incorrect volume)

   G. **Correct:** 5,000 cubic centimeters ÷ (20 centimeters × 20 centimeters) = 12.5 centimeters

   H. Incorrect: 20 centimeters (used the measurement of the base only)

   J. Incorrect: 5,000 cubic centimeters ÷ (20 centimeters × 20 centimeters) = 125 centimeters (incorrectly divided)

   K. Incorrect: 5,000 cubic centimeters ÷ 20 centimeters = 250 centimeters (forgot to divide by the length also)

3. Calculate the amount of space (volume) in each unit. Multiply the answer by the cost per cubic foot. Then multiply that cost by the number of units. *(Lesson 22)*

   A. Incorrect: $800 (cost of only one unit)

   B. Incorrect: $2,000 (decimal point put in the wrong place)

   C. Incorrect: $2,500 (space for one unit was incorrectly calculated)

   D. **Correct:** $20,000; Space for one unit = 8 feet × 8 feet × 10 feet = 640 cubic feet. Cost of one unit is 640 × $1.25 = $800. Total amount is $800 × 25 units = $20,000.

   E. Incorrect: $80,000 (incorrectly calculated the space for one unit)

4. Subtract last quarter's profits from this quarter's profits to find the difference. *(Lesson 20)*

   F. Incorrect: −$1,329. $13,550 − $14,879 = −$1,329 (subtracted last quarter's profits from the next quarter's projected profits)

   G. **Correct:** $13,671 − 14,879 = −$1,208

   H. Incorrect: $121. $13,671 − $13,550 = $121 (subtracted next quarter's projected profits from the current quarter's profits)

   J. Incorrect: $1,208. $14,879 − $13,671 = $1,208 (subtracted the current quarter's profits from last quarter's profits)

   K. Incorrect: $1,329 (subtracted next quarter's projected quarterly profits from last quarter's profits)

5. Find the square footage of the room and then multiply it by the cost per square foot. *(Lesson 26)*

   A. Incorrect: $726 (adds length and width to find the area)

   B. Incorrect: $1,467 (uses the perimeter instead of the area to find the cost)

   C. Incorrect: $5,355 (does not include the fractions when finding area)

   D. **Correct:** $5,808; Area: $14\frac{3}{4}$ feet × $17\frac{1}{2}$ feet = $258\frac{1}{8}$ square feet; Cost: $258\frac{1}{8}$ × $22.50 = $5,807.81

   E. Incorrect: $6,075 (uses the rounded up numbers 15 feet and 18 feet to find the area of the floor)

6. Divide to find the number of kilograms used in 1 hour. Then use that number to calculate how many kilograms would be used in 14 hours. *(Lesson 25)*

   F. Incorrect: 4 kilograms. 96 ÷ 24 = 4 kilograms (number of kilograms per $\frac{1}{2}$ hour)

   G. Incorrect: 8 kilograms. 96 ÷ 12 = 8 kilograms per hour (number of kilograms added per hour)

   H. **Correct:** 112 kilograms. 96 ÷ 12 = 8; 8 × 14 = 112 kilograms

   J. Incorrect: 1,152 kilograms. (number of kilograms if you added 96 kilograms each hour instead of in each 12-hour period)

   K. Incorrect: 1,344 kilograms. (number of kilograms if you added 96 kilograms each hour instead of in each 14-hour period)

7. Convert liters to gallons, then convert gallons to quarts. Subtract 14 to find how many quarts are left. *(Lesson 24)*

   A. **Correct:** 2 quarts. 15.3 liters × 0.264 ≈ 4 gallons; 4 × 4 = 16 quarts − 14 quarts = 2 quarts

   B. Incorrect: 16 quarts. 15.3 liters × 0.264 ≈ 4 gallons; 4 × 4 = 16 quarts (correctly converted the amount of solution that was prepared, but did not subtract the amount used)

   C. Incorrect: 30 quarts. 15.3 liters × 0.264 ≈ 4 gallons; 4 × 4 = 16 quarts + 14 quarts = 30 quarts (converted correctly but added 14 quarts instead of subtracting to find how much is left)

   D. Incorrect: 160 quarts. 15.3 × 2.64 ≈ 40; 40 × 4 = 160 (multiplied by the wrong conversion factor when converting liters to gallons)

   E. Incorrect: 218 quarts. 15.3 ÷ 0.264 ≈ 58; 58 × 4 = 232 − 14 = 218 (divided by the conversion factor instead of multiplying when converting liters to gallons)

8. Use the formula °F = 1.8(°C) + 32 to convert the first hot blast temperature. Then add 24°F to get the present hot blast temperature. *(Lesson 24)*

   F. Incorrect: 1,124°F. 1,100°C + 24°F = 1,124°F (did not convert °C to °F before adding)

   G. Incorrect: 1,998°F. [1.8(1,100°C) + 32] − 24 = 1,998°F (converted correctly but subtracted the increase in temperature instead of adding it)

   H. Incorrect: 2,004°F. [1.8(1,100°C)] + 24 = 2,004°F (partially calculated the conversion formula, but did not add 32)

   J. Incorrect: 2,012°F. [1.8(1,100°C)] + 32 = 2,012°F (correctly converted the current temperature, but did not add the increase in temperature)

   K. **Correct:** 2,036°F. [1.8(1,100°C) + 32] + 24 = 2,036°F

9. Divide to find the cost per slide and compare to find the best deal. *(Lesson 19)*

   A. Incorrect: $100 ÷ 600 = $0.167 → the box of 600, $0.16; 50 ÷ 250 = $0.20; $0.16 < $0.20 (did not round correctly and confused the boxes)

   B. **Correct:** $100 ÷ 600 = $0.167 → the box of 600, $0.17; 50 ÷ 250 = $0.20; $0.17 < $0.20

   C. Incorrect: the box of 250, $0.20. $50 ÷ 250 = $0.20 (found the price per slide, but did not compare to find the better deal)

   D. Incorrect: the box of 250, $0.50. 250 ÷ $50 ≠ $0.50 (set up division incorrectly and incorrectly placed decimal point)

   E. Incorrect: the box of 600, $0.60. 600 ÷ $100 ≠ $0.60 (set up division incorrectly and incorrectly placed decimal point)

10. Double the number of cups in the recipe to find out how many cups are in each tray, then multiply that number by 4. *(Lesson 20)*

   F. Incorrect: $6\frac{1}{2}$ cups. $3\frac{1}{4} \times 2 = 6\frac{1}{2}$ (found the amount for one double batch)

   G. Incorrect: $12\frac{3}{4}$ cups. $3\frac{1}{4} \times 4 = 12\frac{3}{4}$ (used one batch per tray, multiplied incorrectly)

   H. Incorrect: 13 cups. $3\frac{1}{4} \times 4 = 13$ (used one batch per tray)

   J. Incorrect: $24\frac{1}{4}$ cups. $3\frac{1}{4} \times 2 \times 4 = 24\frac{1}{4}$ (multiplied incorrectly)

   K. **Correct:** 26 cups. $3\frac{1}{4} \times 2 \times 4 = 26$

11. Rearrange the formula for finding the area of a circle to solve for the radius: $radius = \sqrt{\frac{area}{3.14}}$. *(Lesson 21)*

   A. Incorrect: 0.14 meter (rearranged the formula for area as $radius = \sqrt{\frac{3.14}{area}}$)

   B. **Correct:** 6.9 meters; radius = $\sqrt{\frac{150 \text{ m}^2}{3.14}}$ = 6.9 meters

   C. Incorrect: 21.7 meters (rearranged the formula for area as $radius = \sqrt{3.14(area)}$

   D. Incorrect: 38.5 meters (rearranged the formula for area as $radius = 3.14\sqrt{area}$)

   E. Incorrect: 47.8 meters (rearranged the formula for area as $radius = \frac{area}{3.14}$)

12. Find the total area of all the rooms. Multiply the cost per square foot. *(Lesson 26)*

   F. Incorrect: $255,600 (did not include dining room in total)

   G. Incorrect: $264,600 (included only 1 bedroom in total)

   H. Incorrect: $277,200 (included only 1 bathroom in total)

   J. **Correct:** $291,600. Kitchen: (15 × 12) × 120 = $21,600; Dining Room: (15 × 20) × 120 = $36,000; Living Room: (21 × 30) × 120 = $75,600; Bedroom: 2(15 × 15) × 120 = $54,000; Bedroom Suite: (21 × 30) × 120 = $75,600; Bathroom: 2(10 × 12) × 120 = $28,800; $21,600 + $36,000 + $75,600 + $54,000 + $75,600 + $28,800 = $291,600

   K. Incorrect: $367,200 (included an extra bedroom suite)

13. Multiply the number of servings by the number of ounces of chicken for each serving. Convert 10 pounds into ounces. Divide the total number of ounces needed by the number of ounces in 1 package, and round up to the nearest package. Determine how many ounces are in 19 packages. Subtract the total amount of chicken from what is needed. Divide the remaining ounces by 5 to determine how many extra servings of chicken there will be. *(Lesson 23)*

   A. **Correct:** 595 × 5 oz. = 2,975 oz.; 10 pounds = 160 oz.; 2,975 oz. ÷ 160 oz. = 18.59 bags → 19 bags; 19 × 160 oz. = 3,040 oz.; 3,040 oz. − 2,975 oz. = 65 oz.; 65 oz. ÷ 5 oz. = 13 servings

   B. Incorrect: 18 (rounded down the number of bags needed to serve the dinner; did not calculate the extra servings of chicken there will be)

   C. Incorrect: 19 (found number of bags needed to serve the dinner, not how many extra servings of chicken there will be)

   D. Incorrect: 45 (subtracted number of ounces in a serving from the number of ounces left over instead of dividing)

E. Incorrect: 65 (found number of ounces left over after serving the dinner, not number of servings)

14. Multiply the inches of shelf space per store by the number of stores. Divide to convert inches to feet. Subtract to find how much shelf space you need to gain. *(Lesson 23)*

   F. Incorrect: $1\frac{1}{2}$ feet (only converted the amount of shelf space in 1 store)

   G. **Correct:** $12\frac{1}{2}$ feet. $18 \times 25 = 450$; $450 \div 12 = 37\frac{1}{2}$ feet; $50 - 37\frac{1}{2} = 12\frac{1}{2}$

   H. Incorrect: $37\frac{1}{2}$ feet (only calculated the amount of space the products occupy in total)

   J. Incorrect: 450 feet (calculated the total number of inches of shelf space, but did not convert to feet)

   K. Incorrect: 600 feet (converted the number of feet occupied by the competitor to inches)

15. In the 4:1 water-to-dye solution, $\frac{4}{5}$ of the solution is water. To determine the amount of water, multiply the total amount of solution by $\frac{4}{5}$. Answers are expressed as fractions. *(Lesson 20)*

   A. Incorrect: $\frac{1}{5}$ liter (used only amount of dye in 1 liter of solution)

   B. Incorrect: $\frac{4}{5}$ liter (found how much water would be used in only 1 liter of solution)

   C. Incorrect: 1 liter (found how much dye would be used in the solution, not how much water)

   D. Incorrect: $3\frac{1}{4}$ liters (multiplied by incorrect ratio [$\frac{3}{4}$])

   E. **Correct:** 4 liters; $\frac{4}{5} \times 5$ liters = 4 liters

16. To find the net cost/profit of each roof, multiply the savings by 10 years and then subtract the cost of installation. Compare the net cost/profit numbers to find the better deal. *(Lesson 19)*

   F. Incorrect: The solar roof because it will net a savings of $2,000. $5,000 - $3,000 = $2,000 (found the difference between 1 year's savings)

   G. Incorrect: The green roof because it will net a savings of $5,000. $30,000 - $25,000 = $5,000 (did not correctly compare to the net profit of the solar roof)

   H. **Correct:** The solar roof because it will net a savings of $10,000. Green roof: ($3,000 × 10) − $25,000 = $5,000 savings; Solar roof: ($5,000 × 10) − $40,000 = $10, 000 savings; $5,000 < $10,000.

   J. Incorrect: The green roof because it will net a savings of $30,000. $3,000 × 10 = $30,000 (did not subtract the cost of installing the green roof)

   K. Incorrect: The solar roof because it will net a savings of $50,000. $5,000 × 10 = $50,000 (did not subtract the cost of installing the solar roof)

17. Convert the measurements to inches. Multiply to calculate the volume. Then use the formula to convert cubic inches to cubic feet. *(Lesson 22)*

   A. Incorrect: 336 cubic feet (does not convert feet to inches)

   B. Incorrect: 384.3 cubic feet (does not convert feet to inches and uses incorrect conversion factor)

   C. **Correct:** 426.9 cubic feet. 8'5" = 101 inches, 6'11" = 83 inches, 7'4" = 88 inches.
   $V = 101 \times 83 \times 88 = 737,704$ cubic inches; $\frac{737,704}{1728} = 426.9$ cubic feet

   D. Incorrect: 577.2 cubic feet (uses incorrect conversion factor)

   E. Incorrect: 737,704 cubic feet (does not divide to convert cubic inches to cubic feet)

18. Convert the formula for amps to solve for watts: *watts = (volts)(amps). (Lesson 22)*

   F. Incorrect: $5 \div 120 = 0.04$ watt (incorrectly solved the electricity formula for watts)

   G. Incorrect: $(120 \times 5) \div 60 = 10$ watts (solved the formula correctly, but divided by Hz)

   H. Incorrect: $\frac{120}{5} = 24$ watts (incorrectly solved the electricity formula for watts)

   J. **Correct:** watts = $120 \times 5 = 600$ watts

   K. Incorrect: $(120 \times 5) \times 60 = 36,000$ watts (solved the electricity formula correctly, but multiplied by Hz)

19. Convert the formula for speed to solve for time ($t = \frac{d}{s}$) for both drivers. Convert answers to minutes by multiplying by 60. Then subtract. *(Lesson 25)*

   A. **Correct:** 6 minutes; You: $\frac{6}{15} \times 60 = 24$ minutes; Evening driver: $\frac{6}{20} \times 60 = 18$ minutes; 24 minutes − 18 minutes = 6 minutes

   B. Incorrect: 18 minutes (time it takes the evening driver)

C. Incorrect: 24 minutes (time it takes the daytime driver)

D. Incorrect: 24 + 18 = 42 minutes (added instead of subtracted)

E. Incorrect: 24 × 18 = 432 minutes (multiplied instead of subtracted)

20. Subtract the rebate from the price and compare results (net prices) to find the better deal. Subtract the net prices to find the difference. *(Lesson 19)*

   F. **Correct:** Solar panel A: $1,395 − $250 = $1,145; Solar panel B: $1,160 − $100 = $1,060; $1,145 − $1,060 = $85

   G. Incorrect: Solar panel A: $1,395 − $250 = $1,145; Solar panel B: $1,160 − $100 = $1,060; $1,145 − $1,060 = $125 (found the net prices correctly, but made a mistake when subtracting to find the difference)

   H. Incorrect: Solar panel A: $250 − $100 = $150 (found the difference in rebates, not net prices)

   J. Incorrect: Solar panel B: $1,395 − $1,160 = $235 (found the difference in prices, not net prices after rebates)

   K. Incorrect: Solar panel A: $1,395 + $250 = $1,545; Solar panel B: $1,160 + $100 = $1,160; $1,545 − $1,160 = $385 (added rebates to prices instead of subtracting, and chose the panel with the greater cost as the better deal)

21. Rearrange the formula for area of a rectangle to solve for width: $width = \frac{area}{length}$. *(Lesson 22)*

   A. Incorrect: 21 ÷ 100 = 0.21 foot (incorrectly rearranged the formula for area)

   B. Incorrect: (21 ÷ 100)(3) = 0.63 foot (incorrectly rearranged the formula for area and multiplied the result by 3 to account for the 3 banners)

   C. **Correct:** $\frac{100}{21}$ = 4.76 feet

   D. Incorrect: 14.29 feet (divided area by 3 to account for the 3 banners, and then divided the sum by the length of the banners)

   E. Incorrect: 33.33 feet (divided area by the number of banners instead of length of each banner)

22. Convert the measurements of the wall to feet. Use the volume formula to calculate the number of cubic feet. Multiply that answer by the rate. *(Lesson 22)*

   F. Incorrect: $162 (uses the volume of one brick)

G. Incorrect: $503 (uses the volume of the brick wall)

H. Incorrect: $1,143 (incorrectly multiplied the number of cubic feet by the rate)

J. **Correct:** 4.5 inches = 0.375 feet; V = 4 feet × 335 feet × 0.375 feet = 502.5 cubic feet; 502.5 cubic feet × $22.75 per cubic foot = $11,431.875 → $11,432

K. Incorrect: $21,204 (converted the cubic inches to cubic feet by mistake)

23. Subtract the area of the circle from the area of the square. *(Lesson 26)*

   A. **Correct:** Area of square = 4 × 4 = 16; Area of circle = 3.14 × 2^2 = 12.56; Area left is 16 − 12.56 = 3.44 square meters

   B. Incorrect: Area of circle = 3.14 × 2^2 = 12.56 square meters (correctly calculated the area of the garden, but did not subtract to find the area of land not incorporated)

   C. Incorrect: Area of rectangle = 4 × 4 = 16 square meters (correctly calculated the area of the rectangular plot, but did not subtract the area of the garden to determine land not incorporated)

   D. Incorrect: Area of square = 4 × 4 = 16; Area of circle = 3.14 × 2^2 = 12.56; 16 + 12.56 = 28.56 square meters (found the sum instead of the difference of the area of the plot and the area of the garden)

   E. Incorrect: Area of square = 4 × 4 = 16; Area of circle = 3.14 × 4^2 = 50.24; 50.24 − 16 = 34.24 square meters (used diameter instead of radius to calculate area of circle)

24. Multiply to find the number of gallons that will be needed using the new cleaner. Use the formula for converting gallons to liters to find the equivalent number of liters. *(Lesson 24)*

   F. Incorrect: 12 gallons × $\frac{1}{3}$ = 4 gallons per week; 4 × 0.264 ≈ 1 liter (multiplied instead of dividing to convert gallons to liters)

   G. Incorrect: 12 gallons × $\frac{1}{3}$ = 4 liters (correctly found the number of gallons needed, but did not convert to liters)

   H. **Correct:** 12 gallons × $\frac{1}{3}$ = 4 gallons per week 4 ÷ 0.264 ≈ 15.1 → 15 liters

   J. Incorrect: 12 gallons ÷ 0.264 ≈ 45 liters (converted the weekly amount of old cleaner to liters, but did not find how much of the new cleaner is used)

K. Incorrect: 12 gallons × 3 = 36 gallons per week; 36 ÷ .0264 ≈ 136 liters (multiplied by 3 instead of by $\frac{1}{3}$ to find the number of gallons needed per week)

25. To find the balance for the period shown on the balance sheet, subtract the numbers with negative signs from the monthly income, and add the number without the negative sign. *(Lesson 20)*

    A. Incorrect: $2,550.45 − $750 − $71.23 − $323.97 − $225 − $50 − $45.10 − $55.90 = $1,079.25 (subtracted the $50 rebate instead of adding it)

    B. **Correct:** $2,550.45 − $750 − $71.23 − $323.97 − $225 + $50 − $45.10 − $55.90 = $1,129.25

    C. Incorrect: $750 + $71.23 + $323.97 + $225 + $45.10 + $55.90 = $1,471.20 (added all expenses together)

    D. Incorrect: $2,550.45 + 50 = $2,600.45 (added both sources of income together, but did not subtract expenses)

    E. Incorrect: $2,550.45 + $750 + $71.23 + $323.97 + $225 + $50 + $45.10 + $55.90 = $4,071.65 (added all numbers on the balance sheet together)

26. Add to find the total number of meters. Multiply to find the total amount of wire in two rolls. Subtract to find the difference. Convert to centimeters. *(Lesson 23)*

    F. Incorrect: 3 + 2.625 + 4.125 = 9.75 meters; 6 meters × 2 rolls = 12 meters; 12 − 9.25 = 2.25 centimeters (expressed the answer in incorrect units)

    G. Incorrect: 3 + 2.625 + 4.125 = 9.75 meters; 9.75 ÷ 3 = 3.25 centimeters; (calculated the average length of wire for each wall and expressed the answer in incorrect units)

    H. Incorrect: 3 + 2.625 + 4.125 = 9.75 centimeters (added to find the amount that was needed, but did not calculate how much was left and expressed the answer in incorrect units)

    J. Incorrect: 6 meters × 2 rolls = 12 centimeters (calculated the amount of wire in two rolls using incorrect units but did not calculate to find out how much wire would be left)

K. **Correct:** 3 + 2.625 + 4.125 = 9.75 meters; 6 meters × 2 rolls = 12 meters; 12 − 9.25 = 2.25 meters; 2.25 meters × 100 = 225 centimeters

27. Find the area of the plot in square yards and convert to square feet. Convert the result from square feet to acres. *(Lesson 26)*

    A. Incorrect: 35.9 acres (did not convert square yards to square feet before dividing)

    B. Incorrect: 2,980 yards × 525 yards = 1,564,500 square yards × 3 = 4,693,500 square feet ÷ 43,560 = 107.7 acres (multiplied by 3 instead of 9 to convert square yards to square feet)

    C. **Correct:** 2,980 yards × 525 yards = 1,564,500 square yards × 9 = 14,080,500 square feet ÷ 43,560 = 323.2 acres

    D. Incorrect: 2,980 yards × 525 yards = 1,564,500 square yards × 27 = 42,241,500 square feet ÷ 43,560 = 969.7 acres (multiplied by 27 instead of 9 to convert square yards to square feet)

    E. Incorrect: 3,232 acres (incorrectly multiplied)

28. Find the volume of the water in cubic feet and convert to cubic inches. Use the formula for converting cubic inches to gallons to determine how much water is needed. *(Lesson 22)*

    F. Incorrect: 300 gallons (used area of pool instead of volume of water)

    G. Incorrect: 1,500 gallons (used volume of pool only)

    H. **Correct:** 15 × 20 × 4.5 = 1,350 cubic feet × 1,728 = 2,332,800 cubic inches ÷ 231 = 10,098.7 → 10,099 gallons

    J. Incorrect: 11,221 gallons (used volume of pool instead of volume of water)

    K. Incorrect: 2,540,769 gallons (multiplied by conversion factor instead of dividing)

Level 7

Lesson 27 (pp. 190–195)
Skill Practice:

    A. 1.32   **B.** 45.45

On Your Own:

1. D	5. B	9. E	13. A
2. K	6. H	10. H	14. J
3. B	7. D	11. A	15. C
4. G	8. F	12. J	16. H

Lesson 28 (pp. 196–201)
Skills Practice:

    A. $17.50   **C.** $2.59 per gallon
    B. $360   **D.** $299.40

On Your Own:

1. D	5. C	9. E	13. C
2. J	6. K	10. G	14. H
3. D	7. A	11. D	15. C
4. H	8. H	12. F	16. F

Lesson 29 (pp. 202–207)
Skills Practice:

    A. 4 to 5, 4:5, or $\frac{4}{5}$ **B.** 8 to 35, 8:35, or $\frac{8}{35}$

On Your Own:

1. B	5. D	9. B	13. C
2. J	6. H	10. G	14. H
3. D	7. C	11. B	15. E
4. F	8. J	12. H	16. H

Lesson 30 (pp. 208–213)
Skills Practice:

    A. 133.97   **B.** 52.28

On Your Own:

1. B	5. A	9. B	13. B
2. J	6. G	10. G	14. K
3. A	7. B	11. B	15. C
4. G	8. G	12. J	16. K

Lesson 31 (pp. 214–219)
Skills Practice:

    A. 6   **B.** 0.008

On Your Own:

1. C	5. C	9. C	13. A
2. K	6. G	10. G	14. F
3. B	7. A	11. D	15. B
4. H	8. G	12. J	16. K

Lesson 32 (pp. 220–225)
Skills Practice:

    A. 63   **B.** 19

On Your Own:

1. C	5. B	9. D	13. A
2. G	6. H	10. G	14. H
3. B	7. A	11. A	15. B
4. J	8. G	12. J	16. H

Level 7 Performance Assessment (pp. 226–232)

1. Convert the weight of the dog from pounds to kilograms by dividing. Calculate the amount of anesthetic needed by multiplying the weight in kilograms by the amount of anesthetic per kilogram. Calculate the amount of solution needed by dividing the amount of anesthetic by the concentration of solution per milligram. *(Lesson 27)*

    A. Incorrect: $45 \div 2.2 = 20.45$; $20.45 \div 12 \div 200 \times 100 = 0.85$ milliliter (divided by 12 instead of multiplying; multiplied by 100 to make answer more reasonable)

    B. **Correct:** 45 pounds ÷ 2.2 pounds per kilogram = 20.45 kilograms; 20.45 kilograms × 12 milligrams/kilogram of body weight = 245.4 milligrams; 245.5 milligrams ÷ 200 milliliter solution/milligram anesthetic = 1.2 milliliters

    C. Incorrect: $45 \times 2.2 = 99$; $99 \times 12 = 1{,}188$; $1{,}188 \div 200 = 5.9$ milliliters (converted pounds to kilograms incorrectly)

    D. Incorrect: $45 \div 2.2 = 20.45$; $20.45 \div 12 = 1.7$; $1.7 \times 200 = 340$ milliliters (divided by 12 and multiplied by 20 instead of multiplying by 12 and dividing by 200)

    E. Incorrect: $45 \times 2.2 = 99$; $99 \div 12 = 8.25$; $8.25 \times 200 = 1{,}650$ milliliters (converted pounds to kilograms incorrectly and divided by 12 and multiplied by 200 instead of the reverse)

2. Rearrange the equation to to solve for volume at altitude (V_a) by dividing both sides by pressure at altitude (P_a). Solve for V_a. *(Lesson 31)*

    F. Incorrect: $V_a = \frac{P_a}{P_a V_s} = \frac{0.12}{(1.0)(75)} = 0.0016$ liter (incorrectly rearranged equation)

    G. Incorrect: $V_a = \frac{P_s}{P_s V_s} = \frac{1.0}{(0.12)(75)} = 0.11$ liter (incorrectly rearranged equation)

    H. Incorrect: $V_a = \frac{P_a V_s}{P_s} = \frac{(0.12)(75)}{1.0} = 9$ liters (incorrectly rearranged equation)

    J. Incorrect: 75 liters (this is the original volume)

    K. **Correct:**
$$V_a = \frac{P_s V_s}{P_a} = \frac{(1.0 \text{ kilogram/centimeter}^2)(75 \text{ liters})}{0.12 \text{ kilogram/centimeter}^2} = 625 \text{ liters}$$

3. Find the total cost for advertising in each newspaper with the planned ad. Compare these costs to the cost of the advertising special. Choose the lowest cost. *(Lesson 28)*

   A. Incorrect: City News: 783 × 3 = $2,349; City Tribune: 585 × 3 = $1,755; $7,200 > $2,349 > $1,755 (used only the number of columns and not the length of each column to calculate cost)

   B. Incorrect: City News: 783 × 5 = $3,915; City Tribune: 585 × 5 = $2,925; $2,925 < $3,915 < $7,200 (used only the length of each column and not the number of columns to calculate cost)

   C. Incorrect: City News: 783 × 8 = $6,264; City Tribune: 585 × 8 = $4,680; $4,680 < $6,264 <$7,200 (added the number of columns and the length of each column instead of multiplying)

   D. **Correct:** City News: $783 per column inch × 5 inches × 3 columns = $11,745; City Tribune: $585 per column inch × 5 inches × 3 columns = $8,775; special is for a larger ad for $7,200; $7,200 is the least expensive option

   E. Incorrect: City News: 783 × 5 × 3 = $11,745; City Tribune: 585 × 5 × 3 = $8,775; $8,775 < $11,745 (didn't consider the cost of the special)

4. Calculate the cost of each ad option and divide by the number of subscribers to that paper. *(Lesson 28)*

   F. **Correct:** $0.29 City News: $783 per column inch × 5 inches × 3 columns = $11,745; 11,745 ÷ 40,000 = $0.29 per subscriber; City Tribune (regular rate): $585 per column inch × 5 inches × 3 columns = $8,775; $8,775 × 22,500 = $0.32; City Tribune (special rate) $7,000 × 22,500 = $0.32; $0.29 < $0.32 < $0.39

   G. Incorrect: 7,200 ÷ 22,500 = $0.32 (assumed that special rate is best deal and did not compare)

   H. Incorrect: 585 × 5 × 3 = 8,775; 8,775 ÷ 22,500 = $0.39 (assumed that lower rate is best deal and did not compare)

   J. Incorrect: 783 × 5 × 3 = 11,745; 11,745 ÷ 40,000 = $2.90 (incorrectly placed decimal point in division)

   K. Incorrect: 585 × 5 × 3 = 8,775; 8,775 ÷ 22,500 = $3.20 (assumed that lower rate is best deal and did not compare and incorrectly placed decimal point in division)

5. Convert the measurements to feet, and then calculate the volume of one basket using the formula for the volume of a cone. Then multiply by 100 baskets and divide by 27 to find the number of cubic yards. *(Lesson 30)*

   A. **Correct:** 18 inches ÷ 12 inches/foot = $1\frac{1}{2}$ feet; Volume $\approx \frac{3.14 \times (1 \text{ foot})^2 \times 1\frac{1}{2} \text{ feet}}{3} = 1.57$ cubic feet; 1.57 × 100 = 157 cubic feet; 157 ÷ 27 = 6 cubic yards

   B. Incorrect: 18 ÷ 12 = $1\frac{1}{2}$; Volume $\approx \frac{3.14 \times (1)^2 \times 1\frac{1}{2}}{3} = 1.57$; 1.57 × 100 = 157 cubic feet; 157 ÷ 9 = 18 cubic yards (converted to cubic yards by dividing by 9)

   C. Incorrect: 18 ÷ 12 = $1\frac{1}{2}$; Volume $\approx \frac{3.14 \times (2)^2 \times 1\frac{1}{2}}{3} = 6.28$; 6.28 × 100 = 628 cubic feet; 628÷27 = 24 cubic yards (used diameter instead of radius)

   D. Incorrect: 18 ÷ 12 = $1\frac{1}{2}$; Volume $\approx \frac{3.14 \times (1)^2 \times 1\frac{1}{2}}{3} = 1.57$; 1.57 × 100 = 157 cubic yards (did not convert from cubic feet to cubic yards)

   E. Incorrect: Volume $\approx \frac{3.14 \times (2)^2 \times 18}{3} = 75.36$; 75.36 × 100 = 7,536 cubic feet; 7,536 ÷ 27 = 279 cubic yards (did not convert depth to feet)

6. Use the ratio to find the width of the playground, and then find the perimeter. Convert all measurements to feet, find how many 48-inch lengths of fencing are needed, and then multiply by $130. *(Lesson 29)*

   F. Incorrect: (40 × 3) ÷ 2 = 120 ÷ 2 = 60; 2(40 + 60) = 2(100) = 200; 48 ÷ 12 = 4; 200 ÷ 4 = 50; 50 × $130 = $6,500 (did not convert yards to feet for the perimeter of the playground)

   G. Incorrect: (40 × 3) ÷ 2 = 120 ÷ 2 = 60; (40 + 60) = 100; 100 × 3 = 300; 48 ÷ 12 = 4; 300 ÷ 4 = 75; 75 × $130 = $9,750 (added length and width instead of finding perimeter)

   H. **Correct:** (40 yards × 3) ÷ 2 = 120 yards ÷ 2 = 60 yards; 2(40 yards + 60 yards) = 2(100 yards) = 200 yards; 200 yards × 3 feet per yard = 600 feet; 48 inches ÷ 12 inches per foot = 4 feet; 600 feet ÷ 4 feet per length of fencing = 150 lengths; 150 lengths × $130 per length = $19,500

   J. Incorrect: (40 × 3) ÷ 2 = 120 ÷ 2 = 60; (40 × 60) = 240; 240 × 3 = 720; 48 ÷ 12 = 4; 720 ÷ 4 = 180; 180 × $130 = $23,400 (multiplied length and width instead of finding perimeter)

   K. Incorrect: (40 × 3) = 120; 2(40 + 120) = 2(160) = 320; 320 × 3 = 960; 48 ÷ 12 = 4; 960 ÷ 4 = 240; 240 × $130 = $31,200 (did not use the ratio correctly; multiplied by 3 to find the width of the playground)

7. Convert the diameter to inches. Divide by 2 to find the radius. Rearrange the formula to calculate the height: *Volume* = $\pi r^2 h$ so height = $\frac{Volume}{\pi r^2}$. *(Lesson 31)*

   A. Incorrect: $\frac{24,416}{3.14 \times 72^2} = \frac{24,416}{16,278} \approx 1.5$ inches (used diameter squared instead of radius squared)

   B. **Correct:** 6 inches; 6 feet × 12 = 72-inch diameter; 72 inches ÷ 2 = 36-inch radius; $h = \frac{24,416}{3.14 \times 36^2} = \frac{24,416}{4,069} \approx 6$ inches.

   C. Incorrect: $24,416/(3.14 \times 6)^2 = \frac{24,416}{355} \approx$ 69 inches (used diameter squared in feet instead of radius squared and did not convert to inches, and performed incorrect order of operations)

   D. Incorrect: $\frac{24,416}{3.14 \times 6^2} = \frac{24,416}{113} \approx 215$ inches (used diameter squared in feet instead of radius squared and did not convert to inches)

   E. Incorrect: $\frac{24,416}{3.14 \times 3^2} = \frac{24,416}{28.3} \approx 864$ feet (did not convert to inches)

8. The ratios are $\frac{1 \text{ bookcase}}{4 \text{ hours}}$ for Gina and $\frac{1 \text{ bookcase}}{6 \text{ hours}}$ for Tom. Write the ratios as fractions with a common denominator: $\frac{3}{12}$ for Gina and $\frac{2}{12}$ for Tom. Add the ratios to find the total number of bookcases made in 12 hours, and then set up a proportion to find the amount of time needed to make 15 bookcases. *(Lesson 29)*

   F. Incorrect: 4 + 6 = 10; 15 ÷ 10 = $1\frac{1}{2}$ hours (added the number of hours it takes Gina and Tom to make 1 bookcase and divided the number of bookcases to be made by that sum)

   G. Incorrect: $\frac{1}{4} + \frac{1}{6} = \frac{2}{10} = \frac{1}{5}$; 15 ÷ 5 = 3 hours (added the ratios incorrectly to find that together Gina and Tom make 1 bookcase in 5 hours working together, then divided the number of bookcases by 5 hours)

   H. **Correct:** $\frac{2}{12} + \frac{3}{12} = \frac{5 \text{ bookcases}}{12 \text{ hours}}$; $\frac{5 \text{ bookcases}}{12 \text{ hours}} = \frac{15 \text{ bookcases}}{x \text{ hours}}$; 5$x$ = 180; x = 36 hours

   J. Incorrect: $\frac{1}{4} + \frac{1}{6} = \frac{2}{10} = \frac{1}{5}$; 15 × 5 = 75 hours (added the ratios incorrectly to find that Gina and Tom make 1 bookcase in 5 hours working together and then multiplied 5 hours by 15 bookcases)

   K. Incorrect: 4 + 6 = 10; 15 × 10 = 150 hours (added the number of hours it takes Gina and Tom to make 1 bookcase and multiplied the number of bookcases to be made by that sum)

9. To find the mean, divide the sum of the readings by the number of readings. *(Lesson 32)*

   A. Incorrect: 16 − 12 = 4 pounds (this answer is the range, not the median)

   B. Incorrect: 13 pounds (this answer is the mode, not the mean)

   C. Incorrect: (13 = 14) ÷ 2 = 13.5 pounds (this answer is the median, not the mean)

   D. **Correct:** $\frac{12 + 13 + 13 + 14.5 + 14 + 13 + 16 + 14.5 + 15 + 13}{10}$ = $\frac{138}{10}$ = 13.8 pounds

   E. Incorrect: $\frac{12 + 13 + 14 + 14.5 + 15 + 16}{6} = \frac{84.5}{6} =$ 14.1 pounds (added one of every number and divided the sum by 6, the number of different responses)

10. Calculate the speed of the winner of each race in feet per second. Subtract to find the difference. *(Lesson 27)*

    F. Incorrect: 1,500-meter race: 1,500 ÷ 0.3048 = 4,921.26; (3 × 60) + 32.94 = 212.94; 4,921.26 ÷ 212.94 sec. = 23.1 feet per second; 1-mile race: 1 mile = 5,280 feet.; (3 × 60) + 35.93 = 215.93; 5,280 ÷ 215.93 = 24.5 feet per second; 24.5 − 23.1 = 1.4 feet per second (matched the times to the wrong races)

    G. **Correct:** 1,500-meter race: 1,500 meters ÷ 0.3048 meters per foot = 4,921.26 feet; (3 × 60 seconds) + 35.93 seconds = 215.93 seconds; 4,921.26 feet ÷ 215.93 seconds = 22.8 feet per second; 1-mile race: 1 mile = 5,280 feet.; (3 × 60 seconds) + 32.94 seconds = 212.94 seconds; 5,280 feet ÷ 212.94 seconds = 24.8 feet per second; 24.8 − 22.8 ft/s = 2.0 feet per second

    H. Incorrect: 1,500-meter race: (3 × 60) + 32.94 = 212.94; 1,500 ÷ 212.94 sec. = 7.0; 1-mile race: 1 mile = 5,280 feet; (3 × 60) + 35.93 = 215.93; 5,280 ÷ 215.93 = 24.5 feet per second; 24.5 − 7.0 = 17.5 feet per second (did not convert meters to feet)

    J. Incorrect: 1,500-meter race: 1,500 ÷ 0.3048 = 4,921.26; 3 + 35.93 = 38.93; 4,921.26 ÷ 38.93 = 126.4 feet per second; 1-mile race: 1 mile = 5,280 feet.; 3 + 32.94 = 35.94; 5,280 ÷ 35.94 = 146.9 feet per second; 146.9 − 126.4 = 20.5 feet per second (calculated seconds incorrectly)

K. Incorrect: 1,500-meter race: 1,500 ÷ 0.3048 = 459.26; (3 × 60) + 32.94 = 212.94; 459 ÷ 212.94 sec. = 2.2 feet per second; 1-mile race: 1 mile = 5,280 feet.; (3 × 60) + 35.93 = 215.93; 5,280 ÷ 215.93 = 24.5 feet per second; 24.5 − 2.2 = 22.3 feet per second (multiplied instead of dividing in conversion from meters to feet)

11. Find the total cost for each option and choose the least expensive option. *(Lesson 28)*

   A. Incorrect: 25 × 25 = $625; 20 × 25 + 15 = $515; 515 < 625 (used wrong amount of fabric)

   B. Incorrect: 25 × 30 = $750; 20 × 30 = $600; 600 < 750 (did not add shipping cost)

   C. Incorrect: 25 × 30 = $750; 20 × 30 + 10 = $610; 610 < 750 (used wrong shipping fee)

   D. **Correct:** $615; $25 × 30 = $750; $20 × 30 + $15 = $615; $615 < $750

   E. Incorrect: 25 × 30 = $750; 30 × 30 + 10 = $910 (used wrong price for amount purchased at catalog store)

12. Find the radius of the sphere and calculate volume using the formula:
   Volume $\approx \frac{4}{3} \times 3.14 \times (radius)^3$. *(Lesson 30)*

   F. Incorrect: 3.14 × 2.5 × 2.5 = 19.6 cm³ (used wrong formula)

   G. Incorrect: $\frac{4}{3}$ × 3.14 × 2.5 × 2.5 = 26.2 cm³ (used square of radius instead of cube)

   H. Incorrect: 3.14 × 2.5 × 2.5 × 2.5 = 49.1 cm³ (used wrong formula)

   J. **Correct:** 65.4cm³; Volume $\approx \frac{4}{3}$ × 3.14 × 2.5 cm × 2.5 cm × 2.5 cm = 65.4³

   K. Incorrect: $\frac{4}{3}$ × 3.14 × 5 × 5 × 5 = 523.3 cm³ (used diameter instead of radius)

13. Use the formula $D = \sqrt{l^2 + h^2}$ to calculate the diagonal measurement and round to the next higher number. *(Lesson 31)*

   A. Incorrect: $D = \sqrt{64 + 36} = \sqrt{100} =$ 10 inches (added dimensions instead of their squares)

   B. Incorrect: 64 − 36 = 28 inches (used incorrect formula)

   C. Incorrect: $D = \sqrt{64 \times 36} = \sqrt{2,304} =$ 48 inches (used incorrect formula)

   D. **Correct:** $D = \sqrt{l^2 + h^2} = \sqrt{64^2 + 36^2} = \sqrt{4,096 + 1,296} = \sqrt{5,392} = 73.4$ inches → 74 inches

   E. Incorrect: 64 + 36 = 100 inches (used incorrect formula)

14. Subtract the number of jeans that are left from the number of jeans that were in stock 2 weeks ago to find how many jeans were sold in 2 weeks. Divide by 2 to find the rate of jeans sold per week, then multiply by 3 to determine how many jeans are needed for 3 weeks. Subtract the number of jeans still in stock to find the number of jeans that need to be ordered, then divide by 32 to find the number of cases to order. Any remainder or decimal indicates an additional case is needed. *(Lesson 29)*

   F. Incorrect: 480 − 24 = 456; 456 ÷ 2 = 228; 228 × 3 = 684; 684 − 24 = 660; 660 ÷ 32 = 20.625 cases → 20 cases needed (misinterpreted the decimal part of the quotient and dropped it)

   G. **Correct:** 480 jeans − 24 jeans = 456 jeans sold in 2 weeks; 456 jeans ÷ 2 weeks = 228 jeans sold in 1 week; 228 jeans × 3 weeks = 684 jeans needed for 3 weeks; 684 jeans − 24 jeans = 660 jeans; 660 jeans ÷ 32 jeans per case = 20.625 → 21 cases

   H. Incorrect: 480 − 24 = 456; 456 ÷ 2 = 228; 228 × 3 = 684; 684 ÷ 32 = 21.375 → 22 cases needed (did not account for the jeans still in stock when finding the number of cases to order)

   J. Incorrect: 480 ÷ 2 = 240; 240 × 3 = 720; 720 ÷ 32 = 22.5 → 23 cases needed (did not account for the jeans still in stock)

   K. Incorrect: 480 − 24 = 456; 456 × 3 = 1,368; 1,368 − 24 = 1,344; 1,344 ÷ 32 = 42 cases needed (multiplied the number of jeans sold in 2 weeks by 3)

15. Convert the length and width measurements of the film to feet. Calculate the area, and then divide the area into the price for each roll. Select the less expensive roll. *(Lesson 27)*

   A. Incorrect: 48 × 100 = 4,800; 108.30 ÷ 4,800 = 0.02; 150 × 75 = 11,250; 300 ÷ 11,250 = $0.03/sq.ft. (did not convert measures)

   B. **Correct:** 48 inches ÷ 12 = 4 ft.; 4 ft. × 100 ft. = 400 square feet; $108.30 ÷ 400 sq. ft = $0.27/square foot; 150 centimeters ÷ 2.54 = 59.1 inches; 59.1 inches ÷ 12 = 4.9 feet; 75 m ÷ 0.3048 = 246.1 feet; 4.9 feet × 246.1 feet = 1,206 square feet; $300 ÷ 1,206 square feet = $0.25/square foot; $0.25/square feet is the less expensive cost per square foot

C. Incorrect: $48 \div 12 = 4$; $4 \times 100 = 400$; $108.30 \div 400 = \$0.27$/square foot (assumed that since \$108.30 < \$300, the cost per square foot would be less also)

D. Incorrect: $150 \times 2.54 = 381$; $381 \div 12 = 31.75$; $75 \times 0.3408 = 22.86$; $31.75 \times 22.86 = 725.8$; $300 \div 725.8 = \$0.41$/square foot (converted metric to customary incorrectly; did not consider other choice)

E. Incorrect: $48 \div 12 = 4$; $4 \times 100 = 400$; $400 \div 108.30 = \$3.69$/sq. ft.; $150 \div 2.54 = 59.1$; $59.1 \div 12 = 4.9$; $75 \div 0.3048 = 246.1$; $4.9 \times 246.1 = 1,206$; $1,206. \div \$300 = \$0.41$ (divided incorrectly to find cost per square foot)

16. Arrange the list of items in order, since the number of items is even, and find the mean of the two values in the middle. *(Lesson 32)*

    F. Incorrect: \$175,000 (one of the two middle values, instead of the average)

    G. **Correct:** \$182,750; $\frac{175,000 + 190,500}{2} = \$182,750$

    H. Incorrect: \$190,500 (one of the two middle values, instead of the average)

    J. Incorrect:
    $$\frac{142,000 + 214,700 + 168,900 + 190,500 + 210,000 + 175,000 + 149,100 + 380,200}{8}$$
    $= \$203,800$ (calculated the mean)

    K. Incorrect: $380,200 - 142,000 = \$238,200$ (calculated the range)

17. Calculate the surface area the cylinder (not including ends) using the formula: Area = $2 \times 3.14 \times radius \times height$. *(Lesson 30)*

    A. Incorrect: Area = $(2 \times 3.14 \times (8)^2) = 402$ centimeters^2 (used incorrect formula)

    B. Incorrect: Area = $3.14 \times 8 \times 50 = 1,256$ centimeters^2 (used incorrect formula)

    C. **Correct:** Area = $2 \times 3.14 \times 8 \times 50 = 2,512$ centimeters^2

    D. Incorrect: Area = $2 \times 3.14 \times 16 \times 50 = 5,024$ centimeters^2 (used diameter instead of radius)

    E. Incorrect: Area = $3.14 \times (8)^2 \times 50 = 10,048$ centimeters^2 (used incorrect formula)

18. Add the initial cost for 125 student editions, 4 teacher editions, and 125 workbooks for the first year and add the cost of 125 workbooks for each of the next five years. Divide by 750 (number of students over 6 years) to find the cost per student for each company. Choose the lowest cost per student. *(Lesson 28)*

F. Incorrect: $64 \times 125 + 107.25 \times 2 + 15.25 \times 125 \times 6 = 19,652$; $75 \times 125 + 125 \times 4 + 8.25 \times 125 = 10,906.25$; $125 \times 6 = 750$; $19,652 \div 750 = \$26.20$; $10,906.25 \div 750 = \$14.54$ (calculated the 2nd option purchasing workbooks for 1 year instead of 6)

G. **Correct:** $\$64 \times 125 + \$107.25 \times 2 + \$15.25 \times 125 \times 5 = \$17,745.75$; $\$75 \times 125 + \$125 \times 4 + \$8.25 \times 125 \times 6 = \$16,062.50$; $125 \times 6 = 750$; $\$17,745.75 \div 750 = \$23.66$; $\$16,062.50 \div 750 = \$21.42$; \$21.42 per student is the least expensive cost per student

H. Incorrect: $64 \times 125 + 107.25 \times 2 + 15.25 \times 125 \times 5 = 17,745.75$; $75 \times 125 + 125 \times 4 + 8.25 \times 125 \times 6 = 16,062.50$; $125 \times 6 = 750$; $17,745.75 \div 750 = \$23.66$; $16,062.50 \div 750 = \$21.42$ (chose the higher cost per student rather than the lower)

J. Incorrect: $64 \times 125 + 107.25 \times 4 + 15.25 \times 125 \times 5 = 17,960.25$; $75 \times 125 + 125 \times 4 + 8.25 \times 125 \times 6 = 16,062.50$; $125 \times 6 = 750$; $17,960.25 \div 750 = \$23.95$; $16,062.50 \div 750 = \$21.42$ (calculated the first option considering 4 teacher editions instead of two; chose the higher cost per student rather than the lower)

K. Incorrect: $\$64 \times 125 + \$107.25 \times 2 + 15.25 \times 125 \times 6 = 19,652$; $75 \times 125 + 125 \times 4 + 8.25 \times 125 \times 6 = 16,062.50$; $125 \times 6 = 750$; $19,652 \div 750 = \$26.20$; $16,062.50 \div 750 = \$21.42$ (calculated the 1st option purchasing 6 years of workbooks instead of 5, chose the higher cost per student rather than the lower)

19. Add to find the total number of chips that were inspected and the total number of defective chips across all three batches. Divide the total number of defective chips by the total number of chips that were inspected, then multiply by 100 to calculate the percentage of defective chips. *(Lesson 32)*

    A. Incorrect: $87 \div 3 \times 100 = 3.4\%$ (probability of defective items in batch 3)

    B. **Correct:** 5.7%; $\frac{5 + 8 + 3}{100 + 96 + 87} = \frac{16}{283} \approx 0.0565$; $0.057 \times 100 = 5.7\%$

    C. Incorrect: $8 \div 96 \times 100 = 8.3\%$ (probability of defective items in batch 2)

    D. Incorrect: $5 + 8 + 3 = 16\%$ (added total number of defective items but did not calculate percent)

E. Incorrect: $\frac{95 + 88 + 84}{100 + 96 + 87} = \frac{267}{283} \approx 0.943$; $0.943 \times 100 = 94.3\%$ (probability of non-defective items)

20. From the given information, find the volume of each unit and the cost per year to verify that it meets the requirements. If the unit meets the requirements, use the cost per month and the volume to calculate the cost per cubic foot per month of each unit. Compare to identify the lowest cost per cubic foot per month. *(Lesson 28)*

F. Incorrect: Unit 1: $10 \times 15 \times 8 = 1{,}200$; $\$250 \div 1{,}200 = \$0.21$ per cubic foot per month; Unit 2: $15 \times 12 \times 10 = 1{,}800$; $415 \div 1{,}800 = 0.23$ per cubic foot per month; Unit 3: $16 \times 18 \times 8 = 2{,}304$; $\$500 \div 2{,}304 = \$0.22$ per cubic foot per month (did not eliminate Unit 1 as too small)

G. **Correct:** Unit 1: 10 feet $\times$ 15 feet $\times$ 8 feet = 1,200 cubic feet (the unit is too small); Unit 2: 15 feet $\times$ 12 feet $\times$ 10 feet = 1,800 cubic feet; $\$415 \div 1{,}800$ cubic feet = $\$0.23$ per cubic feet per month; Unit 3: 16 feet $\times$ 18 feet $\times$ 8 feet = 2,304 cubic feet; $\$500 \div 2{,}304$ cu. ft. = $\$0.22$ per cu. ft. per month; Unit 3 is the lowest cost per cubic foot per month.

H. Incorrect: Unit 1: $10 \times 15 \times 8 = 1{,}200$ per cubic foot per month (the unit is too small); Unit 2: $15 \times 12 \times 10 = 1{,}800$; $415 \div 1{,}800 = \$0.23$ per cubic foot per month; Unit 3: $16 \times 18 \times 8 = 2{,}304$; $500 \div 2{,}304 = \$0.22$ per cubic foot per month (did not choose the unit with the lowest cost per cubic foot per month)

J. Incorrect: Unit 1: $10 \times 15 = 150$ square feet; Unit 2: $15 \times 12 = 180$; $180 \div 415 = \$0.43$ per cubic foot per month; Unit 3: $16 \times 18 = 288$; $288 \div 500 = \$0.58$ per cubic foot per month (found area of floor, not volume of unit; divided in the wrong order to find the cost per unit)

K. Incorrect: Unit 1: $10 \times 15 \times 8 = 1{,}400$; $\$250 \div 1{,}200 = \$0.21$ per cubic foot per month (the unit is too small); Unit 2: $15 \times 12 \times 10 = 1{,}800$; $1{,}800 \div 415 = \$4.34$ per cubic foot per month; Unit 3: $16 \times 18 \times 8 = 2{,}304$; $2{,}304 \div 500 = \$4.61$ per cubic foot per month (divided in the wrong order to find the cost per cubic foot per month)

21. Find the volume of the tower using the formula: Volume $\approx 3.14 \times$ radius$^2 \times$ height. Then find the volume of a cooling tube using the same formula. Subtract the volumes of 10 tubes from the volume of the tower and round to the nearest cubic meter. *(Lesson 30)*

A. **Correct:** 1,052 meters^3. Volume (tower) $\approx 3.14 \times (3 \text{ meters})^2 \times 40 \text{ meters} = 1{,}130.4$ meters^3; Volume (tube) $\approx 3.14 \times (0.25 \text{ meters})^2 \times 40 \text{ meters} = 7.85$ meters^3; $1{,}130.4$ meters$^3 - (7.85 \text{ meters}^3 \times 10) = 1{,}051.9$ meters$^3 \rightarrow 1{,}052$ meters^3

B. Incorrect: Volume (tower) $\approx 3.14 \times (3)^2 \times 40 = 1{,}130.4$ meters^3; Volume (tube) $\approx 3.14 \times (0.25)^2 \times 40 = 7.85$ meters^3; $1{,}130.4 - 7.85 = 1{,}122.65 \rightarrow 1{,}123$ meters^3 (only subtracted one cooling tube)

C. Incorrect: Volume (tower) $\approx 3.14 \times (3)^2 \times 40 = 1{,}130.4 \rightarrow 1{,}130$ meters^3 (did not subtract volume of cooling tubes)

D. Incorrect: Volume (tower) $\approx 3.14 \times (3)^2 \times 40 = 1{,}130.4$ meters^3; Volume (tube) $\approx 3.14 \times (0.25)^2 \times 40$ meters = 7.85 meters^3; $1{,}130.4 + (7.85 \times 10) = 1{,}208.9 \rightarrow 1{,}209$ meters^3 (added volume of cooling tubes)

E. Incorrect: Volume (tower) $\approx 3.14 \times (6)^2 \times 40 = 11{,}120$ meters^3; Volume (tube) $\approx 3.14 \times (0.5)^2 \times 40 = 31.4$ meters^3. $11{,}120 - 31.4 = 11{,}088.6 \rightarrow 11{,}089$ meters^3. (used diameters instead of radii in formulas and only subtracted one cooling tube)

22. Multiply the number of daily doses by the volume in teaspoons and then multiply by the number of milliliters in one teaspoon to find the total number of milliliters. *(Lesson 22)*

F. Incorrect: $3 \times 4 \div 5 = 2.4$ milliliters (divided number of teaspoons by 5 instead of multiplying)

G. Incorrect: $3 \times 4 = 12$ milliliters (calculated number of teaspoons in one day but did not convert to milliliters)

H. Incorrect: $3 \times 5 = 15$ milliliters (found the number of milliliters in one dose instead of total for one day)

J. Incorrect: $4 \times 5 = 20$ milliliters (multiplied the number of doses by the number of milliliters in a teaspoon)

K. **Correct:** 3 teaspoons $\times$ 3 doses per day = 12 teaspoons per day; 12 teaspoons $\times$ 5 = 60 milliliters per day.

23. Convert the interest rate to a decimal and then use the function for compound interest, $B = p(1 + r)^x$, to find the value of the money after 3 years. *(Lesson 31)*

   A. Incorrect: $25,000 × 1^3 + $25,000 × (0.045)^3$ = $25,000 + $2 = $25,002 (did not add 1 and 0.045 before using exponent)

   B. Incorrect: $25,000 × 1.045 = $26,125 (did not use third power of the multiplier)

   C. Correct: $28,529; 4.5% = 0.045; $25,000 $(1 + 0.045)^3$ = .$25,000(1.045)^3$ = $25,000 × 1.1412 = $28,529

   D. Incorrect: $25,000 × $(1.45)^3$ = $25,000 × 3.048 = $76,216 (incorrectly converted percent to decimal)

   E. Incorrect: $25,000 × 1.045 × 3 = $78,375 (multiplied by number of years instead of using number of years as an exponent)

24. Use the exponential function $y = a × b^t$. Replace a with the number of deer, replace b with the percent, in decimal form, and replace t with the time. *(Lesson 31)*

   F. Incorrect: 3 × 15 × 15% = 3 × 15 × 0.15 = 6.75 → 7 (multiplied by 15% and the number of years instead of using the formula)

   G. Incorrect: 15 × 150% = 15 × 1.5 = 22.5 → 23 (multiplied by 150% instead of using the formula)

   H. Correct: $y = a × b^t$; $y = 15 × 1.5^3$ = 50.625 → 51

   J. Incorrect: 3 × 15 × 150% = 3 × 15 × 1.5 = 67.5 → 68 (multiplied by 150% and the number of years instead of using the formula)

   K. Incorrect: $y = 3 × 15 × 150 = 6,750$ (multiplied the numbers in the question by one another instead of using the formula)

25. Convert the building code measurements to mils. Identify which answer lies in the accepted range. *(Lesson 27)*

   A. Correct: 7 mil; 0.15 mm = 0.015 cm; 0.015 cm ÷ 2.54 = 0.0059 inches; 0.0059 inches × 1,000 = 5.9 mil; 0.25 mm = 0.025 cm; 0.025 cm ÷ 2.54 = 0.0098 inches; 0.0098 inches × 1,000 = 9.8 mil; 7 is between 5.9 and 9.8

   B. Incorrect: 0.015 × 2.54 = 0.0381; 0.0381 × 1,000 = 38.1; 0.025 × 2.54 = 0.0635; 0.0381 × 1,000 = 63.5 mils (multiplied by 2.54 instead of dividing to convert cm to inches)

   C. Incorrect: 0.015 ÷ 2.54 = 0.0059; 0.0059 × 1,000 = 59 mil; 0.025 ÷ 2.54 = 0.0098; 0.0098 × 1,000 = 98 mil (multiplied decimal by 1,000 incorrectly)

   D. Incorrect: 0.15 × 2.54 = 0.381; 0.381 × 1,000 = 381; 0.25 × 2.54 = 0.635; 0.0381 × 1,000 = 635 mils (did not convert mm to cm and then multiplied by 2.54 instead of dividing to convert cm to inches)

   E. Incorrect: 0.15 × 10 = 1.5; 1.5 ÷ 2.54 = 0.591; 0.591 × 1,000 = 591; 0.25 × 10 = 2.5; 2.5 ÷ 2.54 = 0.984; 0.984 × 1,000 = 984 mils (multiplied mm to calculate cm instead of dividing)

26. Find how much salt is in the solution you have. Then set up a proportion using the ratio of the amount of salt you have to the unknown amount of water you need, cross-multiply, and solve for the unknown. Finally, subtract the amount of water you already have in the solution to find the amount that needs to be added. *(Lesson 29)*

   F. Incorrect: 4% = 0.04; $\frac{0.04}{x} = \frac{2.5}{97.5}$; 3.9 = 2.5$x$; x = 1.56; 1.56 − (2 − 0.08) = 1.56 − 1.92 = −0.36 liter (did not use the percent to find the amount of salt in 2 liters of solution and did not pay attention to the negative result when choosing an answer)

   G. Incorrect: 4 − 2.5 = 1.5; 2 × 1.5 = 3; 3 − 2 = 1 liter (subtracted the percents, multiplied 2 liters by the difference, and then subtracted 2 liters from the product)

   H. Correct: 4% = 0.04; 2 liters × 0.04 = 0.08 liter; $\frac{0.08 \text{ liter salt}}{x \text{ liters water}} = \frac{2.5 \text{ parts salt}}{97.5 \text{ parts water}}$; 7.8 = 2.5$x$; x = 3.12 liters; 3.12 liters − (2 liters − 0.08 liter) = 3.12 liters − 1.92 liters = 1.2 liters

   J. Incorrect: 4% = 0.04; 2 × 0.04 = 0.08; $\frac{0.08}{x} = \frac{2.5}{100}$; 8 = 2.5$x$; x = 3.2; 3.2 − (2 − 0.08) = 3.2 − 1.92 = 1.28 liters (used the ratio 2.5:100 in the proportion, which compares parts salt to the parts per solution rather than to parts water)

   K. Incorrect: 4% = 0.04; 2 × 0.04 = 0.08; $\frac{0.08}{x} = \frac{2.5}{97.5}$; 7.8 = 2.5$x$; x = 3.12 liters (did not subtract the amount of water that is already in the solution)

27. List the data points in order and find the middle value of the data points. Because there are 16 data points—an even number—the median is the average of the 8th and 9th points. *(Lesson 32)*

   A. Incorrect: $101 - 73 = 28$ (range of data)

   B. Incorrect: 78 (mode of data)

   C. Incorrect: 80 (one of the two middle values, not the average of the two)

   D. **Correct:** 80.5; The 8th point is 80; the 9th point is 81; $80 + 81 \div 2 = 80.5$

   E. Incorrect:

$$\frac{78 + 92 + 78 + 84 + 86 + 73 + 85 + 95 + 101 + 74 + 75 + 80 + 81 + 82 + 78 + 74}{16}$$

$$= \frac{1{,}316}{16} = 82.25 \text{ (mean of the data)}$$

28. Find the sum of all the ages and divide it by the number of participants in the study. *(Lesson 32)*

   F. Incorrect: $101 - 73 = 28$ (range of data)

   G. Incorrect: 78 (mode of data)

   H. Incorrect: $80 + 81 \div 2 = 80.5$ (median of data)

   J. Incorrect:

$$\frac{78 + 92 + 78 + 84 + 86 + 73 + 85 + 95 + 101 + 74 + 75 + 80 + 81 + 82 + 78 + 74}{16}$$

$$= \frac{1{,}316}{16} = 82.25 \approx 82 \text{ (rounded mean to nearest}$$
whole number)

   K. **Correct:** 82.25;

$$\frac{78 + 92 + 78 + 84 + 86 + 73 + 85 + 95 + 101 + 74 + 75 + 80 + 81 + 82 + 78 + 74}{16}$$

$$= \frac{1{,}316}{16} = 82.25$$

Applied Mathematics Formula Sheet

Distance

1 foot = 12 inches

1 yard = 3 feet

1 mile = 5,280 feet

1 mile ≈ 1.61 kilometers

1 inch = 2.54 centimeters

1 foot = 0.3048 meters

1 meter = 1,000 millimeters

1 meter = 100 centimeters

1 kilometer = 1,000 meters

1 kilometer ≈ 0.62 miles

Area

1 square foot = 144 square inches

1 square yard = 9 square feet

1 acre = 43,560 square feet

Volume

1 cup = 8 fluid ounces

1 quart = 4 cups

1 gallon = 4 quarts

1 gallon = 231 cubic inches

1 liter ≈ 0.264 gallons

1 cubic foot = 1,728 cubic inches

1 cubic yard = 27 cubic feet

1 board foot = 1 inch by 12 inches by 12 inches

Weight

1 ounce ≈ 28.350 grams

1 pound = 16 ounces

1 pound ≈ 453.592 grams

1 milligram = 0.001 grams

1 kilogram = 1,000 grams

1 kilogram ≈ 2.2 pounds

1 ton = 2,000 pounds

Rectangle

perimeter = 2 (*length* + *width*)

area = *length* × *width*

Rectangular Solid (Box)

volume = *length* × *width* × *height*

Cube

volume = (*length of side*)^3

Triangle

Sum of angles = 180°

area = $\frac{1}{2}$(*base* × *height*)

Circle

number of degrees in a circle = 360°

circumference ≈ 3.14 × *diameter*

area ≈ 3.14 × (*radius*)^2

Cylinder

volume ≈ 3.14 × (*radius*)^2 × *height*

Cone

volume ≈ $\dfrac{3.14 \times (radius)^2 \times height}{3}$

Sphere (Ball)

volume ≈ $\frac{4}{3}$ × 3.14 × (*radius*)^3

Electricity

1 kilowatt-hour = 1,000 watt-hours

amps = watts ÷ volts

Temperature

°C = 0.56 (°F − 32) or $\frac{5}{9}$(°F − 32)

°F = 1.8 (°C) + 32 or ($\frac{9}{5}$ ×°C) + 32